The Pause

An Overview of the New Testament: Part Three

Bob Evely

To Jill

The wife of my youth.
My best friend.
Most definitely my better half.
An amazing wife, mother, and grandma.

You have made this spiritual journey with me,
Every step of the way.

You have always supported me in all that I do.

I appreciate you far more
than words could possibly express.

With love,

Bob

"The Pause"
Abby Evely

"The Pause"
Lilli Evely

An Overview of the New Testament: Part Three

The Pause

"The Fellowship of ALL Believers"

Acts (Part 2)
Romans
1-2 Corinthians
Galatians
Ephesians
Philippians
Colossians
1-2 Thessalonians
1-2 Timothy
Titus
Philemon

"Callousness, in part, on Israel has come until the
complement of the nations may be entering."
(Romans 11:25)

Bob Evely.

*Scriptures taken from the Concordant Literal New Testament
and the Concordant Version of the Old Testament unless otherwise noted.
Concordant Publishing Concern, 15570 West Knochaven Road,
Santa Clarita, CA 91387 (www.Concordant.org)*

Grace Evangel Fellowship:
P O Box 6, Wilmore, KY 40390
www.GraceEvangel.org

The Pause; An Overview of the New Testament – Part Three
by Bob Evely
Copyright © 2018 by Robert W. Evely

First Printing: 2018

ISBN 978-1-7323228-8-2

Cover created by Cris Evely
Front: Livy Evely
Back: The Evely girls (freeze tag)

Published by:
Robert W. Evely
P.O. Box 6
Wilmore, KY 40390

www.GraceEvangel.org

Table of Contents

Acts (Part 2)	5
Paul's Letters	43
Romans	47
1 Corinthians	91
2 Corinthians	123
Galatians	145
Ephesians	169
Philippians	197
Colossians	207
1 Thessalonians	219
2 Thessalonians	229
1 Timothy	235
2 Timothy	253
Titus	269
Philemon	275
Summary, The Pause	279

𝕬𝖈𝖙𝖘 (𝔓𝖆𝖗𝖙 𝕿𝖜𝖔)

An Overview of the Scriptures, by
BOB EVELY © *2018.*
An Independent Minister of Christ Jesus,
Of the church at Wilmore, Kentucky

Now that we have considered the first part of Acts and the Circumcision letters, all of which were focused on believers from among Israel, we come to a turning point. Israel has rejected their king and crucified Him. Peter continues with the same message to Israel; repent and ready yourselves for the coming kingdom. But once again resistance appears and this kingdom message is rejected.

God now does something not foretold by the prophets, who had foreseen the re-gathering of Israel and the restoration of the kingdom. With the rejection of the kingdom message there is now a *pause* in that agenda. The kingdom will still be restored, and the apostles and the writers of the Circumcision letters instruct the Jewish believers to persevere and wait for that restoration. But in the meantime God will begin a new thing. Saul, who had persecuted and terrorized the believers, and who should rightfully have been struck down, will find grace and a special calling from God. Let us begin with Saul's conversion.

CHAPTER 9

Saul's conversion [(9:1)]

On the road to Damascus, Saul is blinded for three days, and does not eat or drink. A voice from heaven reports, *He is a choice instrument of Mine, to bear My name before both the nations and kings, besides the sons of Israel ...*

> This occurs in 36 A.D. Observe the two parts to Paul's commission. He is to bear Christ's name before:
>
> ✓ Nations and kings (i.e. the nations apart from Israel), and
> ✓ The sons of Israel
>
> Unlike the Twelve who are commissioned to go only to Israel, Paul has a *dual* commission. He is the ONLY apostle commissioned to go to the nations; but note that he is ALSO commissioned to go to the sons of Israel. We must keep this in mind as we continue with our consideration

of Acts and when we read Paul's epistles. We must always ask; is this word being spoken to the nations or to Israel? Paul was commissioned to go to both; and we cannot assume the message he bears will be the same in both cases.

At times Paul will address a mix of individuals from both Israel and the nations. He may use Jewish references for the benefit of his Jewish audience, and non-Jewish references for the benefit of those of the nations. Pay close attention to details as we will see significant differences in the message Paul (and the others) proclaims to those of Israel, and the message Paul proclaims to those of the nations.

Saul's ministry begins (9:19)

Saul comes to be with the disciples in Damascus for some days. Immediately in the synagogues he proclaims Jesus, that He is the Son of God. The Jews of Damascus are confused as Saul *deduces* that Jesus is the Christ, and they consult to assassinate him. The disciples lower Saul thru the wall in a hamper. (See 2 Corinthians 11:32)

Coming to Jerusalem Saul spends time with the disciples. (See Galatians 1:18-19) He speaks boldly with the Hellenists, and they try to assassinate him. The brethren lead him into Caesarea, and they send him to Tarsus.

Not immediately to Jerusalem? From Galatians 1:17 we learn that in these early days Saul went to Arabia and then back to Damascus; before going to Jerusalem. He makes it clear that the evangel he proclaims was not received from men but came thru a revelation of Jesus Christ. (Galatians 1:12)

Had Saul's (Paul's) message been the same as that being declared by the other apostles, he would logically have gone first to spend time with the others. But he makes it very clear that this was not the case. Paul's "my evangel" was not just the same message going to a different group of people (the Gentiles). He was entrusted with the evangel *of* the Uncircumcision, while Peter was entrusted with the evangel *of* the Circumcision. (Galatians 2:7)

Saul spoke with the Jews in Damascus, *deducing* that Jesus is the Christ. (9:22) *Deducing* is *sumbibazo* in the Greek; the same word translated *unite* when speaking of the physical realm. To *deduce* is to unite various facts into a single conclusion. Paul was presenting to the Jews the various evidences in support of the conclusion that Jesus is the Christ. This give us a glimpse into a method used by Saul/Paul as he evangelizes.

Peter's ministry continues (9:31)

The ecclesia enjoys a time of peace and their numbers multiply. Peter heals Eneas the paralytic, and he raises Tabitha from the dead. As a result, many believe.

> The writer turns once again to Peter's ministry to Israel. This portion of Acts has been discussed in greater detail in the previous section when we looked at Acts part one, but we will include here a very brief overview.

CHAPTER 10

Peter is told in a vision to go to Cornelius, a centurion of a squadron called "Italian," devout and fearing God along with his entire house. Peter resists, for Cornelius is a Gentile; though a God-fearing one. But ultimately Peter is obedient and goes.

> From the time of Abraham it was God's plan to *bless all peoples,* but until now God has worked strictly with the Jews. Jesus Himself would go only to the sheep of Israel, and "the church" (ecclesia) up to now is also exclusively Jewish. Everything we have read thus far in Acts has pertained to the JEWISH believers. Has the plan now changed? Will God now go directly to the Gentiles?
>
> Cornelius was no ordinary Gentile. He was devout, feared God, and beseeched God continually. He sought after the God of Abraham, and God now commissions Peter to go to him. As we read on, observe that Peter and the other apostles will continue to go EXCLUSIVELY to the Jews. We remember once again Paul's words; that Paul was entrusted with the evangel of the Uncircumcision, while Peter was entrusted with the evangel of the Circumcision. (Galatians 2:7)

CHAPTER 11

Peter is criticized by those of the Circumcision for going to the uncircumcised. But Peter tells of the vision he has received from God, and the grace God had granted. Upon hearing this report, they glorify God, that the nations have also been given repentance unto life.

Those who are dispersed evangelize as far as Phoenicia and Cyprus and Antioch, speaking the word to no one except TO THE JEWS ONLY. A vast number who believe turn back to the Lord.

> Note that they not only believe, but also *turn back to the Lord.* By inference we see that it is one thing to believe, and another to act (turn back). This is the message proclaimed as a part of the "kingdom evangel" going to the Jews; to believe AND to repent (turn back).

Barnabas and Saul go to Antioch (11:22)

The ecclesia in Jerusalem sends Barnabas to Antioch. He entreats them all with purpose of heart to be remaining in the Lord. Barnabas goes to Tarsus to find Saul, and he brings him to Antioch. They remain there for a year with the ecclesia, teaching a considerable throng.

Agabus (a prophet) signifies thru the spirit that a great famine is about to be on the whole inhabited earth (which occurred under Claudius). As any of the disciples thrive, each designates something to send to the brethren dwelling in Judea, for dispensing.

CHAPTER 12

Major persecution (12:1)

Herod the king mistreats some from the ecclesia. He assassinates James, the brother of John. Peter is arrested and jailed and is then subsequently freed from his chains by a messenger. Herod dies, smitten by a messenger of the Lord for not giving glory to God. The word of God grows.

Barnabas and Saul return to Antioch (12:24)

Barnabas and Saul return from Jerusalem to Antioch, taking along John Mark.

> Here is where we paused in our review of Acts part one to look at the epistles written by the Circumcision writers to the believers from among Israel. To this point in Acts, Peter and James have been the central focus. But now we will observe a change, and from this point on Paul will become the focus.
>
> As stated previously; early in Acts when Judas was replaced it was important to keep the number of apostles at twelve. This makes sense since the apostles represented the ecclesia, the called-out-ones, from among Israel which was comprised of twelve tribes. But when Paul assumes the forefront and is named an apostle, this is a new thing. It will be twelve PLUS Paul. This makes sense since Paul is named apostle to the nations. This, too, is a new thing. Until Acts 13 the nations are only

blessed thru Israel. But in Paul's writings we will see that the believers among the nations will be joint heirs, on the same level as Israel.

It is important to *rightly divide* the word of God, not mixing together things that are different. Doing so leads to confusion and a failure to understand that which God is trying to reveal to us.

The Twelve, and the early church (the "called-out-ones") that we see thru Acts 12 are exclusively believers from among Israel. We within the Body of Christ today cannot reach back and claim that the events recorded and the words spoken pertain to us today; for this was a time when God was working thru ISRAEL as His channel to bless all people.

With Paul, and especially with his later letters, we will see truths not revealed by the prophets, in the four gospel accounts, or in this first part of Acts.

CHAPTER 13

Saul and Barnabas are severed (13:1)

Sever to Me Barnabas and Saul *for the work to which I have called them.* Fasting and praying they place their hands upon Saul and Barnabas and dismiss them.

To SEVER would be to *cut* Saul and Barnabas apart from others in the ecclesia. Had they been taking the same message to the same people (i.e. Israel) there would be no need to *sever* them.

The First Journey (13:4 – 14:28)
48 A.D.

Saul and Barnabas begin their journey (13:4)

They travel to Seleucia, Cyprus (an island 60 miles west of Syria), and Salamis (on the east coast of Cyprus). At Salamis they announce the word of God *in the synagogues.*

Remember Paul's dual commission from Acts 9; the nations AND Israel. In the first part of Acts, and consistent with Jesus' earthly ministry as described in the gospel accounts, God's word went exclusively to Israel. Now Paul has been commissioned to go to Israel and ALSO to the nations. Observe that he will go FIRST to Israel (e.g. announcing the word of God in the synagogues where Israel is assembled) and then, when he is rejected he will go to the nations.

They continue on to Paphos (140 miles across Cyprus, on the west coast).

Sergius Paul and Elymas [(13:6)]

Elymas the Magician (Bar-Jesus) is a false prophet, a Jew. He is with the proconsul Sergius Paul, an intelligent man. Sergius Paul calls for Barnabas and Saul, seeking to hear the word of God. Elymas withstands them, *seeking to pervert the proconsul from the faith.*

Saul, *who is also Paul,* challenges Elymas. Will you not cease perverting the straight ways of the Lord? *You shall be blind, not observing the sun* UNTIL THE APPOINTED TIME. The procounsul believes, astonished at the teaching of the Lord.

> # This is a picture of the stubbornness of Israel, with the Word subsequently going to the nations.

Elymas, a Jew, seeks to stop the word of God from going to Sergius Paul, a Gentile. It seems that this single case is representative of the Jews and Gentiles as a whole. Paul will later say, *Callousness, in part, on Israel has come, until the complement of the nations may be entering* (Romans 11:25). Blindness came upon Elymas so that Sergius Paul of the nations might enter. But observe that this blindness is not permanent, but UNTIL THE APPOINTED TIME (in the case of Elymas) and UNTIL THE COMPLEMENT OF THE NATIONS MAY BE ENTERING (in the case of Israel as a whole).

Observe also ... when blindness comes to a Jew that salvation might come to a Gentile, we are told that Saul *is also Paul.* Saul is his Hebrew name. Paul is the Gentile name given to him by God. From this point on Saul will be referred to as Paul.

On to Perga, of Pamphylia (170 miles). John Mark departs from them and returns to Jerusalem.

> Could Mark's departure have been linked to Paul taking the word directly to a Gentile? When Paul prepares to leave on his second journey he will refuse to take John Mark along (Acts 15:37).

On to Antioch, Pisidia (90 miles to the north).

Paul addresses the Jews [13:14]

Paul is given a chance to speak in the synagogue. He addresses the *Israelites and those who are fearing God.*

To us was the word of this salvation dispatched. Being ignorant of Him and of the voices of the prophets which are read on every sabbath, they judged Him and they asked Pilate to have Him *dispatched.* But God roused Him from among the dead, and He was seen by those who are now His witnesses to the people.

We are bringing to you the evangel, a promise to the fathers, that God has fully fulfilled for our children in raising Jesus, as written in the second Psalm. David could not have been referring to himself, for his body saw decay. Through this One is being announced to you the *pardon* of sins, and from all from which you could not be justified in the law of Moses. In this One everyone who is believing is being *justified.*

> The message to Israel has always been PARDON from sins if there is repentance. Pardon is relieving one who is found guilty from the deserved sentence. But now we see JUSTIFICATION mentioned. To be justified is to be found just, or innocent. There is a big difference between being found innocent and being found guilty and pardoned.
>
> Matthew 18:23 is a parable concerning pardon. Here we see that pardon can be withdrawn if the required conditions are not met. When one is found justified, or innocent, there is nothing to be withdrawn.
>
> Note in the present text the word "and" linking the pardon of sins "and" justification. Paul is presenting two different things; pardon AND justification. Pardon has been presented before, but when Paul speaks of justification it is a new thing!

Beware that that which has been declared in the prophets may not be coming on you. "A work am I working in your days – a work which you should by no means be believing if anyone should be detailing it to you." (Habakkuk 1:5) Habakkuk is telling Israel that God will be raising up the Chaldeans, *a bitter and hasty nation,* to judge Israel.

> As God once used the uncircumcised Chaldeans to judge His people because of their rebellion, so also He will raise up the uncircumcised Gentiles if the Jews continue to reject Him.

Paul is invited back (13:42)

They ask Paul to speak again on the intervening sabbath. Upon leaving the synagogue many of the Jews and reverent proselytes follow Paul and Barnabas, who *persuaded them to remain in the grace of God.*

The Jews oppose Paul; and he turns to the nations (13:44)

On the coming sabbath almost the entire city is gathered to hear the word of the Lord. The Jews contradict the things spoken by Paul, blaspheming.

TO YOU FIRST *was it necessary that the word of God be spoken. Yet, since, in fact, you are thrusting it away, and are judging yourselves not worthy of* EONIAN LIFE, *lo we are turning to the nations. For thus the Lord has directed us: I have appointed Thee for a light of the nations; for Thee to be for salvation as far as the limits of the earth.*

The nations rejoice and glorify the word of the Lord, and believe, *whoever were set for life eonian.*

> Observe the pattern Paul uses. He goes first to the Jews: *To you first was it necessary that the word of God be spoken.* And when he is rejected he turns to the nations. Those of the nations who were *set for life eonian* believe.

The word of the Lord is carried thru the whole country, but the Jews spur on the reverent, respectable women, and the foremost ones of the city, and rouse up persecution for Paul and Barnabas. They eject them from their boundaries. Paul moves on to Iconium (80 miles southeast of Antioch).

CHAPTER 14

Paul in the synagogue in Iconium (14:1)

A vast multitude of both Jews and Greeks believe. Stubborn Jews provoke them against the brethren. They remain a considerable time, speaking boldly in the Lord. The Lord testifies to the word of His grace, granting signs and miracles to occur thru their hands. The city is divided between the Jews and the apostles. They are pelted with stones and flee.

On they go to the cities of Lycaonia; Lystra, Derbe and the surrounding area; bringing the evangel. Lystra (18 miles southwest of Iconium) is the home of Timothy.

A healing; and an opportunity to testify to the nations (14:8)

Paul perceives that a lame man has faith to be *saved*, and he heals the man. They think that Paul and Barnabas are gods; Hermes and Zeus.

> Here *saved* is simply *healed*, one might say saved from death. As stated previously, when we see the word *saved* we must always ask, "saved from what?" Saved or salvation does not always mean the same thing, and we must always examine the context.

We also are men, of like emotions as you, bringing the evangel to you *to turn you back from these vain things to the living God.* He makes heaven and the earth and all that is in them. In past generations He leaves all the nations to go their way, although not without the testimony of good acts; giving showers from heaven and fruit-bearing seasons, filling our hearts with nourishment and gladness.

> Paul grasps this opportunity to *gently* correct ("we are not gods") and to share a word concerning the living God.

The Jews follow Paul and stone him (14:19)

Jews from Antioch and Iconium persuade the throngs, stone Paul, and drag him outside of the city thinking he is dead. Surrounded by the disciples, Paul rises and enters the city.

> This occurs in the Summer of 43 A.D.

On they go to Derbe. They evangelize the city and make a considerable number of disciples.

> Derbe is southeast of Lystra, on the way to Tarsus. They are now within 100 miles of Tarsus; 200 miles of Antioch.

They backtrack and return into Lystra, Iconium and Antioch.

Establishing the disciples (14:22)

They entreat them to remain in the faith. *Through many afflictions must we be entering into the kingdom of God.* Elders are selected for the ecclesia. Praying and fasting, they commit them to the Lord

A word about "church organization." As we study Acts, observe the simplicity within the ecclesia. There is no bureaucracy; just believers living their lives in simplicity and meeting the needs of one another, as the evangel is proclaimed and as new believers enter the fold. Yes there is a structure. Here we see that "elders" are selected to lead the ecclesia. But the structure is minimal and there are no membership vows, articles of religion, or bureaucracies. Much of what we find within the church today (any denomination) are traditions of men. Let us pay close attention to "the church" (ecclesia) as we find it in the Word of God.

They proceed to Pisidia, Pamphylia, Perga, Attalia; and they then return to Antioch.

This first journey took roughly two years; 48-49 A.D.

Gathering the ecclesia in Antioch (14:27)

They inform them of what God does with them, and that He opens to the nations a door of faith. They tarry no brief time with the disciples

CHAPTER 15

Judaizers follow after Paul (15:1)

Some come from Judea, teaching the brethren they must be circumcised to be saved. They prescribe that Paul, Barnabas and some others are to go up to the apostles and elders in Jerusalem concerning this question.

Did Paul "submit" to Jerusalem? It would seem at first that Paul was *required* to appear before the apostles and elders in Jerusalem to defend his position. But when we read Paul's account in Galatians 2:2 we see that he went voluntarily, *in accord with a revelation,* and there he *submitted to them the evangel which I am heralding among the nations, yet privately to those of repute, lest somehow I should be racing or ran for naught.* Paul was not subservient to the leaders in Jerusalem. He was an apostle in his own right, chosen by God as His instrument to be a light to the nations.

> # To Jerusalem (15:1-35 – Gal 2:10)
> # 50 A.D.

They travel to Phoenicia and to Samaria, where they share concerning the "turning about" of the nations. And they arrive in Jerusalem.

The council at Jerusalem (15:4)

They are received by the ecclesia, apostles and elders. They inform them of what God does with them. Some from the sect of the Pharisees who believe rise up, insisting they must be circumcised and must keep the law of Moses. Peter replies: God testifies to them (Gentiles), giving the holy spirit as to us. He discriminates in nothing between us and them. He cleanses their hearts by faith. Why are you trying to place on them a yoke which neither our fathers nor we are strong enough to bear? Thru the grace of the Lord Jesus we are believing, to be saved in a manner even as they.

> Peter notes that salvation is not found by observing the law, as the Jews had found it impossible to do since the time the law was given. Salvation, for Jew and Gentile alike, comes thru believing. Belief comes thru the grace of the Lord Jesus, and salvation follows belief.

Barnabas and Paul tell of the signs and miracles God does among the nations thru them. James then addresses the group, reminding them how Simeon (Peter) tells how God first visits the nations to obtain out of them a people for His name. This agrees with the words of the prophets (Amos 9:11,12). Wherefore *I decide* not to harass those from the nations, but write a letter to them; to be abstaining from ceremonial pollution with idols, and prostitution, and what is strangled, and blood. For Moses has those heralding him, being read on every sabbath in the synagogues.

> James' decision? While Peter addressed the council, it appears that James had authority to make the final decision on behalf of the Jewish ecclesia (15:19). While Peter advised that no yoke be placed upon the Gentile believers, it seems that James' decision was a bit of a compromise. While he basically agreed with Peter, still he took a few things from the law and insisted upon them as *essentials.* His reasoning is given in 15:21, so as not to create a stumbling block for those that were hearing the law of Moses proclaimed on every sabbath. Still, James declared certain "essential" portions from the law to be added to the grace of the Lord. While we understand James' reasoning, was he correct in imposing these *essentials* upon the Gentile believers? We do not read that this was God's decision; it was decided by James. We cannot assume

that James was infallible, or that his decision was correct in this instance.

The apostles, elders and the whole ecclesia agree, choosing men to send along with Paul and Barnabas. They send Judas (called Bar-Sabbas) and Silas. A letter is sent with these representatives; not to be placing one more burden on believers except these essentials; to be abstaining from idol sacrifices, and blood, and what is strangled, and prostitution. They return to Antioch.

The letter is received in Antioch (15:30)

They rejoice at the consolation. Judas and Silas (prophets) entreat and establish the brethren. Paul and Barnabas remain in Antioch, teaching and bringing the evangel of the word of the Lord.

The Second Journey (15:36 – 18:23)
51-54 A.D. (3 years)

Visiting every city (15:36)

They visit the brethren at every city in which was announced the word of the Lord, to see how they are faring. Paul refuses to take John Mark along, creating a disturbance with Barnabas. Barnabas takes John Mark and heads for Cyprus, while Paul chooses Silas to accompany him.

> DOES THIS DISPLAY A TRANSITION IN PAUL'S MINISTRY? Paul had been travelling with Barnabas (a fellow Jew), but because of the disagreement over John Mark, Barnabas departs from Paul. Paul's new companion, Silas, is a Gentile. Could this be symbolic, following the Jerusalem council, of Paul's gradual movement from his ministry to the Jews toward his ministry to the Gentiles? Paul is the apostle to the Gentiles, but remember his commission was to both Jew and Gentile (Acts 9:15) and he has typically gone first into the synagogues.

They travel to Syria, Cilicia, Derbe and Lystra.

CHAPTER 16

Timothy joins Paul (16:1)

Timothy is the son of a believing Jewish woman and a Greek father. Paul circumcises Timothy *because of the Jews who are in those places, for they all were aware that his father belonged to the Greeks.*

> Paul continues to maintain that circumcision is not necessary, but knowing that he is still going into the synagogues he wishes to remove any possible stumbling block. (See Paul's message concerning the use of freedoms that could be stumbling blocks to others in 1 Corinthians 8:9ff.)

Delivering the Jerusalem decrees (16:4)

As they pass thru the cities, they give relay the decrees to maintain which had been decided upon by the apostles and elders in Jerusalem. The ecclesias are stable in the faith and superabound in number day by day.

> DID PAUL AGREE WITH THE DECREE? The decision by James at the Jerusalem council and the resulting epistle being circulated among the ecclesias was, at least to James, a "decree" which delineated certain "essentials" for the brethren. Paul seems to go along with the decree, but it is clear from his writings that he did not consider these things to be "essentials" as it pertains to salvation.
>
> Paul does say that to the Jews he became <u>as</u> a Jew (1 Corinthians 9:20) to be gaining Jews. But while the Jerusalem decree required abstaining from idol sacrifices, Paul points out in 1 Corinthians 8 that there is really nothing wrong with eating meat that was tied to idol sacrifices. But he does go on to say, *Beware lest somehow this right of yours may become a stumbling block to the weak.* (1 Corinthians 8:9) If one exercises his freedom, and this results in injury to others, he is *sinning against brethren* and *sinning against Christ.* (1 Corinthians 8:12)
>
> It seems from Paul's writings that he would not agree that the items in the Jerusalem Decree were "essentials," except in cases where exercising freedoms would cause a stumbling block to others.

Their steps are directed by the spirit (16:6)

They travel to Phrygia, to the Galatian province, and about Mysia. They are forbidden by the holy spirit to speak the word in Asia. They try to go to Bithynia and the spirit of Jesus does not let them. They proceed to Troas.

> Observe these places to which Paul was prohibited from going. These are the places Peter mentioned in his first letter which was addressed to the chosen expatriates of the dispersion of Pontus, Galatia, Cappadocia, the province of Asia and Bythinia. It seems that God's plan at this time was to allow Peter to proclaim the evangel of the Circumcision to the expatriate Jews in these areas, while Paul went to the nations in other places to proclaim the evangel of the Uncircumcision.

Paul's Macedonian vision (16:9)

They seek to come out to Macedonia, deducing that God has called them to bring the evangel to them. They journey on to Samothrace, Neapolis, and Philippi (the foremost city of that part of Macedonia; a colony).

Lydia believes (16:13)

Paul goes outside the gate beside a river where they expect to find a group gathered for prayer. They speak to the women who are coming together. Lydia, a woman who sold purple in Thyatira is among them. The Lord opens up her heart to heed what is spoken by Paul. She and her household are baptized.

> Observe that it is not Lydia's free will that enables her to believe the message spoken by Paul. The Lord opened her heart to heed the message.

Paul casts a spirit from a diviner (16:16)

A woman (a maid) follows Paul, saying: These men are slaves of God most high, announcing to you a way of salvation. She does this for many days. Exasperated, Paul casts out the spirit. But this spirit had brought a vast income to the woman's master. Seeing their income is now gone, they take Paul and Silas to the magistrates; claiming they are announcing customs that Romans are not permitted to assent to. Paul and Silas are cast into jail.

Paul and Silas in jail (16:22)

At midnight they are praying and singing hymns to God. A great quake occurs. The prison doors open and their bonds are slacked. The warden asks Paul, What must I do to be saved? *Believe on the Lord Jesus, and you shall be saved, you and your household.* They speak to him the word of the Lord, with all in his house, and they are baptized.

Paul points out that he and Silas are uncondemned Romans, yet lashed in public. He demands that they come and lead them out. On they journey to Lydia, Amphipolis, Apollonia, and Thessalonica (75 miles from Philippi).

CHAPTER 17

In the synagogues at Thessalonica (17:1)

As was Paul's custom, he enters the synagogue and on three sabbaths he *argues* with them from the scriptures that Christ must suffer and rise from the dead, and that Jesus is the Christ. Some are persuaded; a vast multitude of the reverent Greeks and not a few of the foremost women.

> Paul addresses Jews and those that had accepted the Jewish faith. Note that this occurred in the synagogue, a gathering place for Jews. Paul argues from the scriptures. He has not yet received new revelation not found in the scriptures. He will later receive new truth thru revelation, and he will address the Body of Christ. But for now he continues to address the Jews.

The Jews gather a mob. Not finding Paul, they drag Jason and some brethren to the city magistrates, claiming they are espousing things contravening the decrees of Caesar and saying there is a different king, Jesus. Jason and the others are released after paying bail. They travel to Berea (45 miles from Thessalonica).

Berea (17:10)

Paul goes into the synagogue of the Jews. The Bereans are more noble than those in Thessalonica; they search the Scriptures. Many believe, including not a few of the respectable Greeks.

Jews from Thessalonica come and agitate the throngs. Paul is sent away by the brethren, while Silas and Timothy remain behind.

> Observe the pattern. Paul proclaims to the Jews. Many believe. But then others follow behind to agitate the people and turn them away from Paul.

Athens; Paul appears before the Areopagus (17:15)

Paul's spirit is incited, beholding the city is idol-ridden. He argues in the synagogue and in the market daily with those happening along. Epicurean and Stoic philosophers lead Paul to the Areopagus asking, Can we know what this new teaching is?

Paul addresses the Areopagus. I behold how religious you are, noting the inscription: "To an Unknowable God." This One am I announcing to you; the God Who makes the world and all that is in it. He is not dwelling in temples made by hands. He is not attended by human hands and is not requiring anything. He gives to all life and breath and all. He makes out of one every nation of mankind. He specifies the setting of the seasons and the bounds of their dwelling, for them to be seeking God. Not far from each of us is He inherent. In Him we are living and moving. As your poets declare: For of that race also are we. We ought not to be inferring that the Divine is like gold, silver, stone, a sculpture of art and human sentiment.

Condoning the times of ignorance, God is now charging all to repent. He assigns a day to be judging the inhabited earth by the Man Whom He specifies, raising Him from the dead. When hearing of the resurrection, they jeer. But some ask to hear Paul again, and some join Paul.

> Paul's approach before the Areopagus is an excellent model for us! When Paul went into the synagogues, he argued with the Jews from the Scriptures. Why? Because the Jews respected the Scriptures and accepted that they were a revelation from God.
>
> But the Gentiles did not have the same view of Scripture. And here, before the Areopagus, Paul does not argue from the Scriptures. As a matter of fact when Paul does use a direct quote in support of his argument, the quote comes from Gentile poetry and not from Scripture.
>
> Furthermore, Paul does not condemn his audience as pagans, even though his spirit was *incited* when he first arrived in Athens when he saw the many idols. Instead, Paul builds bridges to his audience. He even compliments them, beholding how "religious" they are. Paul was Christ's Ambassador, and he tailored his approach depending on his audience. *To all have I become all, that I should undoubtedly be saving some.* (1 Corinthians 9:22)

CHAPTER 18

In Corinth (18:1)

He remains with Aquila and Priscilla, fellow tentmakers, and works with them. He argues *in the synagogue* every sabbath and persuades both Jews and Greeks. Silas and Timothy arrive from Macedonia. Paul is *pressed in the word*, certifying TO THE JEWS that Jesus is the Christ.

> THE EDICT OF CLAUDIUS: Acts 18:2 tells us that Aquila and Priscilla departed from Rome due to Claudius prescribing that all the Jews depart. The earliest dating of the edict of Claudius is by Orosius, a 5th century historian, who states that the edict was issued in the ninth year of Claudius (49-50 AD). Orosius claims the date comes from Josephus, but there is no mention in Josephus' works.

---

1 Thessalonians is probably written here.
(50 – 52 A.D.)
Shortly after Paul's arrival in Corinth.

To the nations (18:6)

The Jews resist and blaspheme, and Paul tells them: FROM NOW ON I SHALL GO TO THE NATIONS.

Paul enters the house of Titus Justus who is revering God, and whose house is adjacent to the synagogue. Crispis, chief of the synagogue, believes, with his household. Many Corinthians believe and are baptized.

The Lord promises to protect Paul (18:9)

The Lord tells Paul, Fear not, but be speaking. I am with you and no one shall mistreat you because there are many people of Mine in this city. Paul remains there for 18 months, teaching the word of God.

---

2 Thessalonians is probably written here.
(52 – 53 A.D.)

Gallio refuses to judge Paul [(18:12)]

Paul is accused of inducing men to revere God aside from the law. Gallio replies, If there are questions concerning a word, and names, and a law of yours; you see to it. I am not intending to be a judge of these. They beat Sosthenes, the chief of the synagogue.

> The Gallio inscription is the most certain point in dating Paul's life. According to the inscription at Delphi, Gallio was procounsel during the 12th year of Claudius' tribunal power and after his 26th proclamation as Emperor. The 27th proclamation was in August 52. Procounsels normally took office in mid-Summer. Gallio probably took office in mid-Summer 52, but it may have been mid-Summer 53 allowing time for the procounsel to refer some questions to the Emperor as the inscription mentions he did. Paul probably appeared before Gallio shortly after he assumed office, and probably toward the end of Paul's 18 months in the city.

They travel on to Syria, Ephesus (where Paul *argues with the Jews* in the synagogue), Caesarea and Antioch.

Galatians possibly written here.
(54 A.D. According to the early theory)

The Third Journey [(18:23 – 21:16)]
54-58 A.D. (4 years)

They travel to the Galatian province and to Phrygia; *establishing all the disciples.*

> Here we see Paul's purpose, at least in part, for this third journey; to *establish* the disciples that had previously become believers.

Apollos is corrected by Priscilla and Aquila [(18:24)]

Apollos is a scholarly man, able in the scriptures. He is instructed in the way of the Lord, fervent in spirit, and he speaks and teaches accurately what concerns Jesus. BUT HE IS VERSED ONLY IN THE BAPTISM OF JOHN.

Priscilla and Aquila expound the way of God to him more accurately. He strenuously and thoroughly confutes the Jews in public, exhibiting thru the scriptures that Jesus is the Christ.

> Apollos was teaching *accurately* concerning Jesus. He did have the facts right, but he was only versed in John's baptism and not in truths revealed thereafter.

Here we see a great illustration of the need to "rightly divide" the Scriptures!

> Many today are preaching the message of John the Baptist; Repent, for the kingdom is near. That is certainly an accurate message, as these words were declared by Jesus Himself and by His apostles. But they were declared TO ISRAEL (not the nations) and they pertained to the specific day in which the words were uttered. Let us not, within the Body of Christ today, be versed only in the baptism of John! God has moved on from those truths. No longer water baptism; but baptism of the spirit. No longer things of the flesh; but spiritual things. No longer GOING to the synagogues on the sabbaths but BEING the Body of Christ in all places and circumstances. Let us be sure to distinguish between Biblical truths spoken to Israel in a previous era and Biblical truths intended for us today.

They proceed to Ephesus.

CHAPTER 19

Disciples that had not received the spirit (19:1)

There are about twelve men who had not obtained the holy spirit upon believing. They had not even heard there is a holy spirit. They tell Paul they were baptized *into John's baptism*. They are then baptized in the name of the Lord Jesus. At the placing of Paul's hands on them, the holy spirit comes on them and they speak languages and prophesy.

> Let us not read too much into this. It appears in this instance that evidence of the holy spirit is speaking in languages and prophesying. This was true in the "Pentecostal era" of which we read here, but God works differently from one era to the next. Paul will later speak concerning tongues and prophesying, and he will tell us these are temporary gifts that will pass. More on this later when we review Paul's letters.

All in the province of Asia hear (19:8)

In the synagogue Paul speaks boldly for three months, arguing and persuading that which concerns the kingdom of God. Some are hardened and stubborn, saying evil things concerning *the way*. Paul withdraws and *severs the disciples*, arguing day by day in the school of Tyrannus for two years so all in the province of Asia hear the word of the Lord. God does powerful deeds thru Paul.

> Paul continues his custom, going first to the synagogue. When he is rejected he goes to the Gentiles. But he has not yet ceased going first to the Jews.

Probable letter to the Corinthians written here.
(This letter probably lost – see 1 Corinthians 5:9)

Sons of Sceva (19:13)

Some wandering Jews, exorcists, name the name of Jesus over those having wicked spirits; adjuring *by the Jesus whom Paul is heralding*. Seven sons of Sceva are doing this, and a demon-possessed man leaps on them. Naked and wounded they escape from the house.

> There was danger in calling on the power of God by those not commissioned to employ it.

Many believe and burn their evil scrolls (19:17)

Mightily the word of the Lord grows and is strong.

> # 1 Corinthians is probably written here.
> ### (Spring, 57 A.D.)

Paul plans to go to Jerusalem (19:21)

He travels to Macedonia and then to Achaia, saying: After coming to be there (Jerusalem) I must see Rome also. He attends to the province of Asia, sending Timothy and Erastus to Macedonia.

Demetrius the Silversmith (19:23)

Demetrius stirs up a group against Paul, pointing out that he is hurting their business in all of Asia, associated with the temples of Artemis. They point out that the sanctuary of the great goddess Artemis is being reckoned nothing. The mob becomes full of fury; "Great is Artemis of the Ephesians." They apprehend Paul's associates, Gaius and Aristarchus. The *ECCLESIA* is in confusion. The majority is not aware why they had come together. They unite on Alexander, one of the throng, and he speaks to the mob.

You must possess composure and not commit anything rash. These men are not despoilers of the sanctuary, nor blasphemers of our goddess. If any has a charge against them, court sessions are to be held, and there are proconsuls. In the legal *ECCLESIA* will it be explained. And Alexander dismisses *THE ECCLESIA*.

> Despite the fury of the moment, consider the tact used by Alexander to diffuse the mob. Alexander calmly lays out a very logical argument that is successful in diffusing the situation and dismissing the mob.
>
> *Ecclesia* is translated "church" in most every case in our modern translations. Here we see *ecclesia* used three times where it certainly cannot mean "church." (Acts 19:32,40,41) Even the modern translators use another word here. *Ecclesia* simply means a group of people "called-out" from a larger group (ek = out; klesia = called). *Ecclesia* does not always mean the same thing, as is clearly displayed in the current example. We cannot, therefore, assume the *ecclesia* (church) Jesus spoke of in the Gospels, or the *ecclesia* (church) referred to early in Acts (which was exclusively Jewish), is the same as the *ecclesia* (church) Paul later speaks of. When we read of the *ecclesia* in God's Word, we

should always ask <u>which</u> *ecclesia* (which group of people) is being referred to. We cannot simply take all cases where *ecclesia* is used and use this as the model for our present-day "church."

CHAPTER 20

Further travels (20:1)

They travel to Macedonia and then Greece, where they spend three months. The Jews plot against Paul and he plans to return thru Macedonia.

> # 2 Corinthians probably written here. (Fall, 57 A.D.)
>
> # Galatians probably written here.
> (Winter, 57 A.D. according to the late theory)
>
> # Romans probably written here. (Spring, 58 A.D.)

On to Philippi. After the days of Unleavened Bread they journey to Troas where they stay for seven days.

> Paul was in Philippi during the days of Unleavened Bread. He left for Troas hoping to arrive in Jerusalem by Pentecost. By calculating from the number of days mentioned in Acts 20:6-7 this would place the slaying of the Passover lamb that year on a Thursday. According to Ramsay, Gerhardt, and Michaelis this would be 57, 58 or 56 A.D. respectively.

Eutychus falls from a window (20:7)

Paul argues with them, being about to be off on the morrow. He prolongs the word unto midnight. Eutychus, a young man, falls asleep and falls from the third story. Paul tells them: Make no tumult, *for his soul is in him.*

Traveling toward Jerusalem (20:13)

They travel thru Assos, Mitylene and are abreast of Chios. They continue to Samos, Miletus, and they sail by Ephesus wanting to be in Jerusalem on Pentecost.

Paul addresses the elders from Ephesus (20:17)

From Miletus, Paul calls for *the elders of the ecclesia*. Under no circumstances did I shrink from informing you of anything that was expedient, teaching you in public and at your homes; certifying to both Jews and Greeks repentance toward God, and faith toward our Lord Jesus Christ. Now, bound in spirit, I am going to Jerusalem. The holy spirit certifies that bonds and afflictions remain for me. But I am not making my soul precious to myself, till I should be perfecting my career and the dispensation which I got from the Lord Jesus, TO CERTIFY THE EVANGEL OF THE GRACE OF GOD.

You shall be seeing my face no longer. Under no circumstances do I shrink from informing you of *the entire counsel of God*. The holy spirit appointed you SUPERVISORS to be SHEPHERDING the ecclesia of God. When I am gone wolves will enter among you, not sparing the flocklet. From among yourselves will arise men speaking perverse things to pull away disciples after themselves. Watch! I am committing you to God and to the word of His grace which is able to edify and give the enjoyment of an allotment among all who have been hallowed.

> Here we get a glimpse at the organization of the ecclesia. We have seen that "elders" were appointed as leaders within the ecclesia. Now Paul reminds the elders that they are "supervisors" that have been appointed by the holy spirit, and that they are to be "shepherding" the ecclesia of God. (20:28) No huge bureaucratic structure. No traditions of men. No fancy buildings. Here is the early church, led by elders who are appointed not by men, but by the holy spirit, and who *supervise* and *shepherd* the ecclesia.

I covet no one's silver or gold or vesture. These hands subserve my needs, and of those with me. Thus toiling, you must be supporting the infirm. Remember the words of the Lord Jesus, Happy is it to give rather than to get.

> The believers are to work to support themselves and also the infirm.

CHAPTER 21

Traveling toward Jerusalem (21:1)

They travel to Coos, Rhodes, Patara, Syria, Tyre, Ptolemais, and Caesarea. There they enter the house of Philip the evangelist. Agabus prophesies that the Jews in Jerusalem will bind Paul.

I hold myself in readiness, not only to be bound, but to die also in Jerusalem for the name of the Lord Jesus.

In Jerusalem [(21:15)]

Paul unfolds each of the things which God does among the nations thru his dispensation. They say to Paul, Tens of thousands there are among the Jews WHO HAVE BELIEVED, and all are inherently ZEALOUS FOR THE LAW. They hear that you teach the Jews apostasy from Moses. A multitude must come together, for they will hear you have come. Go with these four men having a vow on them; be purified with them; all will know what they have heard of you is nothing; that you are observing the elements and you yourself are maintaining the law. Paul does as they instruct him.

> # Consider Paul's enemies as he enters Jerusalem!

As Paul sets foot in Jerusalem (58 A.D.) we can understand that the non-believing Jews would be his enemies. They objected to Paul's preaching in the name of Jesus. But Paul has other enemies in Jerusalem as well. In 21:20 Paul is told that the *Jews who have believed* and who are *zealous for the law* are in an outrage over his teachings. As Paul enters Jerusalem, then, it appears that nearly ALL are against him.

Furthermore, this should lead us to ask; at this point is there a single *ecclesia* of God or are there two? We read in 21:20 that there are the Jewish believers that expect Paul to observe "the elements" and maintain "the law." But they did not expect this of the Gentile believers. Of the Gentiles they expected only that they guard themselves from idol sacrifice, blood, what is strangled, and prostitution. (21:25) In modern translations the word *ecclesia* is simply translated "church" as if there is only one homogenized group. But here we see that there were actually two distinct groups; the Jewish *ecclesia* and the Gentile *ecclesia;* and there were different expectations for each. Remember Paul's comment in Galatians 2:7; that he had been entrusted with the *evangel of the Uncircumcision* while Peter was entrusted with the *evangel of the*

Circumcision. There were two evangels, for two different groups; and this accounts for the friction between Paul and the Jewish believers.

This being the case, we must be very careful to observe, when reading the epistles (letters) in the Word of God, WHO they are written to. Peter and the others of the Twelve were writing to the Jewish believers relative to the *evangel of the Circumcision.* Paul was writing to the Jewish believers, but also the Gentiles that came into the *ecclesia* by faith (Body of Christ) in response to his *evangel of the Uncircumcision.* We have no right to mix the two, or as Gentiles to claim things directed to the Jewish believers!

What about Paul's concession? It appears that Paul is here conceding to the Jewish elders in Jerusalem, but from Paul's writings we know that he does not consider observance of the law a necessity. Still, to the Jews Paul is willing to become as a Jew, to be gaining Jews. (1 Corinthians 9:20)

Paul is apprehended (21:27)

Jews from Asia apprehend Paul, saying: This is the man who is teaching all men everywhere against the people, and the law, and this holy place. He led Greeks into the sanctuary and has contaminated this holy place.

As they seek to kill Paul, soldiers and centurions run down to them. They bind Paul and lead him into the citadel. Paul gets permission to speak to the people.

CHAPTER 22

Paul addresses the crowd (22:1)

Hearing Paul speak in Hebrew, they become more quiet. I am a Jew, born in Tarsus, and reared in this city at the feet of Gamaliel. Trained according to the strictness of the law and being inherently zealous for God as you are today, I persecute this *way* to death. Drawing near to Damascus, out of heaven a light flashed and a voice announced: I am Jesus the Nazarene, Whom you are persecuting. The God of our fathers fixes upon you beforehand to know His will, and to be acquainted with the Just One. You shall be His witness to all men of what you see and hear. I shall be delegating you afar to the nations.

They listen until this word, and they raise their voice against him, saying it is not befitting for him to live. The captain orders Paul to be led into the citadel to be interrogated and scourged. Paul asks, Is it allowed you to scourge a Roman man, uncondemned? Learning that Paul is a Roman citizen, the captain is afraid. Paul is loosed, and the chief priests and Sanhedrin are ordered to come together to know the certainty of that of which Paul is being accused.

> It is interesting that they did not object when he proclaims to them that concerning Jesus. Instead they object when Paul says, "I am going to the nations." The Jews who had gathered could very well have included those of the Jewish ecclesia that believed in Jesus, but their objection is that Paul is going to the Gentiles. Note once again Acts 21:20 where we see that many Jews "who have believed" were opposed to Paul, because they were zealous for the law.

CHAPTER 23

Paul addresses the Sanhedrin (23:1)

You are sitting to judge me according to the law, and illegally are you ordering me to be beaten. Knowing that both Sadducees and Pharisees are present, Paul says, A Pharisee, son of Pharisees, am I. Concerning the expectation and resurrection of the dead am I being judged.

There arises a commotion between the Pharisees and Sadducees, for the Sadducees are saying there is no resurrection, nor messenger, nor spirit; while the Pharisees are avowing both. Some of the scribes of the Pharisees say they find no evil in Paul. Fearing for Paul's life the captain orders the troops to snatch him out of their midst, to lead him into the citadel. The Lord tells Paul: Courage! For as you certify that which concerns Me in Jerusalem, thus you must testify in Rome also.

The plot to kill Paul (23:12)

More than 40 Jews vow not to eat or drink until they kill Paul. They ask the chief priests and elders to have Paul led into an ambush. When the captain learns of the plot he arranges to escort Paul in the night with heavy guard to Caesarea; to the governor Felix. The captain writes to governor Felix: Him I found being indicted concerning questions of their law yet having nothing deserving death or bonds. They travel on to Caesarea.

Felix agrees to give Paul a hearing (23:34)

Felix plans to conduct a hearing when Paul's accusers arrive. In the meantime he is guarded in Herod's praetorium.

CHAPTER 24

Hearing before Felix [(24:1)]

Annanias (chief priest), some elders, and an orator (Tertullus) arrive. Tertullus speaks: We find this man a pestilence and stirrer of insurrections among all the Jews on the inhabited earth, who tries to profane the sanctuary also.

Paul responds: I went to worship in Jerusalem not more than twelve days ago, and they did not find me arguing with anyone; not in the synagogues nor the city. Nor can they present evidence to you for that which they are accusing me. According to 'the way,' which they are terming a sect, I am offering divine service to God; believing all that is written according to the law and the prophets, having an expectation in God which these themselves also are anticipating; that there will be a resurrection which is impending for both the just and the unjust. I am exerting myself also to have a conscience which is no stumbling block toward God and men, continually.

Felix makes them postpone to become acquainted more exactly with that which concerns "the way." When captain Lysias comes down he plans to investigate these affairs. Paul is kept, having his ease, and no one is prevented from serving him.

Felix continues to hold Paul. He comes with his wife Drusilla, a Jewess, and sends for Paul. He hears him concerning the faith in Christ Jesus. They argue concerning righteousness, self-control, and the impending judgment. Felix tells Paul he will call for him again. Expecting that Paul will give him money he sends for Paul frequently and talks with him.

Festus succeeds Felix [(24:27)]

The chief priests and foremost of the Jews inform Festus against Paul. Asking Paul to be brought to Jerusalem, they plan an ambush along the way to kill him. Festus invites Paul's accusers to come to Caesarea.

> Eusebius dates Festus' arrival in Nero's second year (between Sept 56 and Sept 57). Many scholars have preferred a later date for the commencement of Festus' procuratorship (59-60 A.D.).

CHAPTER 25

Hearing before Festus [(25:6)]

The Jews make many and heavy charges against Paul which they are not strong enough to demonstrate. Paul responds, Neither against the law of the Jews, nor against the sanctuary, nor against Caesar did I any sin. Festus, wanting to curry favor with the Jews, asks Paul if he is willing to go to Jerusalem to be judged there. Paul responds, At the dais of Caesar I must be judged. If I have committed anything deserving of death, I am not refusing to die. To Caesar am I appealing. Festus tells Paul, To Caesar shall you go.

King Agrippa comes to Caesarea (25:13)

Festus submits Paul's affairs to the king, stating that the people had not brought one charge of the wicked things he had suspected, but had questions concerning their own religion against him; and things concerning a certain Jesus who has died and who Paul is alleging to be alive. Paul has appealed to be kept for the Imperial investigation. Agrippa tells Festus that he intends to hear Paul.

CHAPTER 26

Hearing before King Agrippa (26:1)

Paul makes his defense. I am happy to make a defense before you as you are versed in the customs and questions of the Jews. In expectation of the promise which came by God to our fathers I stand being judged, to which our twelve-tribed people, earnestly offering divine service, is expecting to attain. Why is it unbelievable to you if God is rousing the dead?

Paul tells of his Damascus road experience; that he is to be a deputy and a witness, commissioned to open their eyes and to turn them about from darkness to light and from the authority of Satan to God; for them to get a pardon of sins and an allotment among those who have been hallowed by faith that is in Christ.

Paul reports how he responded to this experience. First in Damascus, and then in Jerusalem, and the entire province of Judea, and to the nations, I reported that they are to be repenting and turning back to God, engaging in acts worthy of repentance. I say nothing outside of what both the prophets and Moses speak of impending occurrences.

Festus interjects, You are mad, Paul. Paul replies, Not mad but making declarations of truth and sanity. The King is adept concerning these things. King Agrippa, are you believing the prophets? I am aware that you are believing. Agrippa asks Paul, Briefly are you persuading me, to make me a Christian? Paul replies: May I ever wish to God, that, briefly as well as greatly, not only you but also all who are hearing me today, become such a kind as I am also, outside of these bonds.

They agree that Paul has done nothing deserving of death or bonds, and that he could have been released if he had not appealed to Caesar.

CHAPTER 27

The trip to Rome (27:1)

They travel thru Sidon, where Paul is permitted to go to friends for care, and then Myra of Lycia, and the Ideal Harbors near Lasea.

A considerable time had elapsed, and sailing was already hazardous. Paul predicts that sailing will be with damage and much forfeit, not only of the lading and the ship, but of *our souls also*. The ship is caught in a hurricane. Paul tells them not one soul will be cast away, as reported to him by a messenger. There were 276 in the ship.

CHAPTER 28

Shipwrecked at Melita (28:1)

The barbarians kindle a fire and take them in. A viper bites Paul, but he does not die. They say he is a god.

The shipwreck occurred in 60 A.D.

The father of Publius is healed (28:7)

Others on the island having infirmities come and are cured.

To Rome (28:11)

They travel thru Syracuse, Rhegium, and Puteoli; and they arrive in Rome. Paul meets with the brethren who had come. He is permitted to remain by himself, together with the soldier who guarded him.

Paul calls for the foremost of the Jews (28:17)

Paul calls together those who are foremost of the Jews. *Because of the expectation of Israel this chain is about me.*

The Jews say they have received no report concerning Paul, or anything wicked concerning him. They ask to hear what Paul has to say. On a set day, more come to him in the lodging and Paul expounds from morning till dusk concerning Jesus, both from the law of Moses and the prophets.

Some are persuaded, yet others disbelieve. There being disagreements, they are dismissed. Paul tells them: The holy spirit speaks thru Isaiah to your fathers. You will be hearing but not understanding. You will be observing but not perceiving. For stoutened is the heart of this people.

Let it be known to you, then, that **TO THE NATIONS** *was dispatched this salvation of God, and they will hear.*

To the nations was dispatched this salvation of God!

This is the same passage from Isaiah that Jesus quoted in Matthew 13:14 as the kingdom evangel was being rejected and He began to speak to the masses only using parables. After the King Himself was rejected (crucified) we read throughout Acts that the kingdom evangel is again proclaimed, and again rejected. Several times Paul has said he would go to the Gentiles, and he then did so. Paul never stopped, however, going to the Jews as well.

Now, however, the Acts of the Apostles has come to a close. We read once again that because of the "stoutened heart" of the Jewish people, salvation is going to the Gentiles. Paul continues to herald the kingdom of God to the end (28:31), but we read his assessment of Israel in Romans 11:25; *Callousness, in part, on Israel has come, until the complement of the nations may be entering. And thus all Israel shall be saved!* In other words; the coming of the Kingdom upon the earth, to Israel, is postponed, while God's salvation now goes to the nations.

This is a turning point!

Consider; Peter had pleaded in Acts 3 with the *men of Israel* to *turn again* in order that Christ might be sent (3:12-21). Now Paul declares, using the words of Isaiah, that stubborn Israel's eyes would be closed lest they should turn again (28:25-27). In Acts 13 we read that it was to Israel that the Word of salvation was sent (13:26,40). But now we read that the salvation of God is sent unto the Gentiles (28:28). And lastly, Paul tells us here that it is for the hope of Israel he had been imprisoned (28:20). But in a later revelation we are told he was the prisoner of Jesus Christ for the Gentiles (Ephesians 3:1-3). All of this points to the fact that here, at the end of Acts, is a turning point. Always the word had gone to Israel; but now it will go to the Gentiles.

Paul remains in Rome for two years [(28:30)]

Paul welcomes all those coming to him; heralding the kingdom of God and teaching that which concerns the Lord Jesus Christ with all boldness, unforbidden.

Whereas in 28:23 Paul proclaimed *the law and the prophets*, after this final rejection by the Jews there is no similar mention; but only the kingdom of God. Paul would always go first to Israel, and only to the nations as he was rejected. Now, with this final rejection, the stage is set for Paul's proclamations concerning the Body of Christ, with no preference to Israel. We see the higher truths revealed to Paul in his prison epistles which were written later in his ministry.

Paul's Captivities in Rome

It is commonly thought that Paul endured two captivities in Rome prior to his death. What follows is based on historical writings and tradition apart from the Scriptures themselves.

First captivity in Rome

Colossians probably written here. (61 or 62 A.D.)

Ephesians probably written here. (61 or 62 A.D.)

Philemon probably written here. (62 or 63 A.D.)

Philippians probably written here. (63 A.D.)

Between captivities

Paul tells of his expectation to be released (Philippians 1:23-27; 2:24; Philemon 22). We see hints of his possible travels in Romans, Philemon, Colossians and Philippians:

✓ Philippi (Philippians 1:26; 2:24)

✓ Colossae (Philemon 22)

> Personnel in the ecclesia at Colossae included Epaphras, Philemon, Apphia, Archippus, Onesimus (Colossians 4:9,12,17; Philemon 1,2,10-11)

✓ Laodicea and Hierapolis

> Paul's expressed concern for these ecclesias and the work of Epaphras (Colossians 2:1; 4:12-13). Those in the ecclesia at Laodicea included Nymphas and Archippus (Colossians 4:15). There is a connection of the letter to the Colossians and the Laodicean ecclesia (Colossians 4:16).

✓ Spain (Romans 15:24,28)

In 64 A.D. there is a great fire in Rome. Nero accuses the Christians, and a terrible persecution begins.

Paul's recorded travels (according to 1 Timothy, Titus, 2 Timothy) ...

✓ Paul and Timothy are in Ephesus. Paul departs to Macedonia where he writes 1 Timothy (1 Timothy 1:3; 3:14-15).

---

1 Timothy is probably written here. (67 A.D.)

Titus is probably written here. (67 A.D.)

Second captivity in Rome

---

2 Timothy is probably written here. (Spring 68 A.D.)

Paul is executed

Tradition is that both Peter and Paul were martyred under Nero. Some suppose that this took place early in the period of persecution (64 A.D.) but other scholars follow Eusebius in placing the martyrdom of Paul toward the end of Nero's reign (Summer, 68 A.D.).

Acts
Part Two: Paul

Saul and Barnabus "severed"   13:1
- "Sever ... to Me Barnabas and Saul for the work to which I have called them" (13:2)

Elymas is blinded *until* the appointed time   13:6
- Elymas (a Jew) kept Sergius Paul from hearing the word of God (13:8)
- "Saul, who is also called Paul..." (13:9)
- "Will you not cease perverting the straight ways of the Lord?" (13:11)
- You shall be blind ... until the appointed time (13:11)
- *[See Romans 11:25 – Israel calloused "until"]*
- John, departing from them, returns to Jerusalem (13:14)

Proclaiming pardon & justification to the Jews   13:14
- Paul addresses the Jews in the synagogue at Antioch, Pisidia (13:14)
- "To us (Jews and those among you fearing God) was the word of salvation given" (13:26)
- "Through this One is being announced to you the pardon of sins, and from all from which you could not be justified in the law of Moses ... everyone believing is being justified" (13:38)

Turning to the nations   13:42
- Paul invited back but the Jews oppose him on the next sabbath (13:42)
- "To you first *[the Jews]* was it necessary that the word of God be spoken." (13:46)
- "Yet, since, in fact, you are thrusting it away, and are judging yourselves not worthy of eonian life, lo! we are turning to the nations." (13:47
- "For thus the Lord has directed us: I have apointed Thee for a light of the nations" (13:47)
- On hearing this the nations rejoiced ... and they believe, "whoever were set" for life eonian (13:48)

In the synagogue in Iconium   14:1
- A vast multitude of both Jews & Greeks believe (14:1)
- The stubborn Jews provoke the nations against them (14:2)
- Signs and miracles accompany the word (14:3)
- Opposition: The city is divided ... Paul is forced to flee (14:4)

Judaizers promote circumcision   15:1
- Teaching that circumcision is necessary for salvation (15:1)
- Paul & Barnabas go to Jerusalem concerning this question (15:2)
- *[Paul went to Jerusalem "in accord with a revelation" – Galatians 2:2]*
- Some from the sect of Pharisees insist they must be circumcised and keep the law (15:5)
- Peter: "Why are you trying to place a yoke on them which neither our fathers nor we are strong enough to bear?" (15:10)
- "Through the grace of the Lord Jesus are we believing, to be saved in a manner even as they" (15:11)

Lydia's heart was opened   16:14
- Paul spoke, and Lydia heard ... "whose heart the Lord opens up to heed what is spoken by Paul" (16:14)

Paul & Silas in jail   16:22
- An earthquake opens the doors and releases the bonds (16:26)
- "**Believe** on the Lord Jesus, **and you shall be saved**..." (16:31)

In the synagogue at Thessalonica   17:1
- As was Paul's custom, he entered the synagogue and on three sabbaths he argues with them from the scriptures ... "This One is the Christ" (17:2)
- Some persuaded ... a multitude of the reverent Greeks and a number of foremost women (17:4)
- Opposition: The Jews are jealous and force Paul out of Thessalonica (17:5)

In the synagogue at Berea   17:10
- Received the word in eagerness, examining the scriptures to see if it is so (17:11)
- Opposition: Jews from Thessalonica come and force Paul out of Berea (17:13)

Athens (The Areopagus)   17:15
- To Whom you are ignorantly devout, this One I am announcing (17:24)
- "Condoning times of ignorance, God is now charging mankind everywhere to repent, as He assigns a day to be judging the inhabited earth in righteousness..." (17:30)
- *[Call to repentance – A day of judging coming – "Impending indignation"]*

Corinth   18:1
- Argued in the synagogue every sabbath ... certifying to the Jews that Jesus is the Christ (18:4)
- Opposition: "From now on I shall go to the nations" (18:6)

Apollos is corrected   18:24
- Versed only in the baptism of John (18:25)
- Priscilla & Aquila expound the way of God to him more accurately (18:26)

Ephesus   19:1
- Paul spoke boldly in the synagogue for three months (19:8)
- Powerful deeds God did thru Paul (19:11)

Calling the elders of the ecclesia in Ephesus   20:17
- "I did not shrink from informing you of anything that was expedient" (20:20)
- "Certifying to Jews & Greeks repentance toward God and faith toward our Lord" (20:21)
- "My dispensation: To certify the evangel of the grace of God" (20:24)

Jerusalem   21:15
- Opposed by "tens of thousands among the Jews who have believed, and are inherently zealous for the law" (21:20)
- *[Paul opposed not by unbelievers, but by believers wanting to add the law to his evangel of grace.]*

Paul's arrest and trials   21:27
- Paul is arrested (21:27)
- Paul addresses the Sanhedrin (23:1)
- Hearing before Felix (24:1)
- Hearing before Festus (25:6)
- Hearing before King Agrippa (25:23)
- Paul describes his commission: "To open their eyes, to turn them about from darkness to light and from the authority of Satan to God, for them to get a pardon of sins and an allotment among those who have been hallowed by faith that is in Me." (26:18)
- "I reported that they are to be repenting and turning back to God, engaging in acts worthy of repentance" (26:20)

The trip to Rome   27:1

- Shipwrecked at Melita (28:1)
- Paul permitted to remain by himself together with the soldier who guarded him (28:16)

Paul calls for the foremost of the Jews   28:17

- "Because of the expectation of Israel this chain is lying about me" (28:20)
- Setting a day, more came to him ... to whom he expounded, certifying the kingdom of God, besides persuading them concerning Jesus, both from the law of Moses and the prophets from morning till dusk (28:23)
- Some believed ... others disbelieved ... disagreements ensued (28:25)
- "Let it be known to you, then, that *to the nations* was dispatched this salvation of God, and they will hear" (28:28) – *[Paul here quoted from Isaiah 6:9,10 just as Jesus did in Matthew 13:14 as the kingdom evangel was opposed and He began to speak only using parables.]*
- Paul remained in Rome for two years, heralding the kingdom of God, *and* teaching that which concerns the Lord Jesus Christ with all boldness, unforbidden. (28:30)

CLOSING THOUGHTS

As we have seen, Acts has two distinct parts. In part one, Peter is primary and his ministry (and that of the other apostles and leaders) is exclusively to Israel. Near the end of part one we see Peter's influence beginning to fade and James appears to take the primary role in leading the Jewish ecclesia. But everything relates exclusively to Israel.

Then comes part two, beginning with the conversion of Saul on the road to Damascus. Saul (Paul) is commissioned to proclaim the evangel to believers of Israel; but he is ALSO commissioned to proclaim to kings and nations aside from Israel. Throughout Acts, though, he goes first to the synagogues to proclaim to those of Israel, and when he is rejected he goes to those of the nations. Clearly his message is different, which leads to his coming to Jerusalem to explain what he is doing. We clearly see Peter and the others from the Jerusalem ecclesia proclaiming to the believers among Israel the *Circumcision evangel* that was entrusted to Peter. And Paul, entrusted with the *Uncircumcision evangel,* goes to the nations. And it is not until Acts ends, and when Paul writes his later letters, that we see some of the amazing new truths God has in store for the Body of Christ.

So, as we turn to Paul's letters let us keep in mind his dual commission; to Israel; and to the nations. We must therefore seek to understand from the context of his letters to whom he is speaking.

Allow me to share a most appropriate quote from Sir. Robert Anderson concerning the book of Acts:

> We must recognize the intensely Jewish character of the Pentecostal dispensation. The Jerusalem Church was Jewish. Their Bible was the Jewish Scriptures. The Jewish temple was their house of prayer and common meeting-place. Their beliefs and hopes and words and acts all marked them out as Jews. My contention is that the Acts as a whole is the record of a temporary and transitional dispensation in which blessing was again offered to the Jews and again rejected. (Sir Robert Anderson 1841-1918; The Silence of God, pg 56.)

𝔓aul's 𝔏etters

An Overview of the Scriptures, by
BOB EVELY © *2018.*
An Independent Minister of Christ Jesus,
Of the church at Wilmore, Kentucky

This is not intended to be a verse by verse commentary on Paul's letters, but an *overview;* an examination of the writer's train of thought. Verse by verse commentaries have a purpose, but care must be taken not to lose sight of the forest as we study the trees. What follows is intended to be an examination of the forest.

Consider the commission Paul received on the road to Damascus: *He is a choice instrument of Mine, to bear My name before both the nations and kings, besides the sons of Israel* (Acts 9:15-16). We know from Acts that Paul did go first to the synagogues to proclaim Christ to the Jews, and then to the Gentiles. Peter, John, James and other New Testament writers had a commission to Israel only. Paul *alone* was commissioned to go to the Gentiles.

We cannot assume Paul's message to the Gentiles is the same as the message proclaimed by the others to Israel. Paul stressed that the gospel he proclaimed was not received from man, but it came through a revelation of Jesus Christ (Galatians 1:11-12). If he preached the same gospel, why would he not have studied under the Twelve who had heard and observed Christ during His earthly ministry? And why would Paul refer to his proclamation as "my evangel" instead of "the evangel" (Romans 2:16; 16:25-26)?

Paul notes that he had been entrusted with the evangel of the Uncircumcision, and Peter had been trusted with the evangel of the Circumcision (Galatians 2:7). He did not say that his was the evangel *to* the Uncircumcision; but *of* the Uncircumcision. It was a different message, and this can be clearly seen if we examine the details. Paul is the only one to have mentioned "the rapture" in 1 Thessalonians 4:13, and the expectation of the Body of Christ in the celestials in Ephesians 2:6. Israel's expectation was always upon the earth, not in the celestials or heavens.

Paul was abandoned by nearly all at the end of his ministry (see 2 Timothy 1:15; 4:16; Acts 21:20). Note in the Acts passage that when Paul returned to Jerusalem he was opposed not by unbelieving Jews, but by believing Jews who were zealous for the law – a clear signal that Paul's message was different than that of the Twelve, and as a result Paul was opposed by Jewish believers.

Paul, in his writings, refers to a MYSTERY that had been previously concealed, but which he was now revealing as God had instructed him. *His body, which is the ecclesia of which I became a dispenser, in accord with the administration of God, which is granted to me for you, to COMPLETE the word of God ... the SECRET which has been concealed from the eons and from the generations, yet now was made manifest to His saints* (Colossians 1:24-16) *... by REVELATION the SECRET is made known to me ... the secret of the Christ, which, in other generations, is not made known to the sons of humanity* (Ephesians 3:3-5).

Clearly Paul was commissioned to address a group not previously addressed by the Twelve (Gentiles), with a different message that had been *revealed* to him not by man but by Christ Himself.

But let us remember Paul's commission. He would be *a choice instrument of Mine, to bear My name before both the nations and kings, besides the sons of Israel* (Acts 9:15). He was commissioned to go to the nations *and* to Israel. So, Paul may at times be speaking to those of Israel who were familiar with the Old Testament prophets and history, while at other times he may be speaking to those from the nations without such background. His audience will most often be mixed. He might reference Israel in his letters knowing that a *part* of his audience is of Jewish ethnicity. But despite the past and the heritage of any given individual, all whom Paul addresses are now within the ecclesia; the called-out-ones of God.

Paul's letters

1 Thessalonians	50-52 AD	During 2nd Journey
2 Thessalonians	52-53 AD	During 2nd Journey
Galatians (early theory)	54 AD	End of 2nd Journey
1 Corinthians	Spring 57 AD	During 3rd Journey
2 Corinthians	Fall 57 AD	During 3rd Journey
Galatians	Winter 57 AD	During 3rd Journey

Romans	Spring 58 AD	During 3rd Journey
Colossians	61-62 AD	During 1st Captivity
Ephesians	61-62 AD	During 1st Captivity
Philemon	62-63 AD	During 1st Captivity
Philippians	63 AD	During 1st Captivity
1 Timothy	67 AD	Between Captivities
Titus	67 AD	Between Captivities
2 Timothy	Spring 68 AD	During 2nd Captivity

In *The Companion Bible,* Mr. Bullinger categories Paul's letters as follows:

Church Epistles

Romans: Doctrine and instruction.
Corinthians I/II: Reproof.
Galatians: Correction.

Ephesians: Doctrine and instruction.
Philippians: Reproof.
Colossians: Correction.

Thessalonians I/II: Doctrine and instruction.

Personal Epistles

Timothy I: Organization in assemblies. Officers.
Timothy II: Organization ignored. Orderly rule succeeded by ruin. Officers replaced by faithful men.
Titus: Organized assemblies (as in 1 Timothy).
Philemon: Practical exhibition of an individual's walk.

Facts about Paul

General

✓ A Jew, born in Tarsus, 5-10 A.D. (Acts 21:39; 22:3; Philippians 3:5)
✓ Circumcised on the eighth day (Philippians 3:5)
✓ Tribe of Benjamin (Acts 13:21; Rom 2:1; Philippians 3:5)
✓ Raised in Jerusalem (Acts 22:3)
✓ Educated in Judaism, studied under Gamaliel (Acts 22:3)
✓ A Hebrew of Hebrews (Philippians 3:5)
✓ A Pharisee, son of a Pharisee (Acts 23:6; 26:4; Philippians 3:5)

- ✓ Kept the law (Acts 26:5)
- ✓ A Roman citizen (Acts 22:25-38)

His family

- ✓ His sister lived in Jerusalem (Acts 23:16)
- ✓ His nephew helped him (Acts 23:16)

His trade

- ✓ A tentmaker (Acts 18:3)

Overall

- ✓ 34 years of ministry
- ✓ 12,000 miles

About Tarsus

- ✓ Capital & chief city of Cilicia in southeastern Asia Minor
- ✓ Queen city of the fertile Cilician plains, cultivated by slave labor
- ✓ On major road from Mesopotamia to Syria; access to Mediterranean and a gap in Taurus Mountains
- ✓ A commercial center; used by camel caravans
- ✓ Location of a university
- ✓ A temple of Baal located there
- ✓ Famous conquerors marched this road (Cyrus of Persia, Alexander the Great, Julius Caesar)
- ✓ Predominantly Hellenistic culture, but within the city was a Jewish community
- ✓ THE BIRTHPLACE OF PAUL

𝕽𝖔𝖒𝖆𝖓𝖘

An Overview of the Scriptures, by
BOB EVELY © *2018.*
An Independent Minister of Christ Jesus,
Of the church at Wilmore, Kentucky

"My evangel" (2:16)

"For God locks up all together in stubbornness, that He should be merciful to all." (11:32)

1 Thessalonians	50-52 AD	During 2nd Journey
2 Thessalonians	52-53 AD	During 2nd Journey
Galatians (early theory)	54 AD	End of 2nd Journey
1 Corinthians	Spring 57 AD	During 3rd Journey
2 Corinthians	Fall 57 AD	During 3rd Journey
Galatians	Winter 57 AD	During 3rd Journey
Romans	**Spring 58 AD**	**During 3rd Journey**
Colossians	61-62 AD	During 1st Captivity
Ephesians	61-62 AD	During 1st Captivity
Philemon	62-63 AD	During 1st Captivity
Philippians	63 AD	During 1st Captivity
1 Timothy	67 AD	Between Captivities
Titus	67 AD	Between Captivities
2 Timothy	Spring 68 AD	During 2nd Captivity

CHAPTER 1

The address on the envelope (1:1)

Paul;
To all who are in Rome, beloved of God, called *saints*.

> *SAINTS* comes from the Greek *hagios* which is translated *holy* when speaking of things other than people. So a saint could be referred to as a holy one. A study of the word holy in Scripture will reveal that God is the acting agent. To be holy means to be set apart by God for some purpose. It is not a trait or behavior of a thing that causes it to be holy; it is the declaration of God as to what *is* holy. We see in Romans 1:7 that these saints (holy ones) in Rome are also referred to as *the called of Jesus Christ*. It is God who does the calling. Abraham did nothing to earn

righteousness. God spoke to him and he believed, and this was *reckoned* to Abraham as righteousness. (Romans 4:3)

How does Paul identify himself? (1:1)

... a called *apostle, severed* for the *evangel of God* ...

The Greek for APOSTLE is *apostello*. When used as a verb it is translated *commission*. An apostle is one who has been *commissioned* by God. But Paul is an apostle? Here is an interesting thought. When God worked thru Israel as His instrument there were twelve apostles; no more, and no less. Just as there were twelve tribes in Israel, there were twelve apostles. When Judas departed there was a need to replace him with just one, to bring the number back to twelve. Not so with Paul, who is a different kind of apostle. The Twelve were commissioned to proclaim the evangel (gospel, or good news) to Israel; the twelve tribes. The good news concerned the coming of the Messiah to reign on David's throne, and the restoration of the kingdom upon the earth; the promises made to Israel thru the Old Testament prophets. Paul was the first commissioned to go to the Gentiles. We see in his writings a message concerning the Body of Christ (Jew and Gentile alike with no barrier or preference). In Paul's writings we hear for the first time of things pertaining to Christ's return to snatch away the Body (1 Thessalonians 4:13), the Body's destiny in the heavenly realm, (Ephesians) justification (as compared with pardon) and reconciliation. Paul was a different kind of apostle, commissioned to go to a different group of people and bearing a different message.

Paul was SEVERED or cut out from his fellow Jews and from the other apostles because God had a special purpose for him. We should not assume that Paul's work and message were the same as that of Peter and the others. Peter and the Twelve went exclusively to the Jews, as we see throughout the book of Acts. Paul was severed to go to a different group; the nations (Gentiles). And if we look carefully we will see that his message was not the same as the message borne by the others. The differences in his message led to Paul's persecution by the others, even as he returned to Jerusalem late in his ministry and was opposed by tens of thousands of the Jews who have believed and who were zealous for the law (Acts 21:20).

What do we learn about the evangel? (1:1)

... concerning His Son Who comes of the seed of David according to the flesh, Who is designated Son of God with power; by the resurrection of the dead; Jesus Christ, our Lord, through Whom we obtained grace and apostleship for *faith-obedience* among *all the nations*.

Paul tells us he was severed *for the evangel of God.* Study the word EVANGEL in its every occurrence throughout the New Testament and you will see that it simply means GOOD NEWS. It is not always the same good news in every instance. Most popular Bible teaching tells us that the gospel (the word evangel in the Greek) is always the same. But clearly this is not so, as can be clearly seen by any who would study the word evangel every time is appears throughout Scripture.

PAUL WAS SEVERED, or set apart from others, for the good news of God *concerning His Son.* Paul proceeds to tell us specifically what this good news consists of. As to the flesh, the Son came of the seed of David (1:4), thereby satisfying the Messianic requirements outlined by the prophets. We remember that the Jews placed great emphasis on satisfying fleshly requirements like circumcision. But the Son was also *designated Son of God with power.* So as it pertains to the Jews, the Son came of the seed of David. And as it pertains to all mankind He was *designated* Son of God.

We recall that Jesus was commissioned to go exclusively to the lost sheep of Israel; the Jews (Matthew 15:24). And Jesus commissioned the Twelve to go only to the lost sheep of Israel (Matthew 10:6). Their message to Israel concerned the nearness of the kingdom; the kingdom that had once belonged to Israel; the restoration of which had been foretold by the prophets.

> # Israel was awaiting the restoration of the kingdom!

Even in Acts, following the resurrection and ascension of Christ, Peter speaks to the Israelites (Acts 2:22; 2:36). Later when Peter is called to go to Cornelius, a Gentile, he resists. And finally when Peter does go to

Cornelius we see that this is a unique case. Cornelius is not just any Gentile; he is devout and fearing God (Acts 10:1). And even after this incident Peter does not re-direct his ministry toward the Gentiles. In Galatians 2:7 we learn that Peter had been entrusted with the evangel of the Circumcision (Israel).

It is Paul who has been chosen by Christ and commissioned as an apostle to go directly to the nations. Paul was entrusted with the evangel of the Uncircumcision; the Gentiles (Galatians 2:7). It is for this that Paul was severed from the others, because his commission was a new direction being established by God.

FAITH-OBEDIENCE *among all the nations* (1:6). This, then, is the purpose for which Paul was given grace and chosen as an apostle; so that those of all the nations might have faith-obedience, just as Abraham had faith and it was reckoned to him as righteousness (Romans 4:3). It is important to recognize that faith obedience is not faith <u>and</u> obedience. This is clearly not what this passage tells us in the original Greek. So what is faith-obedience? It means to obey by having faith, or simply to believe. It is the act of having faith that <u>is</u> the obedience. It is, therefore, FAITH ALONE; and not faith plus works of obedience. We will see this more clearly in Paul's later comments on the subject, but for now we simply note that the Greek in this passage does not read faith plus obedience; it is simply faith-obedience.

PRAYER: Paul concludes the introduction noting that he is making mention of the saints in Rome, always, *in my prayers* (1:8). We see many references to prayer in Paul's letters. Here we see him thanking God for the faith of the saints in Rome, and beseeching God to be able to come to Rome if that be God's will. He prays *unintermittingly* (1:9). The frequency of Paul's mention of prayer should cause us to make prayer a key element in our own lives. Paul's petitions are always God-centered, not self-centered. Paul's desire to come to Rome is for the purpose of sharing some spiritual grace with them, for the saints to be established. But there is also mutual benefit when Paul meets with the saints; *to be consoled together among you through one another's faith, both yours and mine* (1:11). There is benefit to be derived when saints meet together.

The evangel is introduced [(1:14)]

I am eager to bring *the evangel* to you. I am *not ashamed* of the evangel. *It is God's power for salvation to everyone who is believing; to the Jew first, and to the Greek as well. For a righteousness which is of God is being revealed in it, out of faith for faith ...*

> EVANGEL simply means *good news,* and we must look at the context to know what specific good news Paul is referring to. Here in Romans 1 we learn that the evangel is God's power for salvation *for everyone who is believing* (1:16). The focus of the evangel is on God and His power. This power for salvation is *revealed* to those who are believing. Those who do not, or cannot believe, do not recognize God's power; at least not yet.
>
> We also learn that in the evangel *God's righteousness is being revealed, out of faith for faith.* Out of whose faith? And for whose faith? Romans 3:22 sheds light: *A righteousness of God through Jesus Christ's faith, for all, and on all who are believing.* So God's righteousness is brought forth out of Jesus Christ's faith, and it is ON all who are believing. [More on this when we look at 3:22]

Is it our CHOICE to believe or not believe?

> Consider this. Was it Abraham's choice to believe, or was the ability to believe granted to him by God in order that God's purposes might be fulfilled thru Abraham? Did God speak equally to all men, giving all the same chance, but only Abraham believed; or did God speak to Abraham in a way that he had not spoken to others, because Abraham was chosen by God? Think about these passages:
>
> *For you it is graciously granted, for Christ's sake, not only to be believing on Him ...* (Philippians 1:29).
>
> [Lydia] *whose heart the Lord opens up to heed what is spoken by Paul* (Acts 16:14).
>
> *The god of this eon blinds the apprehensions of the unbelieving so that the illumination of the evangel of the glory of Christ, Who is the Image of the*

invisible God, does not irradiate them (2 Corinthians 4:3).

Consider Paul's conversion. He did not simply *choose* to believe and become a follower of Christ. As a matter of fact Paul was the premier opponent of Christ. Yet he was chosen outside of his own "free will." Paul was directly spoken to in a way that others had not been spoken to, because he was the one chosen for this special commission. So it would seem that the saints at Rome, the called of Jesus Christ, were those chosen by God and given the eyes to see and believe in order that God's purposes might be fulfilled thru them.

Now we have seen, from Paul's brief preliminary remarks in Romans, that the evangel is God's power for salvation for everyone who is believing. But is salvation ONLY for Believers? Let us remember what Paul says elsewhere in his writings:

> *God, Who wills that all mankind be saved and come into a realization of the truth* (1 Timothy 2:4).

> (God) *Who is operating all in accord with the counsel of His will ...* (Ephesians 1:11).

> Christ Jesus, Who is giving Himself a correspondent Ransom for all (1 Timothy 2:6).

> God, Who is the Saviour of all mankind, especially of believers (1 Timothy 4:11).

God's will is that all mankind be saved. God is operating all in accord with the counsel of His will. Christ gave Himself as a correspondent ransom for all, not just those that believe. God is the Saviour of all mankind, especially (it does not say exclusively) of believers. Especially of believers, for believers recognize God's power for salvation and His righteousness in this present age while others do not. But while God is the Saviour of believers in a special way, this does not preclude the fact that He is the Saviour of all mankind, and that Christ Jesus gave Himself a correspondent Ransom for all.

This evangel that Paul brings is God's power for salvation, and we who believe can see this power and glorify God for it! This is an evangel not to be ashamed of. It is good news that Christ's ambassadors should be eager to proclaim.

God's indignation is revealed (1:18)

God's indignation is being revealed from heaven on all the irreverence and injustice of men who are retaining the truth in injustice, because that which is known of God is apparent among them, for God manifests it to them. From the creation of the world His invisible attributes are manifested by His achievements and His power.

Knowing God, they do not glorify Him as God or thank Him. Vain were they made in their reasonings. They allege themselves to be wise but they are made stupid. They change the glory of the incorruptible God into the likeness and image of a corruptible human being and flying creatures, quadrupeds and reptiles.

So God gives them over in the lusts of their hearts to the uncleanness of dishonoring their bodies; those who alter the truth of God into the lie; and who offer divine service to the creature rather than the Creator.

And so God gives them over to *dishonorable passions*. Females *alter the natural use* into that which is beside nature. Likewise, males leave the natural use of the female and were inflamed in their craving for one another, males with males effecting indecency, and getting back in themselves the retribution of their deception.

And, as they do not recognize God, He gives them over to a disqualified mind to do that which is not befitting ... injustice, wickedness, evil, greed, envy, murder, strife, guile, depravity, whisperers, vilifiers, detesters of God, outragers, proud, ostentatious, inventors of evil things, stubborn to parents, unintelligent, perfidious, without natural affection, implacable, unmerciful ... deserving of death; not only those doing them, but those endorsing those who are committing these things.

> So while God's righteousness is being revealed in the evangel, we now consider the crucial *need* for the evangel; because God's indignation is revealed upon *mankind's natural state* apart from the grace of God. Let's follow Paul's line of reasoning.
>
> God has revealed Himself to mankind in a way that should be apparent. (1:19)
>
> But man does not glorify God or thank Him. (1:21)
>
> So God causes man's reasoning to be vain. And while men think they are

wise, they are made to be stupid. (1:21)

Man continues to turn away from God, changing God's incorruptible nature into likenesses that are corruptible, like a human being or a creature. (1:23)

God gives man over to his base, fleshly nature; to the lusts of his heart. (1:24) Man gives way to uncleanness, to dishonoring his body (1:24) and to dishonorable passions. (1:26)

Some examples of this uncleanness are given; females altering the natural use of their bodies into that which is beside nature (1:26), and similarly males leaving the natural use of the female as they are inflamed in their craving for one another, males with males effecting indecency and getting back in themselves the retribution of their deception which must be (1:27).

IS THERE A CLEARER CONDEMNATION OF HOMOSEXUAL BEHAVIOR THAN IN THIS PASSAGE?

So man's mind is made to be disqualified, doing things that are not befitting or appropriate (1:28). A lengthy summary list of man's unrighteous behaviors is provided (1:19).

This, then, is the sorry, hopeless state of mankind, before the revealing of God's solution; a righteousness from God which is announced in the evangel. We can clearly see in this description of mankind the desperate need for a righteousness from God, as there is certainly no righteousness to be found within natural man.

Observe in 1:32 that the behavior of man is deserving of death; the same sentence pronounced upon Adam for his sin. Eternal torment (hell) is not the penalty, but death.

CHAPTER 2

Man is not qualified to judge (2:1)

Everyone who is judging another condemns himself, for he is committing the same things. The judgment of God is according to truth.

God's indignation is revealed upon mankind, but when a man judges another he condemns himself because any who judge are committing the same things. Man's judgments, therefore, are hypocritical. Not so when God judges, because the judgment of God is according to truth.

> # Does this mean that one should never judge another's BEHAVIOR?

Consider what Paul has to say in 1 Corinthians about dealing with an immoral brother; that the one who commits this act may be *taken away from your midst* (1 Corinthians 5:2). And: *Expel the wicked one from among yourselves* (1 Corinthians 5:13). It must be remembered, then, that there is a place for judging a brother's immoral BEHAVIOR. We judge behavior, not persons. And behavior is judged not by our own criteria, but God's revelation to us as to behavior He approves of; and that which He does not.

But relative to judging those outside the Body of Christ, and even those within the body in lesser matters (as Paul will address in his other writings); we judge and regulate *ourselves* using our conscience, but we do not judge others.

But why does God permit man's wicked acts to continue? (2:4)

Are you despising the riches of His kindness, forbearance and patience, being ignorant that the kindness of God is leading you to repentance?

Man wants to judge immediately, though he is guilty himself and not qualified to judge according to truth. God is delaying His judgment, showing great patience and kindness, allowing man the opportunity for repentance.

God will judge ... in a day to come (2:5)

You are hoarding for yourself indignation *in the day of indignation* and revelation of the just judgment of God.

The day of indignation.

Despite His great patience and kindness, God will judge. He will not delay judgment forever. This judgment will come in the day of indignation and revelation of the just judgment of God. Many today say that God cannot be just as they observe events in the world around them. But we have not yet seen God's just judgment. We see today only His patience and forbearance.

God will be paying each one in accord with his acts: to those who by endurance in good acts are seeking glory and honor and incorruption, life eonian; yet to those of faction and stubborn as to the truth, yet persuaded to injustice, indignation and fury, affliction and distress.

Without the evangel Paul brings, this would describe God's judgment upon all mankind; based on acts (not faith) and with the sentence being either life eonian (life in the eons to come) or indignation, fury, affliction and distress. Fortunately our destiny is not determined by our acts and abilities. God provides a rescue as we will see later.

But this passage is not referring to eternal life for those who believe in this lifetime and endless torment for those who do not. The judgment and reward here is dependent upon acts, not faith. And EONIAN life refers to life during the EONS to come, not that which follows the conclusion of the eons. We must remember that the Greek *aion* refers to a time period with a beginning and an end; not endlessness. No passage of Scripture, even when talking of judgment, will supersede the final outcome declared by God. Death will one day be abolished, and all will be vivified (given life) when God becomes All in all (1 Corinthians 15:22-28).

Now another point relative to God's future judgment ...

All mankind will be judged by God without partiality. Whoever sinned without law, without law also shall perish; and whoever sinned in law, through law will be judged. When those of the nations do that which the law demands, even though they have no law, they are a law to themselves as they are displaying actions of the law written in their hearts.

God's impartial judgment will come in the day when God will be judging the hidden things of humanity.

> Man cannot judge because he does not see the entire picture. Man can only observe the outer, visible things. But God observes the hidden things of humanity.
>
> Paul uses a phrase in 2:16 that is very interesting: according to MY EVANGEL. We see this several times in Paul's writings. *My evangel* is the good news brought by Paul.
>
> We must remember there is not just a single *gospel* or *evangel* in the Scriptures; but each time the word is used we must examine the context to determine what good news is being referred to. The fact that Paul uses the term *my evangel* instead of *the* evangel should cause us to ask what is unique about the evangel that he brings!
>
> Paul was given revelation directly from Jesus Christ. *For neither did I accept it from a man, nor was I taught it, but it came through a revelation of Jesus Christ* (Galatians 1:12). When Paul was converted, if he was commissioned to deliver the same evangel as the Twelve would it not have made sense for Paul to study under the Twelve who were eyewitnesses of all that Jesus said and did during His earthly ministry? Instead Christ revealed things directly to Paul. This is why Paul can refer to the news he brings as *my evangel.* And if we read the Scriptures carefully we will see that Paul's gospel is different from Peter's.

The Jews dishonor God [(2:17)]

The Jews are resting on law. They have a form of knowledge and the truth but they fail to teach themselves. They teach others not to steal, yet they steal. They teach others not to commit adultery, yet they commit adultery. As a result they dishonor God. And because of them God's name is blasphemed among the nations.

> As we consider the depravity of mankind and the righteousness of God, we recall that God had in the Old Testament chosen Israel. They were His people. They were given the Law. They were set apart from other nations. So at this point in Paul's letter we might ask, "What about Israel?" True, mankind is wicked and deserving of judgment. But what about Israel, God's chosen people?

Circumcision is beneficial if the law is put into practice. But if you [Israel] become a transgressor of the law, circumcision becomes uncircumcision. For circumcision is of the heart, in spirit, not in letter, whose applause is not of men, but of God.

> This does not mean that Gentiles that practiced the law had become "The Circumcision," *replacing* Israel. It is saying that only those among Israel that practiced the law were truly Israel.

CHAPTER 3

What, then, is the prerogative of the Jew and the benefit of circumcision? Much! They were entrusted with the oracles of God. If some disbelieve does this nullify God's faithfulness? No. God is true, though every man is a liar. And if man's unfaithfulness serves to commend God's righteousness, is God unjust for bringing on His indignation? No. Else how shall God be judging the world?

None are just; and the Law cannot justify [3:9]

Not one is just – not even one. Not one is understanding. Not one is seeking out God (3:10 ... from Psalm 14:1-3).

> If no one is just, and if no one is even seeking God, how can ANY find God and be saved?

> This is the bottom line! Since no one seeks out God on his own, how can *any* ever come to know God and be saved? How can any believe God if none are seeking Him? Could it be that God enables some (the called) to believe, even when they were not seeking (as in the case of Paul), so that through this group all mankind will ultimately be blessed?

No one can be justified in God's sight by the law. Through law is the recognition of sin.

> The law revealed to man what sin was. And what a dire picture of mankind! None are just; and the law cannot justify. Yet despite man's helpless condition, Paul's evangel proclaims God's solution ...

God's righteousness is revealed (3:21)

Yet now, apart from law, a righteousness of God is manifest; a righteousness of God through Jesus Christ's faith ...

> This is not righteousness resulting from man's faith. It speaks of God's righteousness, manifest to mankind through <u>Jesus Christ's faith</u>.

... for all, and on all who are believing, for there is no distinction, for all sinned and are wanting of the glory of God.

> God's righteousness is provided to mankind thru Jesus Christ's faith. Its effects are <u>for all</u>, because there is no distinction; all sinned and are wanting of the glory of God. The means thru which man receives this righteousness from God in this present age is thru faith, or belief. God's righteousness is for all, and it is currently received by those who are believing. But there will come a day when Christ reveals Himself by sight to those unable to believe by faith; as in the case of Thomas (John 20:29). Remember: God is the Saviour of all mankind, especially of believers (1 Timothy 4:11). Blessed are they who believe without seeing. In this way believers are *especial.* But as in Adam all died, so also in Christ will all be vivified.

Being justified gratuitously in His grace, through the deliverance which is in Christ Jesus (Whom God purposed for a Propitiatory shelter, through faith in His blood, for a display of His righteousness because of the passing over of the penalties of sins which occurred before in the forbearance of God) ...

To this point sins had simply been "passed over."

> In God's forbearance man's sin had not previously been dealt with. Here we see the meaning of *propitiation*, or the propitiatory shelter (atonement in most Bible translations). The blood of animal sacrifices did not pay for the sins of man; they simply served as a means for God to *pass over* the penalties of sins that had occurred. This was God's patience and forbearance at work, but sin had not been permanently

dealt with. Sin had only been *passed over* until the permanent solution came.

> # But if sins had been passed over and not dealt with, how can God be righteous and just?

Here's how! God justifies man through His grace; His free gift to an undeserving mankind. He provides deliverance through Christ Jesus; toward the display of His righteousness in the current era, for Him to be just and a Justifier of the one who is of the faith of Jesus (3:26). Christ's faith has revealed that God is righteous and just; and that God justifies those who are of the faith of Jesus. In this present age, those of the faith of Jesus are those who believe.

Where, then, is boasting? It is debarred! For we are *reckoning* a man to be justified by faith apart from works of law.

> # If man is able to decide on his own whether to believe or not believe, then those that believe have reason to boast!

But while no man is just or even seeking out God (3:11) man is given deliverance and justification as a gracious gift from God. If man had to do something to earn or receive this grace from God; even weighing the evidence logically and thereupon believing; it would no longer be grace, and man would have a reason to boast! [More evidence in support of the conclusion that man does not *choose* to believe but is *gifted* with belief by God. If this were not the case, man could boast in his belief.]

And He is not God of the Jews only, but of the nations also.

CHAPTER 4

Belief is reckoned for righteousness (4:1)

If Abraham was justified by acts he would have something to boast in. Abraham believes God, and it is reckoned to him for righteousness. To him who is not working yet is believing on Him Who is justifying the irreverent, his faith is reckoned for righteousness.

> Abraham (from Genesis 15:6) is presented as an example. He was RECKONED righteous. He did not WORK for righteousness, thereby earning wages that were owed to him. He simply believed (apart from works), and this belief (same word in the Greek as faith) is reckoned by God as righteousness.

David also spoke of *reckoned* righteousness. Happy they whose lawlessnesses were pardoned and whose sins were covered over! Happy the man to whom the Lord by no means should be reckoning sin!

> This is a reference to Psalm 32:1-2. And this reckoned righteousness applies to the Uncircumcision and the Circumcision. (4:9)

Abraham received the *sign* of circumcision, a *seal* of the righteousness of the faith.

> Circumcision was a *sign.* It was not the physical act of circumcision that made the Jews righteous. The act of circumcision was just a sign given to them by God, and a seal of righteousness that was forthcoming. Abraham received the sign of circumcision; and he is the father of all who are believing.

The promise to Abraham was not thru law; but through faith's righteousness. The law produces indignation. Where no law is, neither is there transgression. But the promise is of faith, in accord with grace; not to those of the law only, but to those also of the faith of Abraham, who is the father of us all.

> Works could bring righteousness if righteousness was in accord with the law. But law is powerless to provide righteousness. It only brings indignation. It is faith that brings righteousness, as it is in accord with grace. No works are required. Grace is all on God's part. And in this present age those who have faith are reckoned righteous.

Abraham believed God when God promised he would become a father of many nations (Genesis 17:5) even though the promise seemed to be beyond expectation. This faith invigorated Abraham. And his belief is reckoned for righteousness.

> So God spoke to Abraham, making a promise that was beyond belief, yet Abraham believed; and it was reckoned to him as righteousness. Again I ask; did this belief come from within Abraham himself, or was the ability to comprehend God's promise and believe a gift from God? Remember the state of mankind apart from the grace of God. None are just. None are seeking out God.

> When God spoke to Abraham, he believed what God told him. What is it we are to believe today? [God] rouses Jesus our Lord from among the dead, Who was given up because of our offenses, and was roused because of our justifying. (4:25) Thru Christ's death we find forgiveness for our offenses. Christ paid the penalty for sin; death. And because we are thereby justified, or reckoned righteous, Christ was resurrected (life). The penalty (death) was reversed!

This reckoned righteousness does not apply only to Abraham; but because of us also, to whom it is about to be reckoned, who are believing on Him.

CHAPTER 5

Peace with God ... conciliated ... justified (4:1)

Being justified, we can have peace with God, and we can glory in expectation of God's glory

> Even when things may appear quite dismal in this life, because of our expectation for what lies ahead we can glory; even in our afflictions.

Affliction produces endurance, which leads to testedness, which leads to expectation. The love of God has been poured out in our hearts, through the holy spirit which He has given to us.

> No conditions are attached. Paul addresses those who believe and tells them the holy spirit has been given to them ... period! First the holy spirit is given. And thru that the love of God is poured out into our hearts.

While we were sinners, Christ died for our sakes. Being now justified; we shall be saved from indignation.

- 62 -

> Again; no conditions are attached! Paul simply tells the believers they are justified.
>
> When we refer back to 2:5 we will see the reference to *the day of indignation* that is coming, from which the believer will be spared.

Thru Christ's death we were *conciliated* to God.

> This *conciliation* (one half of reconciliation) is not just upon believers, but all humanity. It is a one-sided conciliation. God is not reckoning mankind's offenses to him (see 2 Corinthians 5:19). It is not conditioned upon man's acceptance but is an unconditional statement of fact. And the message of Christ's Ambassadors is: *We are beseeching for Christ's sake, 'Be conciliated to God!' For the One not knowing sin, He makes to be a sin offering for our sakes that we may be becoming God's righteousness in Him.* (2 Corinthians 5:20) Those that believe have a two-way conciliation; or reconciliation.

And beyond this conciliation that came through Christ's death, the believer is *saved* in His life.

> Saved from what? As stated previously in this context; the believer is saved from the coming day of indignation and judgment.

Adam and Christ compared (5:12)

Even as through one man sin entered into the world, and through sin death, and thus death passed through into all mankind, on which all sinned.

> # Observe closely the parallel Paul makes between Adam & Christ.

If, by the offense of the one, the many died, much rather the grace of God and the gratuity in grace, which is of the One Man, Jesus Christ, to the many superabounds. The judgment is out of one into condemnation, yet the grace is out of many offenses into a just award.

If, by the offense of the one, death reigns through the one, much rather, those obtaining the superabundance of grace and the gratuity of righteousness shall be reigning in life through the One, Jesus Christ.

> Think about this. If Adam's one offense gave just the *opportunity* to sin, so that some become sinners while others not, then we could say that Christ's work brings justification only to *some*, conditioned upon man's acceptance. But we note that man has no choice as to becoming a sinner. All have sinned. In this parallel then, thus also is the case with ultimate salvation. It is not conditioned on man's acceptance. Belief is the means for man's receiving God's righteousness in this present age, but ultimately all will see, all will be subjected to God, every knee will bow. Ultimately ALL will be justified thru Christ's death.

As it was through one offense for <u>all mankind</u> for condemnation, *thus also* it is through one just award for <u>all mankind</u> for life's justifying. For even as, through the disobedience of the one man, the many were constituted sinners, *thus also*, through the obedience of the One, the many shall be constituted just.

> Note that *the many* is a direct parallel to *all mankind*. *The many* is therefore used to symbolize *the all*. And note the global nature of these statements. Certainly all mankind is condemned as a consequence of Adam's offense. None make a choice to be included in this group, and nothing can be done thru man's will to be excluded. In the parallel, then, the same is true of all mankind who are justified thru Christ's obedience!

> A side note: We do not inherit Adam's sin. We inherit Adam's dying condition (mortality). Because of Adam's sin, death entered the world, and it was death that was then passed to all mankind. Death (mortality) in all mankind then led to sin by all mankind (oh, the weakness of this flesh). At birth we inherit death. Because we have inherited this death condition (mortality), we sin. None are righteous!

We are under grace, not law [(5:20)]

Yet law came that the offense should be increasing. Yet where sin increases, grace superexceeds.

> What, then, was the purpose of the law? The law cannot justify; but it has led to a superexceeding grace from God!

CHAPTER 6

But if grace increases when we sin, should we not just continue sinning? May it not be coming to that! Those who are baptized into Christ Jesus are baptized into His death; so if we have died to sin how shall we still be living in sin? And as Christ was roused from among the dead, so also we should be walking in newness of life. As we were crucified with Him that the body of Sin may be nullified, justifying us, we are not to be slaving for Sin as we once did.

Thus you also, be reckoning yourselves to be dead, indeed, to Sin, yet living to God in Christ Jesus, our Lord.

> Just as God *reckons* us righteous, even when our behaviors are not always righteous; so also we are instructed to *reckon* our old selves to be dead; even though our fleshly bodies may still be alive. Remember, when God spoke to Abraham He called that which was not as if it were.

Let not Sin, then, be reigning in your mortal body, for you to be obeying its lusts. Nor yet be presenting your members, as implements of injustice, to Sin, but present yourselves to God as if alive from among the dead, and your members as implements of righteousness to God.

> Man could not save himself. The law cannot justify. None are seeking after God. Yet God, through Christ, has become conciliated to the world. And He has gifted a part of humanity with faith; the ability to believe, and to thereby be reckoned righteous. Why? As we read others of Paul's writings we will see the reasons God has called His "church" (ecclesia in the Greek; literally called-out-ones). But for now let us note that we who believe should reckon our old selves dead, and should offer ourselves to God as His implements. No longer should we slave for Sin as the rest of humanity, apart from God, does.

But since we are not under law, is it permissible to sin? May it not be coming to that! We are slaves to whoever we obey; Sin (for death), or Obedience (for righteousness). Now, being freed from Sin, you are enslaved to Righteousness.

> This is stated as a fact! We who believe are freed from Sin, and we are now slaves to Righteousness. But while this is a fact, we make choices as we live that cause us to either be in harmony with our Master or in opposition to Him. It is not "anything goes" but behaving worthily, in accord with and in harmony with life choices God has revealed as acceptable in His eyes.

Present your members as slaves to Righteousness for holiness. When you were slaves of Sin what fruit had you then? – of which you are now ashamed, for, indeed, the consummation of those things is death.

> Paul is not saying to the believer that persisting in these wrong behaviors will lead to death, as opposed to eonian life. He is reminding the believers that these behaviors (fruit) found in mankind apart from grace are such that would lead to death; and they are behaviors not appropriate for the one rescued. They are behaviors that cause believers to be ashamed. (6:21)

Yet now, being freed from Sin, yet enslaved to God, you have your fruit for holiness. Now the consummation is life eonian. For the ration of Sin is death, yet the gracious gift of God is life eonian, in Christ Jesus, our Lord.

> Paul is not threatening those believers who stray in their behavior that they will lose their eonian life. Eonian life is a gracious gift from God. Paul is reminding the believers that because of this gracious gift they now produce fruit for holiness and righteousness, and their proper behavior in response to God's grace is to present themselves to God to be used as implements of righteousness.

CHAPTER 7

The law lords it over a man as long as he is living. A wife is bound to a man by law. But if the man dies she is exempt from the law of the man.

Bear fruit (7:4)

You died to the law thru the Body of Christ to become another's. Be bearing fruit to God. Before, in the flesh, the passions of sins operated in our members, bearing fruit to death. But now we are exempt from the law, so that it is for us to be slaving in newness of spirit and not in oldness of letter.

The law taught us about sin (7:7)

But sin I knew not except through law. I had not been aware of coveting except the law said, "You shall not be coveting." Now Sin, getting an incentive through the precept, produces in me all manner of coveting. But apart from law, sin is dead.

> The law has served the purpose of making us aware of sin. And the law has displayed to us the futility of seeking righteousness thru our own

efforts. But the law, itself, is not sin. The law is holy, and the precept holy and just and good.

Man's struggle under the law (7:14)

The law is spiritual, yet I am fleshly, having been disposed of under Sin. For what I am affecting I know not, for not what I will, this I am putting into practice, but what I am hating, this I am doing.

> The problem is not the law, but man. Without God's grace coming to the rescue, man faces a hopeless struggle as he seeks to gain righteousness thru the law.

For it is not the good that I will that I am doing, but the evil that I am not willing, this I am putting into practice. It is no longer I who am affecting it, but Sin which is making its home in me.

> Paul is not talking of a struggle he then faced, but is speaking of man under the law:

Good is not making its home in my flesh. It is not the good that I will that I am doing, but the evil that I am not willing; this I put into practice. So since I am not willing what I am doing, it is not I who am affecting it but Sin that makes its home in me.

> The struggle exists because of a friction between spirit and flesh.

For I am gratified with the law of God as to the man within, yet I am observing a different law in my members, warring with the law of my mind, and leading me into captivity to the law of sin which is in my members.

> All seems lost and hopeless.

A wretched man am I! What will rescue me out of this body of death?

GRACE is God's solution! (7:25)

> Most English Bible translations appear to leave the question in 7:24 unanswered. The Concordant Version provides the response: Grace! Some ancient manuscripts omit the word grace, thereby leaving the question unanswered. But evidence seems to support those manuscripts which contain the response. Grace is what will rescue man in his hopeless state. Grace fits with Paul's line of thought throughout Romans, providing evidence that the manuscripts that include this response are the correct ones.

CHAPTER 8

No condemnation for those "in Christ Jesus" (8:1)

Nothing, consequently, is now condemnation to those in Christ Jesus. Not according to flesh are they walking, but according to spirit, for the spirit's law of life in Christ Jesus frees you from the law of sin and death.

> So nothing condemns those in Christ Jesus. And especially (based on the context) the Law and its provisions cannot condemn the one in Christ Jesus.

Who is "in" Christ Jesus?

> Is it just those who manifest acceptable behaviors? Or, upon believing as we are reckoned righteous does this place us in Christ Jesus as a matter of fact; because of what God has accomplished thru His grace?

> As we consider how Paul uses the phrase *in Christ Jesus* it is quite clear that he refers to ALL WHO BELIEVE. At times he must admonish errant behaviors (as in the Corinthian church), but never does he condemn a believer so as to exclude him from the Body of Christ because of behavior. Paul admonishes and encourages, but he does not hold condemnation as a threat to those who do not believe.

Walk in accord with the spirit (8:3)

For what was impossible to the law, which was infirm through the flesh, God did; sending His own Son in the likeness of sin's flesh. He condemns sin in the flesh, that the just requirements of the law may be fulfilled in us, who are not walking in accord with flesh but in accord with spirit.

> Again, this is a statement of fact, not based on the believer's achievements. This is something God accomplished. Upon believing WE ARE WALKING in accord with the spirit. Christ condemns sin, having defeated it.

For those who are in accord with flesh are disposed to that which is of the flesh, yet those who are in accord with spirit to that which is of the spirit. Now those who are in flesh are not able to please God.

> But then Paul tells the believers in Rome ...

Yet you are not in flesh, but in spirit, if so be that God's spirit is making its home in you. Now if anyone has not Christ's spirit, this one is not His. Now if Christ is in you, the body, indeed, is dead because of sin, yet the spirit is life because of righteousness.

> Now we remember back to Romans 5:5, before any discussion of behavior took place, Paul told ALL of the believers ... the love of God has been poured out in our hearts through the holy spirit which is being given to us. It is a FACT, not dependent upon man's response, that those who believe have been given the holy spirit. Therefore it is a matter of fact that ALL who believe are not in flesh, but in spirit; because God's spirit is making its home in them (8:9). Paul admonishes the believer to present himself to God and to walk worthily; but he does not threaten a loss of position in Christ for those that are not exhibiting proper fruit. The solution to man's dilemma is 100% God, given to man freely thru His grace. Despite how we may appear in the flesh, God has justified us in Christ. And the future judgment has been delegated to Christ, the very One Who died for us and Who pleads for us at God's right hand.

The effect of God's spirit on the believer (8:11)

Now if the spirit of Him Who rouses Jesus from among the dead is making its home in you, He Who rouses Christ Jesus from among the dead will also be *vivifying your mortal bodies* because of His spirit making its home in you.

> So having been given the holy spirit, what is the effect of God's spirit upon the believer? Vivifying! This vivifying (bringing life) is not the same as rousing (resurrection). The holy spirit brings life within the believer even in this present age. The spirit generates within us the ability to be led by God's spirit, and not our fleshly nature.

If in spirit you are putting the practices of the body to death, you will be living.

Sons of God (8:14)

Whoever are being led by God's spirit, these are sons of God.

> Remember that the spirit has been given to all believers.
>
> We know of the many references to Christ Jesus being the son of God. And through what Christ has accomplished we see now that we who believe are sons of God! God, thru His grace, has conciliated us, justified us, saved us, and given us His spirit; and He now declares that we are sons of God!

No longer burdened by slavery's spirit, causing us to fear; you got the spirit of sonship, in which we are crying, 'Abba, Father!' We are children of God, with an allotment. We suffer together and will be glorified together.

We await redemption [(8:18)]

The sufferings of the current era do not deserve the glory about to be revealed for us.

> While we await the full effects of what God is accomplishing, we live in these mortal bodies. At times we suffer, but we have the expectation of what is coming. And the glory that lies ahead will far exceed these temporary afflictions.

To vanity was the creation subjected, not voluntarily, but because of Him Who subjects it, in expectation that the creation itself, also, shall be freed from the slavery of corruption into the glorious freedom of the children of God. For we are aware that the entire creation is groaning and travailing together until now.

> And we also groan ...

We ourselves also, who have the firstfruit of the spirit, we ourselves also, are groaning in ourselves, awaiting the sonship, the deliverance of our body.

> While we have been given the spirit of sonship, in this present age we do not have the full realization of the sonship that will one day come. For now we live in expectation of what lies ahead. When our bodies are delivered from this present bondage, when the Lord descends from heaven to snatch us away (1 Thessalonians 4:13) He will transfigure these bodies to conform to His glorious Body (Philippians 3:21). In the meantime ...

That which we are not observing we are awaiting with endurance. And as we await our expectation, the spirit also is aiding our infirmity, for what we should be praying for, to accord with what must be, we are not aware, but the spirit itself is pleading for us with inarticulate groanings.

> # Paul's model for prayer in this present age

An examination of prayer during the days when the kingdom evangel was being proclaimed unto Israel, with its message of the kingdom to come upon the earth, will reveal a different model for prayer; one of persistence, and belief without wavering as to the object of prayer. If you should be having faith and not be doubting; all, whatsoever you should be requesting in prayer, believing, you shall be getting (Matthew 21:21-22). But in the present age as the evangel of grace is proclaimed, with its message not in reference to this earth but the celestial realm (the heavens), we see a different model for prayer; inconsistent with the kingdom model. Here we see weakness and ignorance, and total reliance upon the spirit of God in even knowing how to pray. We are not disposed to the terrestrial things (Philippians 3:19). Sufficient for you is My grace, for My power in infirmity is being perfected (2 Corinthians 12:9).

God is working all together for good [8:28]

God is working all together for the good of those who are loving God, who are called according to the purpose, that whom He foreknew He designates beforehand also, to be conformed to the image of His Son.

Does this mean that God only works for the good of SOME of mankind? Clearly we see throughout this section that God is the acting agent; not man. It is not men who choose God, but God who chooses men, to accomplish His purposes.

Now whom He designates beforehand, these He calls also, and whom He calls, these He justifies also; now whom He justifies, these He glorifies also. How shall we respond to these things? If God is for us, who is against us? Who will indict God's chosen ones? Nothing will be able to separate us from the love of God in Christ Jesus our Lord.

GOD CHOOSES <u>SOME</u>? No man is just; and none are even seeking God (2:11). God, knowing this to be the case, designates beforehand a group of mankind that He calls, and justifies, and glorifies. It is not that this group is more deserving than the remainder of mankind. God has made a choice in order that He can accomplish His purpose. In this current age God is working all together for the good of those He has called. Ultimately this will benefit all mankind. But for now God has a purpose for calling some. And nothing can condemn nor separate from His love those whom He has chosen (8:31-38).

CHAPTER 9

What about Israel? ^(9:1)

At this point we might ask, what about Israel? Once God's chosen, has God now rejected Israel forever? Many today take Bible passages pertaining to Israel and claim these passages now refer to the Church. But has Israel been rejected permanently, with the Church now taking her place as Israel's substitute? Paul says of Israel …

Whose is the sonship and the glory and the covenants and the legislation and the divine service and the promises; whose are the fathers, and out of whom is the Christ according to the flesh …

But not all born out of Israel are Israel. The children of the flesh are not the children of God, but the children of the promise He is reckoning for the seed.

God chose Jacob before he was born; that the purpose of God may be remaining as a choice, not out of acts, but of Him Who is calling. And to Moses God said: 'I shall be merciful to whomever I may be merciful, and I shall be pitying whomever I may be pitying.' Consequently, then, it is not of him who is willing, nor of him who is racing, but of God, the Merciful.

God rose up Pharaoh that He should be displaying His power, and so that His name should be published in the entire earth.' Consequently, then, to whom He will, He is merciful, yet whom He will, He is hardening.

We clearly see the sovereignty and the choices of God are in control, and not the choices and the will of man.

Has not the potter the right over the clay? God chooses one vessel, indeed, for honor, yet one for dishonor. If God, wanting to display His indignation and to make His powerful doings known, carries with much patience, the vessels of indignation, adapted for destruction, it is that He should also be making known the riches of His glory on the vessels of mercy.

> # Remember that God's ultimate objective is to bless all mankind!

Since the time God chose Abraham as His instrument, His ultimate objective has been TO BLESS ALL MANKIND (Genesis 12:3; 22:18; 26:5; 28:14). We must remember that this is His intent and His purpose as we consider His interactions with man. Thru God's wisdom He chooses vessels of various kinds to accomplish His purpose. And even when some of His vessels appear to be working against Him (such as Pharaoh, those that mistreated Joseph, or those that had a hand in crucifying Christ), they are actually playing a part in fulfilling God's ultimate purpose. Not all are chosen by God, or given the measure of faith, to be His vessels of honor ... His ecclesia ... the Body of Christ. But all are vessels of some kind, all are serving a purpose, and all will one day be reconciled to God; because from the time He chose Abraham His purpose was for all peoples to be blessed.

Having pursued righteousness thru the law, Israel stumbles. As a result the nations overtook righteousness; a righteousness that is out of faith; even though they were not pursuing righteousness.

What wisdom! Israel sought to establish her own righteousness, rather than becoming subjected to God's righteousness. Man's pride and shortcomings prevent him from finding righteousness, and in response God graciously gives righteousness where it is not even sought.

Remember that the climax of history will be when all are subjected to God (1 Corinthians 15:28). Rather than becoming subject to God's righteousness, Israel sought to establish her own righteousness thru the law. Israel failed to recognize that Christ is the consummation of law for righteousness to everyone who is believing (10:4). Law was not the solution; but faith, that it might accord with God's grace.

CHAPTER 10

Israel has a zeal for God, but not in accord with recognition. They are ignorant of God's righteousness and seek to establish their own righteousness. Christ is the consummation of law for righteousness, to everyone who is believing.

If you should be avowing with your mouth the declaration that Jesus is Lord and should be believing in your heart that God rouses Him from among the dead, you shall be saved.

> Let us not turn this passage into a formula to achieve salvation. We are not commanded to present this as an offer to humanity; that if they will believe and profess they can be saved. Instead, this is the response of those who are given the gift of faith in this present age.
>
> As stated previously, without God's grace to ENABLE us to believe, we COULD NOT and WOULD NOT believe. God chooses SOME and ENABLES them to believe in order that those who DO believe can serve His purpose; to ultimately bless ALL.
>
> Those who believe that man has a "free will" to make choices that determine his ultimate eternal destiny will here label me as a Calvinist; a determinist. I was raised a Methodist and for many years interpreted Scripture thru a Methodist lens, including a belief that man has the free will to make his choices. Please do not label me based on what I am saying. I seek only to escape any bias or lens, and to objectively understand what God is revealing thru His Word. That which God reveals I will believe. There are many earnest believers who read Scripture and who believe it is saying different things. I am merely presenting to the reader how I understand Scripture as fitting together, one portion in relation to other portions, in order to understand what God is saying.

There is no distinction between Jew and Greek, for the same One is Lord of all. Everyone who should be invoking the name of the Lord shall be saved.

How, then, should they be invoking One in Whom they do not believe? Yet how should they be believing One of Whom they do not hear? Yet how should they be hearing apart from one heralding? Yet how should they be heralding if ever they should not be commissioned?

Is the church proclaiming
the right message?

God's means for opening the eyes of believers is thru the commissioning of those who herald the evangel. In this present age it is the Body of Christ that has a commission to be Christ's ambassadors (2 Corinthians 5). But let us be sure we proclaim the correct message for this present age; not a message that has been crafted by organized religion and that has been in error for centuries, a message it thinks is biblically-based but is in actuality taken out of its Biblical context, having been directed to a different people group (Israel) and in a different age that has now passed.

But not all obey the evangel. For Isaiah says, *Lord, who believes our tidings?*

So *obeying the evangel* simply means *believing* it.

First Moses is saying, I shall be provoking you to jealousy over those not a nation (10:19 - from Deuteronomy 32:21). Isaiah is very daring and is saying, 'I was found by those who are not seeking Me; I became disclosed to those who are not inquiring for Me' (10:20 - from Isaiah 65:1). But Israel is a stubborn and contradicting people.

So as Israel stumbles, the nations find God. This is clearly referring to entire nations, and not to individuals within the nations. All within Israel did not stumble, and all within the nations did not have faith. The point is that God had once worked thru Israel as His instrument in dealing with mankind. Now God is working directly thru the Gentile nations.

CHAPTER 11

Israel is not permanently discarded (11:1)

So then, does God thrust away His people? No. As in Elijah's day there is a remnant according to the choice of grace. And if it is of grace, it is no longer out of works. Some of Israel have faith. But the rest were calloused. God gives them a spirit of stupor, eyes not to be observing, and ears not to be hearing. And thru Israel's offense the nations find salvation, provoking jealousy in Israel. And if their casting away is the conciliation of the world, what will the taking back be if not life from among the dead?

Callousness, in part, on Israel has come until the complement of the nations may be entering. And thus all Israel shall be saved ... (11:25)

> # Callousness, in part, has come upon Israel <u>UNTIL</u> the complement of the nations may be entering!

So Israel's casting away is not permanent, but only UNTIL the complement of the nations enters the ecclesia (literally called-out-ones; commonly translated church). And the temporary casting-away of Israel serves a grand purpose; salvation to the nations.

There is stubbornness; and then mercy. Even this stubbornness in man is used by God for the good of mankind.

Even as you once were stubborn toward God, yet now were shown mercy at their stubbornness, thus these also are now stubborn to this mercy of yours, that now they also may be shown mercy.

FOR GOD LOCKS UP ALL TOGETHER IN STUBBORNNESS, THAT HE SHOULD BE MERCIFUL TO ALL (11:30).

O the depths of the riches and the wisdom and the knowledge of God. How inscrutable are His judgments, and untraceable His ways!

God's ways are untraceable. Man cannot "trace" the ways of God using his own reasoning or logic, but can only know that which God has *revealed.* We note that God's judgments and ways may be inscrutable or untraceable, but His overall objective to bless all mankind and to reconcile all of His creation to Himself is very clear in His Word.

Out of Him and through him and for Him is all (11:36).

> ALL is out of God; not just SOME of His creation. And one day, when the purpose of the eons has been achieved (Ephesians 3:11) God will be All in all (1 Corinthians 15:28).

CHAPTER 12

How then shall we live? (12:1)

Present your bodies a sacrifice, living, holy, well pleasing to God, your logical divine service, and not to be configured to this eon, but to be transformed by the renewing of your mind, for you to be testing what is the will of God, good and well pleasing and mature.

> Paul speaks of the appropriate conduct for believers. "I am entreating you, then" links Paul's discussion on behavior to that which he has previously said. It is as if he is saying, "In light of what God has done, live like this."
>
> Note the language; I am ENTREATING you. Grace does not threaten or punish. It can only entreat. Paul begins with a general principle to guide behavior ...

Be of a sane disposition, as God parts to each the measure of faith.

"Measures of faith"

> We are to use the measure of faith given to us. So we observe that believers may have different measures of faith, as given by God. Mature believers must be patient with those having a lesser measure of faith.

One body; many members (12:4)

In a body there are many members. All members in the body do not have the same function. Each are individually members of one another. Thus we who are many are one body in Christ. We are to function in accord with the grace which is given to us.

> Some of the gracious gifts from God are itemized here: prophecy, dispensing, teaching, entreating, generosity, presiding and mercy.

Appropriate behavior within the body [(12:9)]

Paul provides a series of instructions as to the behavior to be expected within the body.

- ✓ Let love be unfeigned
- ✓ Abhor what is wicked; cling to what is good
- ✓ Have fond affection for one another; brotherly fondness
- ✓ Deem one another first
- ✓ Have diligence
- ✓ Be fervent in spirit
- ✓ Be slaving for the Lord
- ✓ Be rejoicing in expectation
- ✓ Endure affliction
- ✓ Persevere in prayer
- ✓ Contribute to the needs of the saints
- ✓ Pursue hospitality
- ✓ Bless those persecuting you
- ✓ Rejoice with those rejoicing; lament with those lamenting
- ✓ Be mutually disposed to one another; humility
- ✓ Don't hold yourself up as prudent
- ✓ Don't render evil for evil
- ✓ Make ideal provision in the sight of all men; if possible out of yourselves
- ✓ Be at peace with all mankind
- ✓ Be not avenging yourselves; vengeance is the Lord's
- ✓ Treat your enemy with kindness
- ✓ Conquer evil with good

CHAPTER 13

Be subject to authorities [(13:1)]

Be subject to the superior authorities. Those in authority have been set under God. So to resist authority is to resist God's mandate. Authority is God's servant for your good.

> In other words, God uses authority as His instrument; an avenger for indignation to him who is committing evil.

Wherefore it is necessary to be subject, not only because of indignation, but also because of conscience.

Taxes are God's ministers, perpetuated for this self-same thing. Render to all their dues, to whom tax, tax, to whom tribute, tribute, to whom fear, fear, to whom honor, honor.

Love one another (13:8)

Love one another; love is the fulfillment of law. To no one owe anything, except to be loving one another, for he who is loving another has fulfilled law.

> # Love fulfills the law.

> When one considers the law concerning such things as adultery, murder, stealing; it is summed up like this: *You shall love your associate as yourself.* If one lived by this standard; loving all associates; there would be no adultery, murder, or stealing.

Love is not working evil to an associate. The complement, then, of law, is love.

Walk respectably (13:11)

Being aware of the era in which we live; it is already the hour for us to be roused out of sleep, for now is our salvation nearer than when we believe. The night progresses, yet the day is near.

Therefore ... We, then, should be putting off the acts of darkness, yet should be putting on the implements of light. As in the day, respectably, should we be walking, not in revelries and drunkenness, strife or jealousy. Put on the Lord Jesus Christ and be making no provision for the lusts of the flesh.

CHAPTER 14

Bear with those of weaker faith (14:1)

Be taking to yourselves the *infirm in the faith*, but not for discrimination of reasonings.

> As we deal with those who may have lesser faith than ourselves, we are to receive the infirm in faith; but not for *discrimination of reasonings.* We bear with those weaker in faith, but we do not look to them for an understanding of spiritual things.

One is believing to eat all things, yet the infirm one is eating greens. Let not him who is eating be scorning him who is not eating. Yet let not him who is not eating be judging him who is eating. Who are you who are judging another's domestic? To his own Master is he standing or falling.

Some place one day over another day (14:5)

One is deciding for one day rather than another day, yet one is deciding for every day. Let each one be fully assured in his own mind. He who is disposed to the day is disposed to it to the Lord. Not one of us is living or dying to himself. If we should be living and if we should be dying, we are the Lord's.

> The strong in faith are not to judge the weak in faith; and the weak in faith should not judge those who are stronger in faith (concerning, for example, eating different foods or observing different days). We do not judge a brother on these issues, as each is responsible only to His Master. It is a matter of conscience; Let each one be fully assured in his own mind (14:5). Each of us is guided by our conscience, with the help of the holy spirit that has been given to us. We take responsibility for ourselves, as opposed to judging others.

> Relative to deciding for one day rather than another day (14:5); we observe that the Sabbath was never given as a command to the Gentiles. It was a part of the Law given to the Israelites. To keep the Sabbath as an observance of God's Law is to put ones-self under the Law. Furthermore, there is nowhere in Scripture a reference to a Sunday Sabbath for Christians! This is based purely on the traditions of men and not the Word of God. It is not wrong for a Believer to set aside Sunday, or any other day, to the Lord, if he chooses to do so. But God's Word should not be distorted in calling for any required observances on any particular day. Such mandatory observances may have been required for Israel in times past, but never for the Body of Christ in this present age. To enforce a Sabbath day or any other portion of the Law would be to reject Christ (see Galatians).

All will give an account to God (14:10)

Why are you judging or scorning your brother? For all of us shall be presented at the dais of God. Each of us shall be giving account concerning himself to God. By no means, then, should we still be judging one another.

Place no stumbling blocks before others (14:13)

Decide this, not to place a stumbling block for a brother, or a snare.

As we exercise the measure of faith given to us, a major consideration must be the possibility of causing others to stumble. That which is right or wrong is determined by our individual conscience; but we are not to place stumbling blocks before others.

Nothing is contaminating of itself, except that the one reckoning anything to be contaminating, to that one it is contaminating. If because of food your brother is sorrowing, you are no longer walking according to love. Consequently we are pursuing that which makes for peace and that which edifies others.

It is ideal not to be eating meat, nor to be drinking wine, nor to do anything by which your brother is stumbling or is being snared or weakened.

Now he who is doubting if he should be eating is condemned, seeing that it is not out of faith. Now everything which is not out of faith is sin.

While certain foods, for example, are not contaminating and would be acceptable for the believer to eat, we are to be guided by a higher principle; seeking to edify others.

CHAPTER 15

Now we, the able, ought to be bearing the infirmities of the impotent, and not to be pleasing ourselves. Let each of us please his associate, for his good, toward his edification. For Christ also pleases not Himself.

Scripture is for our benefit (15:4)

Whatever was written before, was written for this teaching of ours, that through the endurance and the consolation of the scriptures we might have expectation.

Distinction between Israel and the nations (15:8)

As Paul concludes his presentation of the evangel, he makes the distinction between how God was dealing with Israel as compared to the Nations.

Christ has become the Servant of the Circumcision, for the sake of the truth of God, to confirm the patriarchal promises. Yet the nations are to glorify God for His mercy.

> Confirmation of the patriarchal promises was the expectation of Israel. What was unanticipated prior to Paul's evangel was the mercy God was showing to the nations.

May the God of expectation be filling you with all joy and peace in believing, for you to be superabounding in expectation, in the power of holy spirit.

Closing (15:14)

I write in part to *prompt* you because of the grace given to me from God; for me to be *the minister of Christ Jesus for the nations.* I dare not speak any of what Christ does not affect through me for the obedience of the nations, in word and work, in the power of signs and miracles, in the power of God's spirit. I am ambitious to bring the evangel where Christ is not named.

> Paul is taking a contribution to Jerusalem for the poor of the saints there, after which he intends to pass thru Rome and to Spain. Paul asks the saints to ...

Struggle with me in prayers for me, that I should be rescued from the stubborn in Judea, that my dispensation for Jerusalem is well received, and that I may be coming to the saints in Rome.

CHAPTER 16

> Paul commends 28 different people by name.
>
> ECCLESIA AT THEIR HOUSE: We receive a glimpse of the structure (or non-structure) of the church (ecclesia) in that day. Referring to Prisca and Aquila, Paul makes note of *the ecclesia at their house.* And Paul also passes along greetings from *all the ecclesias of Christ.*
>
> APOSTLES: Paul makes reference to Andronicus and Junias as notable among the apostles. So again we note that the apostles are no longer limited to the 12 in Jesus' day.
>
> Two final notes relative to appropriate behavior ...

Avoid those making dissentions and snares. Be wise for good, yet artless for evil.

> Paul's amanuenses, who has recorded Paul's letter, records his own greeting.

I, Tertius, the writer of the epistle, am greeting you in the Lord.

The letter concludes with a benediction.

Now to Him Who is able to establish you in accord with *my evangel,* and the heralding of Christ Jesus in accord with the *revelation of a secret hushed in times eonian, yet manifested now* and through prophetic scriptures ... according to the injunction of the eonian God being made known to all nations for faith-obedience ... (16:25-27).

Truly Paul's writings are a revelation of things that had been a secret in times past, as God calls him to be a different kind of apostle; commissioned to go directly to the Gentiles with a message Paul received directly from Christ Jesus.

Romans
The gospel according to Paul ("My evangel" 2:16)

The evangel introduced   1:14
- God's power for salvation to everyone who is believing (1:16)
- In it God's righteousness is being revealed (1:17)

God's indignation is being revealed   1:18
- God has revealed Himself to man
- But man does not glory or thank Him
- God gives man over to his lusts
- So God causes man's reasonings to be vain
- Man's mind is made "disqualified"
- Doing things deserving of death

God will judge   2:1
- Man not qualified to judge
- Those judging do the same things
- God's patience leads to repentance
- God will judge in the day of indignation
- In accord with man's acts
- Life eonian or indignation and fury
- No partiality with God's judgment
- Judging the "hidden things of humanity"

Israel has dishonored God   2:17
- They rest on the law
- They have the *form* of truth in the law
- But they do not teach themselves
- Boasting in law, they dishonor God
- Circumcision only benefits if practiced
- Though some disbelieve, God is still faithful

None are just   3:9
- No one is understanding
- Not one is seeking out God
- No flesh justified by works of law
- Through law is the recognition of sin

YET - God's righteousness is manifest   3:21

- Apart from law ... thru Jesus Christ's faith
- For all, and on all who are believing
- Justified gratuitously in His grace
- No distinction, for all sinned and are wanting
- Display of His righteousness in current era
- Where then is boasting?

Belief is reckoned for righteousness   4:1

- Abraham believes God ... reckoned righteous
- Abraham received the "sign" of circumcision
- It is of faith that it may accord with grace
- The promise was not thru law, but faith
- Not Abraham only ... we who are believing

Conciliated ... now justified   5:1

- Conciliated to God thru Christ's death
- Now justified in His blood
- We may be having peace with God
- We shall be saved from indignation

Adam and Christ compared   5:12

- Judgment out of one to condemnation
- One offense for all mankind to condemnation
- Grace out of many offenses to a just award
- One disobedience ... the many are sinners
- One just award for all mankind for justifying
- One obedience ... the many are just

We are under grace, not law   6:1

- We died to sin ... baptized into Christ's death
- Should be walking in newness of life
- No longer slaving for Sin
- Reckon yourselves dead to sin
- Let not sin be reigning in your mortal body
- Now enslaved to Righteousness
- Present members as slaves to Righteousness
- We died to the law ... are exempt from law

The struggle under the law   7:7

- The law made us aware of sin
- It produces in me all manner of coveting
- The law is spiritual ... I am fleshly
- I do what I do not wish to do
- Sin makes its home in me
- Captive to the law of sin
- A wretched man am I
- What will rescue me?

Grace!   7:25

- Nothing is condemnation to those in Christ
- What was impossible to the law; God did
- He condemns sin in the flesh
- Law's just requirements fulfilled in us
- We are not walking in accord with flesh
- Walking in accord with spirit
- The holy spirit given to us
- The spirit will be vivifying our mortal bodies

We await redemption   8:18

- Sufferings not deserving of glory to come
- Creation was subjected to vanity
- All creation groans, awaiting redemption
- We groan also, awaiting deliverance of our body
- That which we expect, we await with endurance
- The spirit helps our infirmity
- God is working all together for our good
- Nothing can separate us from God's love

What about Israel? (God's sovereignty)   9:9

- God chose Jacob before he was born
- "I shall be merciful to whomever I may"
- God rose up Pharaoh to display His power
- Israel zealous; but not in accord with recognition
- Christ is the consummation of law
- God locks all in stubbornness; that He should be merciful to all
- Israel stumbles ... the nations find God
- In their offense is salvation to the nations
- To provoke Israel to jealousy

- Israel calloused *UNTIL* nations enter
- Thus all Israel shall be saved

How shall we live, in light of God's grace?   12:1
- Present bodies a sacrifice
- As God parts to each the measure of faith

One body ... many members   12:4
- Not all members have the same function
- Prophecy, dispensing, teaching, entreating, generosity, presiding mercy
- In accord with the grace given us

Behavior within the Body   12:9
- Let love be unfeigned
- Abhor what is wicked; cling to good
- Fond affection for one another
- Deem one another first
- Be slaving for the Lord
- Rejoice in expectation
- Endure affliction
- Persevere in prayer
- Contribute to the needs of the saints
- Pursue hospitality
- Bless those persecuting you
- Be mutually disposed to one another
- Don't render evil for evil
- Be at peace with all mankind
- Vengeance is the Lord's
- Treat enemies with kindness
- Be subject to authorities
- Love one another
- Love is the complement of the law
- Walk respectably
- Receive the infirm in faith
- Place no stumbling block
- Bear with the weakness of others
- Superabound in expectation

CLOSING THOUGHTS

Romans is largely a presentation of DOCTRINE, centered on God's righteousness that has been provided in Christ Jesus as contrasted with the law. In his commentary, A.E. Knoch observes that Romans reveals God's present grace, in preparation for the higher unfoldings in Ephesians. *The Companion Bible* describes Romans as, "The ABC of the believer's education. Until its lesson is learned, we know and can know nothing."

This letter tells us that correct doctrine is important. Romans speaks of God's wrath against sin, and how righteousness is provided solely by God's grace, apart from any works of man.

But the letter is not entirely focused on doctrine. Beginning with chapter 9 Paul begins to talk about proper behavior in response to God's grace. Salvation is not dependent upon works; but Paul entreats the ecclesia to exhibit good works in response to grace.

"The Roman Road" is an evangelism tool used by many churches today. It is an attempt to delineate how one can be saved, using Romans as a basis. The formula goes like this:

1. All have sinned and fall short of the glory of God (Romans 3:23)

2. The wage of sin is death (Romans 6:23a)

3. But the gift of God is eternal life through Jesus Christ our Lord (Romans 6:23b)

4. God demonstrates His own love for us, in that while we were yet sinners Christ died for us (Romans 5:8)

5. Whoever will call on the name of the Lord will be saved (Romans 10:13)

6. If you confess with your mouth Jesus as Lord and believe in your heart that God raised Jesus from the dead, you shall be saved; for with the heart man believes, resulting in righteousness, and with the mouth he confesses, resulting in salvation (Romans 10:9,10).

The problem is that the "Roman Road" as presented by most Christians today is an *offer* resulting in an eternal destiny of *heaven* for those who accept the terms, or *hell* for those who do not.

But the real "Roman Road" is far more glorious than that!

1. None are righteous, and none are even seeking out God;

2. Yet God provides the solution entirely of Himself so that no man can boast.

3. Salvation in this present age comes not by works of any kind, but through faith that it may accord with grace.

4. Those able to believe in this age of faith recognize the grace and the love of God and are a part of the ecclesia; those called-out from humanity to serve a specific purpose in the plan of God.

5. God has conciliated the world to Himself, not counting man's sins against him.

6. The message of Christ's Ambassadors today is, *Be conciliated to God* (2 Corinthians 5).

We do not present an *offer* to mankind resulting in an eternal destiny of heaven or hell. We present a *proclamation* of what God has done, and what He is in the process of doing. Ultimately all will be saved, even those not recognizing God in this present age. All will be reconciled to God when He becomes All in all.

1 Corinthians

An Overview of the Scriptures, by
BOB EVELY © *2018.*
An Independent Minister of Christ Jesus,
Of the church at Wilmore, Kentucky

"For even as, in Adam, all are dying, thus also, in Christ, shall all be vivified. Yet each in his own class ..." (15:22)

1 Thessalonians	50-52 AD	During 2nd Journey
2 Thessalonians	52-53 AD	During 2nd Journey
Galatians (early theory)	54 AD	End of 2nd Journey
1 Corinthians	**Spring 57 AD**	**During 3rd Journey**
2 Corinthians	Fall 57 AD	During 3rd Journey
Galatians	Winter 57 AD	During 3rd Journey
Romans	Spring 58 AD	During 3rd Journey
Colossians	61-62 AD	During 1st Captivity
Ephesians	61-62 AD	During 1st Captivity
Philemon	62-63 AD	During 1st Captivity
Philippians	63 AD	During 1st Captivity
1 Timothy	67 AD	Between Captivities
Titus	67 AD	Between Captivities
2 Timothy	Spring 68 AD	During 2nd Captivity

CHAPTER 1

The address on the envelope (1:1)

Paul, a called apostle of Christ Jesus;

To the ecclesia of God which is in Corinth, hallowed in Christ Jesus, called saints, together with all in every place who are invoking the name of our Lord, Jesus Christ.

> ECCLESIA: Generally translated "church," *ecclesia* in the Greek literally means called-out-ones. The called-out-ones of God would be those whom God has called out from humanity to serve some purpose. The called-out-ones may not always be the same group from one age to the next. During Jesus' earthly ministry the called-out-ones were believers among Israel. Paul introduced an ecclesia with a different make-up; the Body of Christ, which included Jews and Gentiles on an equal basis.

> HALLOWED/HOLY: Paul describes the ecclesia as *hallowed,* called *saints.* Both *hallowed* (hagiazo) and *saints* (hagion) are from the same Greek root word most often translated holy. When holy refers to people, it is often translated saints. The ecclesia are those made holy or set apart by God.

In everything you are enriched in Him, in all expression and all knowledge; not deficient in any grace, awaiting the unveiling of our Lord Jesus Christ.

> As we await Christ to come and snatch us away (1 Thessalonians 4:17) to extricate us out of the present wicked eon (Galatians 1:4), we are not lacking in any grace; and we are *enriched* in Christ in all things.

Let there be no schisms (1:10)

I am entreating you that all may be saying the same thing, and there may be no schisms among you, but you may be attuned to the same mind and to the same opinion. There are strifes among you. Some are saying "I am of Paul," and others "I am of Apollos" or "I am of Cephas" or "I am of Christ."

> Strife had entered the ecclesia, much like denominational differences and the differences between individual churches today. Paul entreats the ecclesia to all be saying the same thing, and with no schisms, attuned to the same mind and to the same opinion.

> Truth is truth, and once one understands truth he will be attuned to all others who see truth. All will be of the same mind; the mind of Christ. But schism is not eliminated by simply consenting, without debate, to the loudest voices in the ecclesia. We should not be lobbying for our opinions as to the things of God. All within the ecclesia, the Body of Christ, should be seeking, and working together to understand the mind of God as revealed in His word.

> Remember that in Paul's day there was not a Baptist Church, a Methodist Church, etc. There was simply one ecclesia. They met together in smaller groups, or ecclesias, often in peoples' homes, and likely very informally, but all were a part of the single ecclesia. How complicated and divided the ecclesia has become in our present world of denominations, independent churches, articles of religion, membership covenants, rituals and ceremonies. How the ecclesia has been systematized, fragmented and split apart; far from the unity Paul called for.

The evangel ^(1:13)

You were not baptized into the name of Paul. I thank God that I baptize none of you except Crispus and Gaius and the household of Stephanas. Christ does not commission me to be baptizing, but to bring the evangel.

> Paul's commission is to bring the evangel; not to baptize. Notice how unimportant baptism seems to be from Paul's perspective.

Our "Great Commission"

> But what about "The Great Commission" found in Matthew? *"Going, then, disciple all the nations, baptizing them ..."* (Matthew 28:19). While most believers in the church today see "The Great Commission" as *their* commission, obviously Paul does not. He is not commissioned to be baptizing. "The Great Commission" is taken out of context today. It speaks of Israel discipling the nations, as will be done in the end times upon the earth. (Revelation) It does not speak to the church today at all. We have a different commission; not the one found in Matthew 28.

The word of the cross is stupidity to those who are perishing. But to us who are being saved it is the power of God. Where are the wise? Does God not make stupid the wisdom of this world? God delights, through the stupidity of the heralding, to save those who are believing.

The Jews seek signs, and the Greeks seek wisdom. But we are heralding Christ crucified; a snare to the Jews and stupidity to the nations. But to those who are called, both Jews and Greeks, Christ is the power and wisdom of God.

> So only *those who are called* recognize the evangel as the power of God.

God chooses *the stupidity of the world*; the weak; the ignoble; the contemptible; so that no flesh at all should be boasting. Yet you, of Him, are in Christ Jesus; Who became to us wisdom from God, righteousness, holiness and deliverance.

> The world often ridicules the idea of the crucifixion; and even a belief in God who is to be recognized and respected and worshipped. The world

trusts in worldly power, worldly knowledge, and so-called wisdom. But God humbles the world by showing how useless these worldly things are; and He introduces wisdom and power through something that seems weak and unintelligent; the evangel that Paul brings.

CHAPTER 2

I come not with superiority of word or wisdom; but only Jesus Christ and Him crucified. I came to you in weakness and fear; not with the persuasive words of human wisdom but with demonstration of spirit and power; that your faith may not be in the wisdom of men but in the power of God.

Much of what Paul states here concerning the evangel is a re-statement of his presentation in Romans. It is God's power and righteousness (Romans 1:16; 3:21). It is deliverance (Romans 3:24). There is no room for boasting (Romans 3:27). As Paul prepares to address some issues within the Corinthian ecclesia, he begins by reminding them of his evangel.

Maturity is needed to understand spiritual things (2:6)

We speak wisdom among the mature; but not wisdom of this eon. We speak God's wisdom in a secret, which has been concealed, which God designates before; before the eons, for our glory.

If wisdom "not of this eon" is being spoken, how can we understand?

To us God reveals; through His spirit. Humanity is only acquainted with things of the spirit of humanity. No one knows that which is of God except the spirit of God.

We have been given the spirit of God that we may perceive that which is being graciously given to us by God. We speak of this, not with words taught by human wisdom but with words taught by the spirit; matching that which is spiritual with those who are spiritual. The soulish man is not receiving those things which are of the spirit of God; they are stupidity to him.

Who knew the mind of the Lord? Who will be deducing from Him? Yet we have the mind of Christ.

Only those called; those who have eyes to believe; those who have been given the spirit of God; can understand spiritual things.

CHAPTER 3

But the Corinthians were not mature (3:1)

But you are still fleshly. I could not speak to you as to spiritual things, but only as to fleshly things.

> Despite the fact that God has revealed, and the believers have the holy spirit and should be able to understand, they were minors in Christ and could not understand spiritual things. How does Paul discern that these believers are fleshly, and unable to understand spiritual things?

Where there is jealousy and strife among you, are you not fleshly and walking according to man? For whenever anyone may be saying, "I am of Paul" or "I am of Apollos" is he not fleshly?

> Division is the manifestation of man's walking according to the flesh. Men were being elevated and followed, creating divisions much like those seen in the Church today; I follow the Methodists; I follow the Baptists, etc.

Based on what Paul is saying here, we should not expect the more advanced truths that he would share with the mature, which we find in his later "perfection epistles" (Ephesians, Colossians, Philippians)

Who is Apollos or Paul? Servants as God gives to each! I plant and Apollos waters, but God makes it grow. He who plants or waters is nothing; but only God who makes it grow. We are God's fellow workers. You are God's farm; His building.

Building on the one foundation (3:10)

According to the grace of God which is being granted to me, as a wise foreman I lay a foundation, yet another is building on it. Let each one beware how he is building on it. No other foundation can one lay beside that which is laid; Jesus Christ.

If anyone is building on this foundation gold and silver, precious stones, wood, grass, straw, each one's work will become apparent, for the day will make it evident, for it is being revealed by fire. And the fire will be testing each one's work; what kind it is. If anyone's work is remaining which he builds on it, he will get wages. If anyone's work is burned up, he will forfeit it, yet he shall be saved, yet as through fire (3:13).

> The works of a believer will be evaluated by God at some future time (Romans 14:12; 2 Corinthians 5:10). We note that the absence of good works does not jeopardize one's salvation, but it will affect the wages (rewards) received.

Remember you are a temple of God (3:16)

Are you not aware that you are a temple of God and the spirit of God is making its home in you? If anyone is corrupting the temple of God, God will be corrupting him, for the temple of God is holy, which you are.

Don't delude yourself. Don't presume to be wise. The wisdom of this world is stupidity with God. Let no one be boasting in men.

> God's spirit resides in the believers; for they are His temple. Don't corrupt the temple. Don't delude yourselves, presuming to be wise. Don't boast. From these remarks we can develop some idea of the issues within the ecclesia at Corinth that prompted Paul to write this letter.

CHAPTER 4

Administrators of God's secrets (4:1)

Let a man be reckoning with us as deputies of Christ and administrators of God's secrets. An administrator should seek to be found faithful and is examined by the Lord and is not concerned with how he might be examined by men.

Don't judge before the season (4:5)

Be not judging anything before the season, till the Lord should be coming. He will illuminate the hidden things of darkness and manifest the counsels of the hearts. And then applause will be coming to each one from God.

> A close parallel to Romans 2, Paul speaks to the issue of judging our fellow brethren. God will judge at the appropriate time (when the Lord comes). We who believe will appear before the dais of God to give an

account for our actions (Romans 14:10; 2 Corinthians 5:10). Then reward ("applause") will come from God.

No grounds for boasting (4:6)

Learn not to be disposed above what is written, that no one may be puffed up; one against another. What you have was given to you, so there are no grounds for boasting.

> # Be not disposed above what is written.

Perhaps we judge one another because we presume to know things beyond what God has revealed; beyond what is written.

God demonstrates with us, the last apostles, as death-doomed. We became a theatre to the world and to messengers and to men. We are stupid because of Christ, weak, dishonored, hungering, thirsting, naked, buffeted, unsettled, toiling, working with our own hands. But you are prudent, strong, and glorious.

Being reviled, we are blessing; being persecuted, we are bearing with it; being calumniated, we are entreating.

I am entreating you; become imitators of me. I am sending Timothy to remind you of my ways which are in Christ Jesus, according as I am teaching everywhere in every ecclesia.

Paul points out the differences between what he is modeling, and what he is seeing in the Corinthian believers.

CHAPTER 5

Dealing with immoral behavior (5:1)

There is prostitution among you, and such prostitution which is not even named among the nations, so that someone has his father's wife. And you do not mourn but are puffed up.

Are we to judge, or not?

Paul has warned against judging before the season. But here he says there is a place for judging within the ecclesia, at least concerning immoral behavior. Rather than mourning the immoral behavior in their midst, the ecclesia is "puffed up;" apparently having justified the behavior thru reason.

Remove the one committing this act. Give up such a one to Satan for the extermination of the flesh, that the spirit may be saved in the day of the Lord Jesus.

Observe that discipline of the immoral brother is not vindictive, but toward the goal of his salvation. Correction is brought to the Body of Christ, and the welfare of the individual being disciplined is considered. This expresses God's heart; that none are punished endlessly, and that correction is accomplished.

Are you not aware that a little leaven is leavening the whole kneading? Clean out, then, the old leaven.

Addressing matters of immorality within the ecclesia also serves to preserve the ecclesia itself.

Do not be commingling with paramours. It is not as to the paramours of this world, or the greedy and extortionate, or idolaters, else you ought to come out of the world. Yet now I write to you not to be commingling with anyone named a brother, if he should be a paramour, or greedy, or an idolater, or a reviler, or a drunkard, or an extortioner. With such a one you are not even to be eating.

Judgment within the ecclesia.

Judge only inside the ecclesia. These actions against the one with immoral behavior relate only when the behavior is found WITHIN the ecclesia, not in the world outside the ecclesia.

What is it to me to be judging those outside? You are not judging those within! God is judging those outside. Expel the wicked one from among yourselves.

> In the church today the reverse seems to be more prevalent. Sin within the Church is tolerated, and sin in the world outside the Church is condemned. Those within the ecclesia should remember that abortion is wrong, as is homosexuality, adultery, greed, etc. But we are instructed to regulate these things WITHIN the Body of Christ; not among those of the world outside the body.

CHAPTER 6

Settling disputes within the ecclesia (6:1)

Do you, having business with each other, dare to be judged before the unjust as opposed to the saints? Are you not aware that the saints will judge the world? You will be judging messengers, not to mention life's affairs. Is there not one wise man able to adjudicate amidst his brethren? Brother is suing brother, and before unbelievers!

Bad enough that there are lawsuits among yourselves. Would it not be better if you are injured or cheated? But you are injuring and cheating brethren!

> It would seem appropriate that if a dispute arises in the ecclesia, another Believer should be asked to mediate. And if resolution is not possible, the aggrieved party should drop the dispute and suffer loss, rather than to bring disgrace to Christ by litigating the matter before unbelievers. Everything the believer does should be done to glorify God.
>
> Paul now admonishes the believers to deal with one another justly ...

Are you not aware that the unjust shall not be enjoying the allotment of God's kingdom? Be not deceived. Neither paramours, nor idolaters, nor adulterers, nor catamites, nor sodomites, nor thieves, nor the greedy, nor drunkards, nor revilers, nor extortioners shall be enjoying the allotment of God's kingdom. Some of you were these, but you are bathed off; hallowed; justified.

> Paul is not talking here about an eternal destiny of heaven or hell. If enjoying the allotment of God's kingdom refers to "going to heaven," what part does faith play in this passage? Only man's works are discussed.

> # Remember, the believer has been justified; reckoned just. He is not unjust!

Knowing that salvation comes by grace through faith (God's gracious gift), Paul is stating as an example to believers that without God's grace freely given to them these behaviors would have prevented them from participating in the kingdom that is to come upon the earth. This would have been their expectation before the revelation Paul brings concerning their destiny in the heavens. This earthly kingdom allotment does not pertain to them. Paul is simply pointing out those things that please and displease God, to encourage proper behavior within the ecclesia. In other words, "You know that those of the world exhibit these behaviors and will not enter the kingdom, so you who have been saved by God's grace should not exhibit these behaviors as they are objectionable to God. You should know better!"

This interpretation is supported by verse 11. *Some of you were these, but you are bathed off, but you are hallowed, but you were justified in the name of our Lord Jesus and by the spirit of our God.* Paul reminds the believers that they are not as those of the world. They are not unjust as those who will not enjoy the allotment of God's kingdom. They are just (or justified). They were called and hallowed. Paul asks them to remember this as they live their life within the ecclesia. And having been hallowed and justified ...

All is allowed me, but not all is expedient. All is allowed me, but I will not be put under its authority by anything.

All may be permitted through our freedom in Christ, but not all things operate for our good; and we should be aware of those things that may addict us and cause us to be under their authority.

Coping with fleshly passions (6:13)

The body is for the Lord, not prostitution. Are you not aware that your bodies are members of Christ? Should I be taking the members of Christ and making them members of a prostitute? No! Are you not aware that he who joins a prostitute is one body? For He says that the two will be one flesh. He who joins the Lord is one spirit. Flee from prostitution.

He who is committing prostitution is sinning against his own body. Are you not aware that your body is a temple of the holy spirit in you, which you have from God, and you are not your own? For you are bought with a price. By all means glorify God in your body.

> Just as in Old Testament times, God dwells in His temple, and that place is hallowed by His presence. As the holy spirit indwells the believer, his body becomes God's temple. Our bodies are no longer ours, but God's. Like the temple of old in Jerusalem, nothing should be permitted to enter God's temple that would defile it.

CHAPTER 7

Deal with passions thru marriage (7:1)

It is ideal for a man not to be touching a woman. Yet because of prostitutions, let each man have a wife for himself and each woman have her own husband. Let the husband render to the wife her due, and likewise the wife also to her husband. Do not deprive one another except sometime by agreement for a period, that you have time for prayer. But then be the same once again, lest Satan be trying you.

This is a concession not an injunction. I want all men to be as myself, but each has his own gracious gift from God. I say this to the unmarried and widows, that it is ideal for them to remain as I. But if they are not controlling themselves, let them marry.

> So Paul is not married, and he states this as his preference. But he recognizes that not all have the gift (chastity) and so he speaks of this concession for those needing to be married to fulfill their passions appropriately.

A wife is not to be separated from her husband. Yet if she should be separated let her remain unmarried or be conciliated to her husband. And a husband is not to leave his wife.

As for marriage to unbelievers; a believer with an unbelieving spouse should not leave the spouse if he/she approves of making a home with him/her. The unbelieving husband/wife is hallowed by the believing spouse. Yet if the unbeliever is separating, let him separate.

It is better to remain as you were when God called you; whether circumcised or uncircumcised (circumcision is nothing), slave or free. If you were called when a slave, let it not be causing you concern. Though if you are able to become free, do so. For in the Lord a slave is the Lord's freedman. And the one free when he is called is the slave of Christ. But do not become slaves of men. With a price you were bought.

Let each remain as when he was called. You are bound to a wife? Do not seek to be loosed. You have been loosed from a wife? Do not seek a wife. Yet if you ever should be marrying, also, you did not sin.

The era is limited. (7:29)

> This appears to be what is driving Paul's dissertation. Since he believes the era is limited and the return of Christ is near, it is better to remain as-is for the limited time remaining, focusing on spiritual things. Clearly Paul did not yet understand that Christ would not be returning in his lifetime.

The unmarried one is solicitous about the things of the Lord, how he should be pleasing the Lord. Yet he who marries is solicitous about the things of the world, how he should be pleasing his wife.

> The reason being unmarried is preferred (if one has that gift and does not burn with passion) is that it allows full focus on pleasing the Lord.

CHAPTER 8

Love builds up (8:1)

Concerning idol sacrifices: We are aware that we all have knowledge. Knowledge puffs up yet love builds up. If anyone is *presuming* to know anything, he knows not as he must know. If anyone is loving God, he is known by Him.

Do not become a stumbling block (8:4)

Concerning the eating of idol sacrifices; an idol is nothing. There is no other God except One. Even if there are others being called gods in heaven or on earth; even as there are many gods and many lords, for us there is one God, the Father, out of Whom all is; and one Lord, Jesus Christ, through Whom all is; and we through Him.

> *God* is simply a title that means *subjector*. This is *elohim* in the Hebrew Old Testament. We can find cases in the Scriptures where *men* were referred to as elohim, or gods. Likewise *lord* is simply a title denoting

> authority over others. And so there are other gods and lords, but for us within the ecclesia there is only ONE God the Father and ONE Lord. (Observe the distinction between these two entities; the Father distinct from the Son.)
>
> Another note. In Romans 11:36 Paul wrote that all is out of God. Similarly we see in 1 Corinthians 8:6 that all is out of God (He is the source of all things), and all is through Christ (He is the channel of all things). God deals with mankind only thru Christ, and even creation was carried out thru Christ. Christ is the way to the Father, and the only means thru Whom we can know God.

But not all have this knowledge concerning idols. Some are eating of an idol sacrifice and their conscience, being weak, is being polluted. Food does not give us a standing with God; whether we eat it or not does not matter.

But do not let your rights become a stumbling block to the weak. Will not the conscience of him who is weak be hardened to the eating of the idol sacrifices? For the weak one is perishing by your knowledge; the brother because of whom Christ died. In thus sinning against brethren, and beating their weak conscience, you are sinning against Christ. So if food is snaring my brother, I may not be eating meat for the eon.

> We should be prepared to give up rights at times so as not to snare a weaker brother.

CHAPTER 9

Paul's example; all things to all men ^(9:1)

Am I not free? Am I not an apostle? Have only I and Barnabas no right not to be working? Who is warring and supplying his own rations? The Lord prescribes that those who are announcing the evangel are to be living of the evangel.

> As an apostle Paul could have insisted upon certain rights. But he forfeited rights for the sake of the evangel.

Nevertheless we do not use this right. We are forgoing all, lest we may be giving any hindrance to the evangel of Christ.

> Paul was entrusted with an administration; bringing the evangel. He will not let anything stand in the way of that commission, even if it required him to forfeit certain rights and freedoms.

Woe to me if I should not be bringing the evangel! For if I am engaging in this voluntarily, I have wages, yet if involuntarily, I have been entrusted with an administration.

> Paul brought the evangel without expense, so as not to use up his authority in the evangel.

I enslave myself to all, that I should be gaining the more. To the Jews I became as a Jew. To those under law I became as under law, to be gaining those under law. To all have I become all; that I should undoubtedly be saving some.

I do this to become a joint participant. I am racing for an incorruptible wreath. Every contender is controlling himself in all things to obtain a corruptible wreath; yet we race for an incorruptible wreath. I discipline my body. Thus am I racing, not as dubious, thus am I boxing, not as punching the air, but I am belaboring my body and leading it into slavery, lest somehow, when heralding to others, I myself may become disqualified.

CHAPTER 10

Facing trials (10:1)

The majority of your fathers fell in the wilderness. This became types of us, for us not to be lusters after evil things, according as they lust. And do not become idolaters, as some of them; nor commit prostitution, nor put the Lord on trial, nor murmur. These things befell them typically; but it was written for our admonition.

> "Your fathers" shows Paul is talking with the Jewish believers at Corinth. There were also Gentiles in the group, but this comment is for the benefit of the Jewish believers.

No trial has taken you except what is human. God is faithful. He will not be leaving you to be tried above what you are able, but, together with the trial, will be making the sequel also, to enable you to undergo it.

> God does not provide an escape from trials, as some Bible translations will tell us. If we escaped our trials, we would not need to be enabled to "undergo" them. Instead God provides a SEQUEL; a positive conclusion to the trial. Ours is not to seek escape from trials, but grace to endure. And we can contemplate the positive outcome that the trial is designed to produce.

The cup we are blessing is the communion of the blood of Christ. The bread we are breaking is the communion of the Body of Christ. We who are many are one bread, one body, for we all partake of the one bread. Observe Israel according to the flesh. That which the nations are sacrificing they sacrifice to demons and not to God. Do not become participants with the demons.

We have freedom; but consider others (10:23)

All is permitted, but not all is edifying. Let one not seek his own welfare, but the welfare of another.

Eat anything that is sold at the meat market. Examine nothing because of conscience. For the Lord's is the earth and that which fills it.

If an unbeliever invites you and you want to go, be eating everything that is placed before you, examining nothing because of conscience. Yet if anyone should be saying to you, 'This is a sacred sacrifice,' do not eat, because of that one who divulges it, and conscience. Yet conscience, I am saying, not that of yourself, but that of another.

Why is my freedom being decided by another's conscience? Whether you are eating or drinking, or anything you are doing, do all for the glory of God. And become not a stumbling block. I seek not my own expedience but that of the many, that they may be saved. Become imitators of me, as I also am of Christ.

> Some may see "that they may be saved" as an inference that all will not be ultimately saved. Let us keep in mind what Paul means in this letter when he uses the term *saved*. Remember from Romans that mankind is headed toward a future day of God's judgment, when His indignation will be unveiled. The believer will be saved from that coming day, as his faith is reckoned as righteousness. But we must remember that even the coming indignation is intended to accomplish God's overall objective; the reconciliation of all, that He might become All in all (we will see this in 15:28). So for Paul, to be *saved* is to be saved from the day of indignation. But in the end, all will be reconciled, and saved from what orthodoxy claims is an eternal torment.

CHAPTER 11

God's hierarchy (11:1)

God is the head of Christ.
Christ is the head of every man.

Man is the head of the woman.

Man is inherently the image and glory of God.
Woman is the glory of the man.

Woman was created out of man.
Woman was created because of the man.

Man and woman are not apart from each other.
As the woman is *out of* the man, thus the man is *through* the woman.

Yet all is of God.

> The discussion of men and women wearing, or not wearing, head coverings is simply an outward, physical demonstration of these basic truths concerning "headship" that Paul has shared. And the bottom line; all is of God!

Courtesies when coming together (11:17)

You are coming together, not for the better. I am hearing of schisms.

Assembling is not always a good thing!

> Something to keep in mind when the Body of Christ assembles. Assembling for the sake of assembling is not necessarily a good thing. It is possible to come together, but not for the better.

At your coming together in the same place, it is not to be eating the Lord's dinner, for each one is getting his own dinner before in the eating, and one, indeed is hungry, yet one is drunk.

As often as you are eating the bread and drinking the cup you are announcing the Lord's death until He should be coming. Whoever should be eating the bread or drinking the cup of the Lord unworthily, will be liable for the body and the blood of the Lord. Now let a man test himself first, and thus let him eat of the bread and drink of the cup. For he who is eating and drinking unworthily is eating and drinking judgment to himself, not discriminating the body of the Lord. Therefore many among you are infirm and ailing, and a considerable number are reposing. For if we adjudicated ourselves, we would not be judged. Yet, being judged, we are being disciplined by the Lord, that we may not be condemned with the world.

> Now comes the bottom line ...

So that, my brethren, when coming together to eat, be waiting for one another. If anyone is hungry let him eat at home.

CHAPTER 12

You are the Body of Christ ^(12:1)

Concerning spiritual endowments (gifts); there are apportionments of graces and services; yet the same spirit and the same Lord. There are apportionments of operations yet the same God Who is operating all in all.

> God is operating *all in all* but He is not yet All in all. That will happen at the climax of history, as noted by Paul in 15:28.

To each one is being given the manifestation of the spirit, with a view to expedience.

> "Expedience" would mean that which is appropriate, or which is promoting one's interests; in this case the interests of God. Paul now provides a list of gifts given thru the spirit ...

Through the spirit one is given the word of wisdom, the word of knowledge, faith, graces of healing, operations of powerful deeds, prophecy, discrimination of spirits, species of languages, translation of languages. All these one and the same spirit is operating, apportioning to each his own, according as He is intending.

The body is not one member, but many; yet all the members are one body. In one spirit we all are baptized into one body, whether Jews or Greeks, slaves or free. Not all are an ear or an eye. If the whole body were an eye, where would be the hearing? God places the members in the body as He wills.

There are many members, yet one body. The eye cannot say to the hand, I have no need of you. God blends the body together, giving to that which is deficient more exceeding honor that there may be no schism in the body, but the members may be mutually solicitous for one another. And when one member is suffering, all the members are

- 107 -

sympathizing. When one member is being esteemed, all the members are rejoicing with it.

> Paul lists the various members God has placed in the ecclesia ...

God placed in the ecclesia; first apostles, second, prophets, third, teachers, thereupon powers, thereupon graces of healing, supports, pilotage (steering/governing), species of languages. Not all members are the same. Not all are apostles. Not all are prophets. Yet be zealous for the greater graces.

And still I am showing you a path, suited to transcendence.

> *Transcendence* is a state of being or existence above and beyond the limits of material experience. Compare the list of spiritual gifts found here with the list in Paul's later revelation in Ephesians 4:11. Could the difference be accounted to Paul's statement in 12:31; "a path suited to transcendence?" In the later list, some of the "lesser" gifts (powers, healing, languages) are omitted. The termination of some gifts was foretold in 13:8.

Are some of these gifts now extinct?

> Remember that Paul could not share deeper spiritual truths with the Corinthians as they were not mature (3:1). Yet he was able to share these secrets with the more mature believers (Ephesians 4:13; Philippians 3:14; Colossians 1:28; Colossians 4:12). Furthermore, Paul "completed" the Word of God as noted in Colossians 1:25; so there would appear to be no longer a need for prophecy to provide a word from God. Miracles and healings were manifestations that accompanied the kingdom evangel, as signs of what was to come when the kingdom came upon the earth. But the expectation of the Body of Christ is not upon the earth. We do not look for Christ to come to reign upon His throne in Jerusalem; that is Israel's expectation. We listen for the trumpet to sound, and for Christ to snatch us away and meet us in the air, to take us to be with Him in the celestials (1 Thessalonians 4:13ff).

Could it be that by the time Paul wrote to the Ephesians, some of the gifts had ceased; accounting for their absence from the Ephesians list?

A note concerning the church today. The *church* is not the many ecclesiastical organizations that exist; but a single invisible unified Body of Christ, comprised of all who have the spirit of God. All the members of the invisible Body are dependent on one another, with each equipped to perform different functions; all toward the edification of the Body. No one can choose his place within the Body. We should instead seek to discover our place as determined by God.

CHAPTER 13

Love is most important [13:1]

If I speak in the languages of men and of the messengers but should not have love, I am just resounding copper or a clanging cymbal. If I should have prophecy and should be perceiving all secrets and all knowledge, and if I should have all faith so as to transport mountains, yet have no love, I am nothing.

Love is patient, kind, not jealous, not bragging, not puffed up, not indecent, not self-seeking, not incensed, not taking account of evil, not rejoicing in injustice, yet is rejoicing with the truth, forgoing all, believing all, expecting all, enduring all.

> # Some gifts will cease ...

Prophecies will be discarded, languages will cease, knowledge will be discarded; but love is never lapsing. Out of *an instalment* we know and are prophesying. When maturity may be coming, that which is out of an installment shall be discarded.

We remember that Paul had previously accused the Corinthians of being less than mature. We discern from this letter that they were fighting over "lesser gifts" and were lacking in love.

Presently we observe by means of a mirror, in an enigma, yet then, face to face. At present I know out of an instalment, yet then I shall recognize according as I am recognized also. Yet now are remaining faith, expectation, love – these three. Yet the greatest of these is love. Be pursuing love.

Be zealous for spiritual endowments (14:1)

Be zealous for spiritual endowments; that you may be prophesying. He who is speaking in a language is not speaking to men, but to God. In spirit he is speaking secrets. But he who is prophesying is speaking to men for edification and consolation and comfort. He who is speaking in a language is edifying himself, but he who is prophesying is edifying the ecclesia. I want you all to be speaking in languages; but *rather* that you may be prophesying. Greater is the one who is prophesying than the one speaking in languages, unless he may be interpreting that the ecclesia is edified.

> Remember that love is the most important thing and is to be pursued. Other gifts are only effectual in *an installment* (temporary) and will, at some point, cease. At this point Paul is speaking, prophecy is preferred over languages as it is speaking to men for edification, consolation and comfort, and is edifying the ecclesia.

If I come to you speaking in languages, how does that benefit you if I am not speaking in revelation, or knowledge, or prophesy, or teaching? If you should not be giving an intelligible expression through the language, how will it be known what is being spoken?

Since you are zealots for spiritual endowments, seek to the edification of the ecclesia. If one speaks in a language let him pray that he may be interpreting. I thank God that I speak in a language more than all of you, but in the ecclesia do I want to speak five words with my mind so as to instruct others, or ten thousand words in a language?

Become mature.

> Languages without interpretation do not edify. What is the purpose of languages and prophecy?

Languages are for a sign, not to believers but to unbelievers. Prophecy is not for the unbelievers but for believers. If the whole ecclesia comes together in the same place and all are speaking in languages, if unbelievers enter will he not declare you are mad? If all should be prophesying and an unbeliever enters, he is being exposed and examined by all. The hidden things of his heart become apparent and he will fall on his face, worshiping God and reporting that God is among you.

> Again I ask, since Paul "completed" the Word of God (Colossians 1:25) is prophecy needed to bring the Word of God to believers? And do languages still serve a purpose as a demonstration to non-believers? Or could it be that both of these gifts have now ceased, as Paul foretells in 13:8?

Seek to edify when coming together (14:26)

When you come together let all occur to edification. If any is speaking in a language, by two or at the most three instalments let one also interpret. If there should be no interpreter let him hush in the ecclesia. As for prophets, let two or three speak and let the others discriminate. Let it be that all may be learning and all may be consoled. God is not for turbulence, but peace, as in all the ecclesias of the saints. Let all occur respectably and in order.

> Comments in this section pertaining to women not speaking in the ecclesia would appear to relate to the context, and toward the overall objective of order within the gathering. The women of Corinth were apparently such that they were not edifying when speaking, but disorderly.

CHAPTER 15

The evangel (15:1)

Now I am making known to you, brethren, the evangel which I bring to you, which also you accepted, in which also you stand, through which also you are saved, if you are retaining what I said in bringing the evangel to you.

Christ died for our sins according to the scriptures, He was entombed, and He has been roused the third day according to the scriptures.

> The basic evangel Paul brings concerns the death and resurrection of Christ. And there were numerous witnesses to Christ's resurrection.

He was seen by Cephas, by the twelve, by over 500 brethren at once, of whom the majority are remaining hitherto, by James, and thereafter by all the apostles.

> And now, most recently Paul was also a witness.

Yet, last of all, even as if a premature birth, He was seen by me also. For I am the least of the apostles, who am not competent to be called an apostle, because I persecute the ecclesia of God. Yet, in the grace of God I am what I am.

> If Paul is the last of all to see the risen Christ, why does he refer to his experience as a premature birth instead of an "after-the-fact" occurrence? While many others had seen the risen Christ, Paul's case was different, and it signaled a new direction God was taking. While the others (disciples) were seeking after and following Christ, Paul was Christ's enemy. He persecuted the ecclesia of God. Paul's experience was as a "premature birth" in terms of GRACE! In the past the kingdom evangel went to the sheep of Israel, requiring repentance. Paul had no repentance; he was Christ's enemy. Yet it was GRACE that found Paul and caused him to become an apostle, and God's instrument.
>
> Paul is a different kind of apostle, called to proclaim a different evangel. His message was not, *Repent, for near is the kingdom.* The kingdom had been rejected, and its coming delayed. Paul now proclaims directly to the nations (Gentiles) a new evangel, founded purely on grace; *Be conciliated to God; for God was in Christ conciliating the world to Himself, not reckoning their offenses to them* (2 Corinthians 5:18-21).
>
> But some were saying there was no resurrection ...

How are some among you saying that there is no resurrection of the dead? Now if there is no resurrection of the dead;

- ✓ Neither has Christ been roused,
- ✓ Our heralding is for naught,
- ✓ Your faith is for naught,
- ✓ We are false witnesses of God,
- ✓ You are still in your sins,
- ✓ Those who sleep in Christ have perished,
- ✓ More forlorn than all men are we.

Yet Christ HAS been roused from among the dead, the Firstfruit of those who are reposing.

THE RESURRECTION OF ALL (15:21)

Since, in fact, through a man came death, through a man, also, comes the resurrection of the dead. For even as, in Adam, all are dying, thus also, in Christ, shall all be vivified.

> # Consider the direct one-for-one, all-for-all parallel between Adam and Christ!

Yet each in his own class ...
- ✓ The Firstfruit, Christ;
- ✓ Thereupon those who are Christ's in His presence;
- ✓ Thereafter the consummation.

> Here we see the order of the resurrection. First Christ; second those who are Christ's (believers); and third the consummation. Paul now describes this final stage of the resurrection; the consummation ...

Whenever He (Christ) may be giving up the kingdom to His God and Father, whenever He should be nullifying all sovereignty and all authority and power. For He must be reigning until He should be placing all His enemies under His feet. The last enemy being abolished is death. For He subjects all under His feet. Whenever all may be subjected to Him, then the Son Himself also shall be subjected to (God); that God may be All in all.

> # This is the climax of the Scriptures and of the entire history of mankind!

> AS PAUL SPEAKS OF THE CONSUMMATION, HE SPEAKS OF THINGS NOT REVEALED BY GOD THROUGH THOSE WHO PROCLAIMED THE KINGDOM EVANGEL; not even John when he penned that which Christ revealed to him in the book of Revelation.
>
> For any who might conclude that Revelation is the latest revelation from God as to His plans for future times, consider the following:

In Revelation 22:5 we read of His slaves who are reigning, and in Revelation 21:24 we read of kings of the earth. But in 1 Corinthians 15:24 we are told of a time when all sovereignty, authority and power are nullified.

In Revelation 21:5 we see Christ seated on the throne. But in 1 Corinthians 15:28 we read that Christ will reign UNTIL all enemies are under His feet, at which time He Himself becomes subject to God the Father.

In Revelation 21:8 we read that the lake of fire is in operation, and it is referred to as the "second death." But in 1 Corinthians 15:27 we read that the last enemy, death, is abolished.

In Revelation 22:2 we read of leaves on the tree which are for the "cure" of the nations. This implies bodies that are in need of the leaves to sustain health. But in 1 Corinthians 15:42-44 we read of an incorruptible body.

In Revelation 21:12,14,24 we read of the twelve tribes, the twelve apostles (which would not include Paul) and the nations outside the city, respectively. But in Galatians 3:28 Paul speaks of no distinction between Jew or Greek; and we see no distinction anywhere in 1 Corinthians 15.

Revelation has a distinct Jewish character. It is a continuation of the kingdom evangel to the sheep of Israel, after the Body of Christ has been removed from the earth (1 Thessalonians 4:13). Revelation speaks of a physical realm when the kingdom comes upon the earth; much like our present world but with Christ reigning and keeping evil in check. But 1 Corinthians 15 is very obviously referring to a spiritual realm, with no corruption, reign or power. All are subjected. There are no enemies, no death, no sin, no rebellion. The purpose of the eons has been achieved, and God is now All in all.

Revelation speaks of the final age (eon) upon the earth. 1 Corinthians 15 (the consummation) speaks of a time after the ages have concluded; when God's purpose of the eons (Ephesians 3:11) has been accomplished.

If the dead are not being roused, we may be eating and drinking, for tomorrow we are dying. Be not deceived: evil conversations are corrupting kind characters. Sober up justly and do not be sinning.

> This is the adverse effect of those disputing the resurrection; corruption of those within the ecclesia. Paul admonishes them to sober up and not to be sinning.

How will the dead be raised? (15:35)

But someone will be protesting, How are the dead being roused? With what body are they coming?

> Some amongst the Corinthian believers were questioning how the dead could be raised. It will be a different kind of body.

You are not sowing the body which shall come to be, but a naked kernel, perchance of wheat or some of the rest. God is giving it a body according as He wills, and to each of the seeds its own body. Not all flesh is the same flesh, but there is one, indeed of men, yet another flesh of beasts. There are bodies celestial as well as bodies terrestrial.

Sown in corruption ... dishonor ... infirmity ... a soulish body;
Roused in incorruption ... glory ... power ... a spiritual body.

The first man, Adam, became a living soul;
The last Adam a vivifying Spirit.
First the soulish, then the spiritual.

> An incorruptible body will be needed in the celestial kingdom.

Flesh and blood is not able to enjoy an allotment in the kingdom of God, neither is corruption enjoying the allotment of incorruption.

A secret to you am I telling! We all, indeed, shall not be put to repose, yet we shall be changed, in an instant, in the twinkle of an eye, at the last trump. For He will be trumpeting, and the dead will be roused incorruptible, and we shall be changed. For this corruptible must put on incorruption, and this mortal put on immortality.

> Some within the Body of Christ will still be living when the trumpet sounds. They will be CHANGED and given an incorruptible, immortal body.

> Compare this to 1 Thessalonians 4:13-18 when the trumpet sounds and those IN CHRIST are SNATCHED AWAY to be with Him.

So; superabound in the work of the Lord (15:58)

So, my beloved brethren, become settled, unmovable, superabounding in the work of the Lord always, being aware that your toil is not for naught in the Lord.

In light of the complete reconciliation of all things that Paul has described, and the incorruptible bodies that will be given, Paul now encourages the Corinthian believers as they live in the present situation.

CHAPTER 16

A collection for the believers in Jerusalem (16:1)

I prescribe to the ecclesias of Galatia, thus you also do. On one of the sabbaths let each of you lay aside by himself in store that in which he should be prospered.

Paul is speaking of a collection for the saints.

The ecclesias (plural) would be those small groups of believers scattered about Galatia. It does not suggest a formal structure of "churches" in Galatia as we know them today. These groups may not have formally met together except for those, for example, living together in a home. We must be careful not to read into the Scriptures the characteristics and forms of "the church" as we know it today.

This collection would be taken by Paul to the saints who were in need in Jerusalem. It is an illustration of how the body works together when some are in need.

We might ask why Paul refers to "one of the sabbaths" if he has proclaimed freedom from the law? We must remember that Paul has noted the immaturity of the Corinthians, and the fact that he must speak to them as "minors in Christ" (3:1). And we remember that Paul speaks of forfeiting his rights for the sake of a weak brother. For these reasons Paul may be speaking to them in terms relating to their world, and in this case relative to their observance of the sabbaths. Remember also that some of the Corinthians were followers of Apollos (3:4). In Acts 18:25 we learn that Apollos was versed only in the baptism of John, at least until Priscilla and Aquila expounded the way of God to him more accurately. It could be, then, that at this point in time many of the Corinthians were following the teachings of Apollos, and it could be that Apollos was still teaching observance of the sabbaths. Recognizing the immaturity of the Corinthians, Paul speaks to them as minors, keeping in mind their recognition of the sabbaths.

Paul's plans to visit (16:5)

Paul speaks of his plans to visit, expecting to stay some time if the Lord permits. He will remain in Ephesus till Pentecost, *for a door has opened for me, great and operative, and many are opposing.*

Closing admonitions (16:13)

Watch! Stand firm in the faith! Be manly! Be staunch! Let all your actions occur in love!

Greetings from others (16:15)

You are acquainted with the house of Stephanas and Fortunatus, that it is the firstfruit of Achaia, and they set themselves to the service of the saints.

> A glimpse of "the church." Paul does not refer to a church in Achaia, but simply points to these two individuals and their house. They were the first to believe in Achaia, and they set themselves to serving others who came to believe. No formal structure to the church here; just individuals and those of their house.

Greeting you are the ecclesias of the province of Asia; Aquila and Prisca, together with the ecclesia of their house; and all the brethren.

> Here we see reference to multiple ecclesias that are a part of the one ecclesia (the Body of Christ). At least in the case of Aquila and Prisca, their ecclesia either was a group that met at their home, or perhaps simply those living in their house and who are referred to as the ecclesia of their house. Either way we observe the simplicity of the ecclesia in that day, in contrast to the many churches built upon the traditions of man in our day.

1 Corinthians
Questions & Issues concerning the evangel

THE EVANGEL   1:17
- Paul commissioned to bring the evangel
- Not to baptize
- Wisdom, righteousness, holiness, deliverance from God
- The power of God to those being saved
- No boasting

Maturity is needed   2:6
- To us God reveals ... thru His spirit
- We have the spirit of God
- But you are fleshly (jealousy & strife)
- Building on the one foundation

Remember you are a temple of God   3:16
- Do not corrupt the temple of God
- Don't presume to be wise
- Let no one boast
- We are deputies ... administrators
- Seeking to be found faithful
- Examined only by the Lord

Do not judge before the season   4:5
- Judge nothing until the Lord comes
- God will reward

Do not be "puffed up"   4:6
- Not disposed above what is written
- What you have was given to you
- No place for boasting

Deal with immoral behavior   5:1
- There is prostitution among you
- You are puffed up and do not mourn
- Remove the one committing this act that his spirit may be saved
- And to preserve the ecclesia
- Do not commingle with the wicked brother
- Judge only inside the ecclesia

Settling disputes within the ecclesia   6:1
- There are disputes
- Brother suing brother in front of unbelievers
- Believers will one day judge the world
- Are none able to judge within the ecclesia?
- Bad enough there are disputes
- The unjust will not enjoy the allotment
- You have been hallowed and justified
- All is permitted ... not all is expedient

Coping with fleshly passions   6:13
- The body is for the Lord
- Your body is a temple; it is not your own
- Dealing with passions thru marriage
- Better to remain as called

Love builds up   8:1
- Knowledge puffs up ... love builds up
- Not all have knowledge
- Do not let rights become stumbling blocks
- You are sinning against Christ

Paul's example: All things to all men   9:1
- Foregoing rights for the sake of the evangel
- Bringing the evangel without expense
- Paul enslaved himself to all
- Becoming all things to all men

Facing Trials   10:1
- Many of our Fathers fell in the wilderness
- A "type" for us
- When facing trials, God provides the sequel

Freedom ... but consider others   10:23
- All is permitted, but not all edifies
- Seek the welfare of others, not yourself
- Do all for the glory of God
- Become not a stumbling block

God's hierarchy 11:1
- God is the head of Christ
- Christ is the head of man
- Man is the head of woman
- Yet all is of God

Courtesies when coming together 11:17
- Coming together, but not for the better
- Schisms
- Though eating together, not the Lord's dinner
- Eating & drinking unworthily ... judgment
- We are being disciplined by the Lord
- When sharing a meal, wait for one another

Gifts within the body 12:1
- Spiritual gifts; with a view to expedience
- Apportioned as God intended
- One body; many members
- Place in the Body as God wills
- All members necessary
- Members mutually solicitous for one another
- Not all members are the same

Love is most important 13:1
- Prophecy, languages, knowledge; will cease
- Love is never lapsing
- When maturity comes ... some gifts discarded
- Be zealous for spiritual endowments
- Seek to be edifying to the ecclesia
- Become mature
- Be pursuing love

Seek to edify when coming together 14:26
- Let everything be toward edification
- God is not for turbulence, but peace
- Let all occur respectably and in order

THE EVANGEL   15:1
- Through which you are saved
- Concerns Christ's death and resurrection
- Witnesses to His resurrection
- Christ HAS been roused; the Firstfruit
- As in Adam all are dying
- Thus also in Christ shall all be "vivified"
- The resurrection order
- THE CONSUMMATION

Doubts about the resurrection   15:35
- How will the dead be raised?
- A body according as God wills
- *Incorruptible*

Therefore ... (How shall we live in response?)   15:58
- Superabound in the work of the Lord
- Being aware that your toil is not for naught

CLOSING THOUGHTS

The goal of Romans was to define proper doctrine. Paul presented *his* evangel; the evangel revealed to him and entrusted to him. Despite man's inability to be righteous, God imparts His righteousness. The believer is justified and reckoned righteous. *Doctrine* was outlined in Romans.

But the ecclesia at Corinth had issues they were dealing with. In light of Paul's evangel, how are these issues to be addressed? This is the purpose of 1 Corinthians.

We might say that Romans presents doctrine, and 1 Corinthians elaborates on that doctrine and addresses practical issues and questions concerning that doctrine. *The Companion Bible* states that the Corinthian letters are about reproof of the practical failure to exhibit the teaching of Romans; through not seeing one's standing as having died and risen with Christ. In these letters we can develop a picture of the numerous specific issues and questions that were present in the ecclesia at Corinth.

2 Corinthians

An Overview of the Scriptures, by
BOB EVELY © 2018.
An Independent Minister of Christ Jesus,
Of the church at Wilmore, Kentucky

"For Christ, then, are we ambassadors, as of God entreating through us. We are beseeching for Christ's sake, 'Be conciliated to God!'" (5:20)

1 Thessalonians	50-52 AD	During 2nd Journey
2 Thessalonians	52-53 AD	During 2nd Journey
Galatians (early theory)	54 AD	End of 2nd Journey
1 Corinthians	Spring 57 AD	During 3rd Journey
2 Corinthians	**Fall 57 AD**	**During 3rd Journey**
Galatians	Winter 57 AD	During 3rd Journey
Romans	Spring 58 AD	During 3rd Journey
Colossians	61-62 AD	During 1st Captivity
Ephesians	61-62 AD	During 1st Captivity
Philemon	62-63 AD	During 1st Captivity
Philippians	63 AD	During 1st Captivity
1 Timothy	67 AD	Between Captivities
Titus	67 AD	Between Captivities
2 Timothy	Spring 68 AD	During 2nd Captivity

CHAPTER 1

The address on the envelope (1:1)

Paul, an apostle of Christ Jesus … and brother Timothy;
To the ecclesia of God which is in Corinth,
Together with all the saints who are in the whole of Achaia.

God consoles, and enables us to console (1:4)

God is consoling us in our every affliction to enable us to be consoling those in every affliction, through the consolation with which we ourselves are being consoled by God. As you are participants of the sufferings, thus of the consolation also.

> God's consolation enabled the believers to console others. This was greatly needed, as there was great affliction.

We were inordinately burdened, over our ability, so that we were despairing of life also.

> It was important to place confidence in God and not in self.

We have the rescript of death in ourselves, that we may be having no confidence in ourselves, but in God, Who rouses the dead, Who rescues us from a death of such proportions, and will be rescuing; on Whom we rely that He will still be rescuing also.

> Prayer assisted those in affliction.

You also assisting together by a petition for us, in order that, from many faces He may be thanked by many for us for the gracious gift given to us.

Our example to the world (1:12)

In holiness and sincerity of God, not in fleshly wisdom, but in the grace of God, we behaved ourselves in the world, yet more superabundantly toward you.

I had intended to come to you (1:15)

I intended formerly to come to you, and through you to pass into Macedonia, and to come again from Macedonia to you, and by you to be sent forward into Judea. Am I planning according to flesh, that it may be with me 'Yes, yes,' and 'No, no?' Whatever promises are of God, are in Him 'Yes.'

> It is not Paul's plans, but God's will that will come to pass.

He Who is confirming us together with you in Christ, and anoints us, is God, Who also seals us and is giving the *earnest of the spirit* in our hearts.

> The holy spirit, given by God to believers, is an "earnest deposit" that confirms them, and consoles them in their affliction.

Stand fast in the faith.

> Again, a needed word in times of affliction. They needed consolation, but also a reminder to stand fast in the faith.

CHAPTER 2

I decide not to come again to you in sorrow. I write to you lest, coming, I may have sorrow. Out of much affliction and pressure of heart I write to you through many tears, not that you be made sorrowful but that you may know the love I have for you.

> Paul must tell them things that will make them sorrow, but that is not his intent. Still, it is a necessity if he is to carry out his charge faithfully.

Deal graciously with offenders (2:5)

Deal graciously and console, lest somehow such may be swallowed up by the more excessive sorrow. Ratify your love to him. I also have dealt graciously, because of you in the face of Christ, lest we may be overreached by Satan, for we are not ignorant of the things he apprehends.

> The enemy is Satan, not the fallen brother. In 1 Corinthians 5, Paul had instructed the ecclesia to expel the one who had immoral behavior. Now he gives further instructions for dealing with offenders in the ecclesia.

We are a fragrance of Christ to God (2:14)

Thanks be to God, Who always gives us a triumph in Christ, and is manifesting the odor of His knowledge through us in every place. We are a fragrance of Christ to God, in those being saved (an odor of life for life) and in those perishing (an odor of death for death).

> Here is a hint as to the purpose of the ecclesia; to bring a knowledge of God wherever we go.

God makes us competent dispensers (2:17)

For this, who is competent? For we are not as the majority who are peddling the word of God, but as of sincerity.

Peddling the Word of God?

> Unlike those who were "peddling" the word of God, Paul notes his sincerity; and the fact that his competency comes from God (since apart from God no man is competent to dispense the evangel). Could it be that the same is still true today; that the majority within the organized church are simply "peddling" the word of God?

CHAPTER 3

Need we not, even as some, commendatory letters? You are our letter; read by all men.

> Could it be that this is still a problem today? Much weight is given to the commendations of man (degrees, experience).

Not that we are competent of ourselves; but our competency is of God, Who also makes us competent dispensers of a new covenant, not of the letter, but of the spirit, for the letter is killing, yet the spirit is vivifying.

The dispensation of righteousness; not law (3:7)

If the dispensation of death, by letters chiseled in stone, came in glory; how shall not rather the dispensation of the spirit be in glory? For if in the dispensation of condemnation is glory, much rather the dispensation of righteousness is exceeding in glory.

> Could it be that the organized church today still needs this reminder; that the dispensation we are given is not of the law? Much weight seems to be given to adherence to certain aspects of the law (sabbath observance, tithing, do's and don'ts from the law).

Israel is calloused; the truth is veiled (3:12)

As Moses covered his face so that Israel could not look intently upon that which is being nullified; Israel's apprehensions are veiled. Their apprehensions were calloused, for until this very day the same covering is remaining at the reading of the old covenant, not being discovered that in Christ is it being nullified. Yet if ever it should reach a turning back to the Lord, the covering is taken from about it.

> Israel continues to read and observe the old covenant. They fail to recognize Christ. Their understanding is calloused.

But we are being transformed (3:17)

The spirit of the Lord brings freedom. Now we all, with uncovered face, mirroring the Lord's glory, are being transformed into the same image, from glory to glory, even as from the Lord, the spirit.

CHAPTER 4

We manifest the truth (4:1)

Therefore, having this dispensation, according as we were shown mercy, we are not despondent. We spurn the hidden things of shame, not walking in craftiness, not adulterating the word of God.

> That is; we are not to contaminate the word of God by proclaiming something other than our commission. We are not to mix the law with grace, as those in Paul's day were guilty of doing; thereby "adulterating" the word of God entrusted to us.

By manifestation of the truth, commending ourselves to every man's conscience in God's sight.

The evangel is covered (4:3)

If our evangel is covered, it is covered in those who are perishing. The god of this eon blinds the apprehensions of the unbelieving so that the illumination of the evangel of the glory of Christ, Who is the Image of the invisible God, does not irradiate them.

> Unbelievers are blinded by *the god of this eon.* But to the believer, God illuminates.

The God Who says that, out of darkness light shall be shining, is He Who shines in our hearts, with a view to the illumination of the knowledge of the glory of God.

If unbelievers are blinded by the god of this eon, how can they ever come to believe?

> Those who are unbelievers are blinded by the god of this eon and cannot apprehend (understand) the evangel. All of mankind would be such, had God not chosen to reveal and enlighten the ecclesia (called-out-ones). With the god of this eon blinding the apprehensions of man, who can believe except those God has called and enlightened?

> Note the sequence. It is not that unbelievers fail to believe and are thereby blinded and perishing. Instead, they are blinded by the god of this eon and therefore do not believe. With the god of this eon blinding mankind, who CAN believe? God, in His grace and wisdom, breaks thru the power of the god of this eon and ENABLES SOME TO BELIEVE; in order

that the evangel is proclaimed thru these believers; leading to the ultimate goal ... ALL mankind is ultimately blessed.

This treasure in earthen vessels [4:7]

Now we have this treasure in earthen vessels, that the transcendence of the power may be of God and not of us.

> The reason we are given the treasure in earthen vessels is so we can clearly see the power is of God, and not of us.

We are afflicted, but not distressed; perplexed but not despairing; persecuted but not forsaken; cast down but not perishing; that the life of Jesus may be manifested in our body. Death is operating in us, yet life in you.

We are believing, wherefore we are speaking also. Being aware that He Who rouses the Lord Jesus will be rousing us also, through Jesus, and will be presenting us together with you.

> This is the treasure we carry; the *knowledge* that as Jesus was roused, we will also be roused.

Wherefore we are not despondent, but even if our outward man is decaying, nevertheless that within us is being renewed day by day. For the momentary lightness of our affliction is producing for us a transcendently transcendent eonian burden of glory, at our not noting what is being observed, but what is not being observed, for what is being observed is temporary, yet what is not being observed is eonian.

> So in the weakness of these earthen vessels, our weakness displays God's glory and power. That which we see while in these vessels is temporary, but we focus on that which cannot be seen; that which is eonian.

> Some will point to this passage to prove that *eonian* means "endless," since eonian is contrasted with temporary. But by examining every usage of the word *aion* and *aionian* in Scripture we clearly see that the word cannot refer to endlessness but is a finite period of time. Here the contrast made by Paul is between that which is of a short duration (in the present eon only - temporary) and that which will endure for a longer period of time (in the coming eons - eonian).

CHAPTER 5

Groaning in these earthly tabernacles [(5:1)]

We are aware that if our terrestrial tabernacle house should be demolished, we have a building of God, a house not made by hands, eonian, in the heavens.

> Here we see a discussion very similar to that found in Romans 8. We groan in this temporal condition, as all creation groans; awaiting redemption. And the spirit helps us in our infirmity (Romans 8:26). But we have a building of God in the heavens.

We are groaning and are burdened; not wanting to be stripped and found naked, but to be dressed in our habitation that is out of heaven, that the mortal may be swallowed up by life. God gives us the earnest of the spirit.

Being at home in the body, we are away from home from the Lord (for by faith are we walking, not by perception), yet we are encouraged and are delighting rather to be away from home out of the body and to be at home with the Lord.

When a believer dies, does he go immediately to heaven?

> This passage is often used to support the thinking that upon death the believer immediately goes to heaven. Note, though, that Paul mentions three states; in the body, at home with the Lord, and naked/stripped/undressed (5:4). Paul is in the body and he longs to be with the Lord, and as he writes to the Corinthians he is thinking the time is short before the resurrection occurs. But until the resurrection those who have died are "naked," or without a body. The Scriptures teach that upon death, we sleep in hades (unseen state) with no consciousness until the Lord calls and we are resurrected.

But whether at home or away from home, our ambition is to please God.

We will give an account to God (5:10)

All of us must be manifested in front of the dais of Christ, that each should be requited for that which he puts into practice through the body, whether good or bad. Being aware, then, of the fear of the Lord, we are persuading men, yet we are manifest to God.

> The actions of believers, good or bad, do not go un-judged. Believers will appear before the dais of Christ. Works do not affect salvation, but they are judged when determining reward or loss of reward in the ages to come.

Any in Christ are a NEW CREATION (5:14)

The love of Christ is constraining us. If One died for the sake of all, consequently all died. And He died for the sake of all that those who are living should by no means still be living to themselves, but to the One dying and being roused for their sakes.

So that we, from now on, are *acquainted with no one according to flesh.* Yet even if we have known Christ according to flesh, nevertheless now we know Him so no longer.

Acquainted with no one according to flesh!

> Even Christ is no longer known "according to flesh," yet most in the church today look primarily to Christ's teachings according to flesh as found in the "kingdom evangel" He proclaimed during His earthly ministry (while in flesh); His message that the kingdom to be restored unto Israel was near, and repentance was required to enter.

So that, if anyone is in Christ, there is a *new creation*: the primitive passed by. Lo! There has come new!

Born again? Or new creation?

Israel was told they must be BORN AGAIN. The Body of Christ is not to be born again but is instead a NEW CREATION.

God conciliated the world (5:18)

All is of God.

Observe that it is not just things that are good that are of God, but ALL is of God.

[God] conciliates us to Himself through Christ, and is giving us the dispensation of the conciliation, how that God was in Christ, conciliating the world to Himself, not reckoning their offenses to them, and placing in us the word of the conciliation.

> # God is conciliating the world to Himself, not reckoning their offenses to them!

God conciliated the world to Himself. Observe the one-sided nature of what God has done. Regardless of man's actions or beliefs, God was, in Christ, conciliating the world to Himself; not reckoning man's offenses to Him. Upon believing and becoming conciliated to God on our part, we have a two-sided "reconciliation." But we see here that even with respect to unbelievers, God is conciliated and not reckoning, or counting, their offenses.

For Christ, then, are we AMBASSADORS, as of God entreating through us. We are beseeching for Christ's sake, 'Be conciliated to God!' For the One not knowing sin, He makes to be a sin offering for our sakes that we may be becoming God's righteousness in Him.

> ## This is the Great Commission to the Body of Christ! It is <u>our</u> commission in this present day.

The message given to Christ's ambassadors to proclaim is simply, Be conciliated to God. God is conciliated to the world, not reckoning man's offenses against Him; therefore, Be conciliated to God. Today we hear a much different message proclaimed by most churches. The kingdom is being proclaimed, based upon Jesus' words in the four gospels. But that message pertained to Israel. Today we often hear a mixture of law with grace. But that is the DIFFERENT gospel that Paul warns about in Galatians 1:7. And many of Christ's ambassadors today are concocting their own message or proclaiming a message from somewhere in Scripture that pertains to a different group of people.

> ## Christ's ambassadors need to take care to proclaim the correct message for the present era.

CHAPTER 6

Don't receive God's grace for naught (6:1)

Don't receive God's grace for naught. For He is saying, In a season acceptable I reply to you, and in a day of salvation I help you (6:2; from Isaiah 49:8). Now is a most acceptable era! Now is a day of salvation!

> The ecclesia had received God's grace. It should not be misused, abused, or taken for granted. And the manner in which the believer lives should be in response to the grace of God.

> What a wonderful era this is; as God has brought salvation to the ecclesia despite any man's ability to be righteous on his own!

Give no one cause to stumble (6:3)

We are giving no one cause to stumble in anything, lest flaws be found with the service, but in everything we are commending ourselves as servants of God, in much endurance.

> We see this repeated often in Paul's writings. There is freedom granted to the ecclesia through God's grace. We are freed from the law. But we must take care that we do not exercise our freedom in such a way as to cause others to stumble.

Be not yoked with unbelievers (6:14)

Do not become diversely yoked with unbelievers. For what partnership have righteousness and lawlessness; a believer with an unbeliever?

You are the temple of the living God, as God said that I will be making My home and will be walking in them. Wherefore, Come out of their midst and be severed, the Lord is saying. And touch not the unclean, and I will admit you, and I will be a Father to you, and you shall be sons and daughters to Me, says the Lord Almighty.

> These comments are in reference to a believer yoking himself to an unbeliever in a partnership. This does not infer a total removal from those of the world (see 1 Corinthians 5:9-13).

CHAPTER 7

Be holy (7:1)

Having, then, these promises, beloved, we should be cleansing ourselves from every pollution of flesh and spirit, completing holiness in the fear of God.

Joy in affliction (7:4)

I am filled full with consolation, I am superexceeding in joy in all our affliction. For even at our coming into Macedonia, our flesh has no ease, but we are afflicted in everything: outside fightings; inside fears.

God, Who is consoling the humble, consoles us by the presence of Titus, yet not only by his presence but by the consolation also with which he was consoled over you, informing us of your longing, your anguish, your zeal for my sake.

Here we see God using man to provide consolation to others.

Glad you were sorry to repentance (7:8)

For I am observing that that epistle makes you sorry, even if it is for an hour. Now I am rejoicing, not that you were made sorry, but that you were made sorry *to repentance*. For you were made sorry according to God. For sorrow according to God is producing repentance for unregretted salvation, yet the sorrow of the world is producing death.

In everything you commend yourselves to be pure in this matter. Consequently, even if I write to you it is not on account of the one who injures, but neither on account of the one being injured, but on account of manifesting to you your diligence for our sake in God's sight.

> Paul had previously written to the Corinthians, and his letter had made them sorry. Paul rejoiced not that he caused the Corinthians to have sorrow; but that it led to their repentance. His purpose in writing is not simply to address a single episode, but to encourage diligence in the life of the believers at Corinth.

Therefore we are consoled; I am encouraged in you.

CHAPTER 8

Giving gleefully (8:1)

According to their ability; and beyond their ability; of their own accord [the Macedonians] give first to the Lord, and to us through the will of God. Even as you are superabounding in everything; in faith and word and knowledge and all diligence and the love that flows out of you into us; that you may be superabounding in this grace also.

I am not saying this as an injunction, but, through the diligence of others, testing also the genuineness of this love of yours.

> Giving is not a requirement. It is to be genuine. God does not require a tithe as He did of Israel under the law. Giving should be voluntary and is an expression of genuine love. Now Paul invokes the example of Christ ...

Christ became poor because of you. For you know the grace of our Lord Jesus Christ, that, being rich, because of you He became poor.

For it is not, that, to others ease, yet to you affliction, but by an equality, in the current occasion, your superabundance is for their want, that their superabundance also may be coming to be for your want, so that there may be coming to be an equality, according as it is written: the one with much increases not, and the one with few lessens not.

Thru giving there would come to be equality in the ecclesia.

Let no one find flaws in us in this exuberance which is being dispensed by us, for we are providing the ideal, not only in the sight of the Lord, but in the sight of men also.

CHAPTER 9

He who is sowing sparingly shall reap sparingly, and who is sowing bountifully shall reap bountifully, each according as he has proposed in his heart. Not sorrowfully, nor of compulsion, for the gleeful giver is loved by God.

Superabound in good work. God is able to lavish all grace on you that, having all CONTENTMENT in everything always, you may be superabounding in every good work.

May He Who is supplying seed to the sower, and bread for food, be furnishing and multiplying your seed and be making the product of your righteousness grow, being enriched in everything, for all the generosity which is producing through us thanksgiving to God.

Subjection to the evangel (9:12)

The dispensation of this ministry not only is replenishing the wants of the saints. We give thanks also at the subjection of your avowal to the evangel of Christ; and in the generosity of the contribution. Thanks be to God for His indescribable gratuity!

Providing for the needs of the saints is not the only purpose of Paul's ministry; but it is a *part* of his purpose. Subjection to the evangel is a part of Paul's purpose. Observe God's intent that all become subjected to Christ (1 Corinthians 15:27) in order that all will then become subjected to God (1 Corinthians 15:28). Christ is therefore assigned the commission of bringing all in subjection to God. This subjection is brought about thru the evangel. Therefore Paul gives thanks when the ecclesia subjects itself to the evangel.

Christ is the one bringing all in subjection to God; that God becomes All in all. And the ecclesia is Christ's complement (Ephesians 1:23). By proclaiming the correct evangel for our day (*Be conciliated to God*) we act as Christ's complement, and ultimately ALL will become subjected to Christ through the evangel; and subjected ultimately to God.

CHAPTER 10

Spiritual warfare (10:1)

Walking in flesh, we are not warring according to the flesh. For the weapons of our warfare are not fleshly, but powerful to God; toward the pulling down of bulwarks; pulling down reckonings and every height elevating itself against the knowledge of God and leading into captivity every apprehension into the obedience of Christ, and having all in readiness to avenge every disobedience, whenever your obedience may be completed.

> # Some things appear to be obvious based on what we can see, but there are spiritual forces at work!

Are you looking at that which is on the surface? If anyone is presuming to have confidence in himself to be Christ's, let him be reckoning again with himself, that, according as he is Christ's, thus also are we.

Some criticized Paul (10:9)

Some say his epistles are weighty and strong, yet his bodily presence is weak and his expression to be scorned. We are not daring to judge ourselves by, or compare ourselves with, some who are commending themselves. But they, measuring themselves by themselves, and comparing themselves with themselves, do not understand.

Not he who is commending himself is qualified, but whom the Lord is commending.

> The commendation of man is found everywhere within the organized church today. Emphasis is placed upon degrees, titles, ordinations, popularity, eloquence, ability to grow in number. We must remember that it is only the commendation of the Lord that matters.

CHAPTER 11

Be not deluded (11:1)

I fear that somehow, as the serpent deludes Eve by its craftiness, your apprehensions should be corrupted from the singleness and pureness which is in Christ.

For if he who is coming is heralding another Jesus whom we do not herald, or if you are obtaining a different spirit which you did not obtain, or a different evangel, which you do not receive, you are bearing with him ideally.

> Others were proclaiming a different; an incorrect evangel. This will be the primary reason Paul writes Galatians. Here we get a small taste of his warning against being deluded by an incorrect evangel.

Paul defends his apostleship (11:5)

I am reckoning to be deficient in nothing pertaining to the paramount apostles. Even if I am plain in expression, I am not in knowledge, but in everything being made manifest in all for you.

Do I sin in humbling myself that you may be exalted, seeing that I bring the evangel of God to you gratuitously? From other ecclesias I get rations for dispensing to you. And being present with you and in want, I am not an encumbrance to anyone; for the brethren coming from Macedonia replenish my wants. In everything I keep myself that I be not burdensome to you.

There are false apostles, fraudulent workers, being transfigured into apostles of Christ. And no marvel, for Satan himself is being transfigured into a messenger of light. It is no great thing, then, if his servants also are being transfigured as dispensers of righteousness – whose consummation shall be according to their acts.

Since many are boasting according to the flesh, I also shall be boasting. Hebrews are they? I also! Israelites are they? I also! The seed of Abraham are they? I also! Servants of Christ are they? Above them am I!

> We see that Paul's primary opposition was from the Jewish element within the ecclesia that was resting upon things of the flesh; their genealogy and the law. Paul proceeds to give an account of that which he has suffered for the sake of the evangel ...

✓ In weariness more exceedingly
✓ In jails more exceedingly
✓ In blows inordinately
✓ In deaths often
✓ By Jews five times I got forty save one
✓ Thrice am I flogged with rods
✓ Once am I stoned
✓ Thrice am I shipwrecked
✓ A night and a day have I spent in a swamp
✓ In journeys often
✓ In dangers of rivers
✓ In dangers of robbers
✓ In dangers of my race
✓ In dangers of the nations
✓ In dangers of the city
✓ In dangers in the wilderness
✓ In dangers in the sea
✓ In dangers among false brethren
✓ In toil and labor
✓ In vigils often
✓ In famine and thirst
✓ In fasts often
✓ In cold and nakedness
✓ In Damascus, lowered through a wall to escape the king's hands

CHAPTER 12

Paul's apparitions and revelations (12:1)

If boasting must be, though it is not expedient, I shall also be coming to apparitions and revelations of the Lord. I am acquainted with a man in Christ, fourteen years before this (whether in a body I am not aware, or outside of the body, I am not aware – God is aware) such a one was snatched away to the third heaven. And I am acquainted with such a man; that he was snatched away into paradise and hears ineffable declarations, which it is not allowed a man to speak. Over such a one I shall be boasting; yet over myself I shall not be boasting, except in my infirmities.

Consider only what you see and hear from me. No one should be reckoning me to be above what he is observing of me or anything he is hearing of me.

Grace is sufficient (12:7)

Wherefore also, lest I should be lifted up by the transcendence of the revelations, there was given to me a splinter in the flesh, a messenger of Satan, that he may be buffeting me, lest I may be lifted up. For this I entreat the Lord thrice, that it should withdraw from me. And He has protested to me, 'Sufficient for you is My grace, for My power in infirmity is being perfected.'

Wherefore I delight in infirmities, in outrages, in necessities, in persecutions, in distress, for Christ's sake, for, whenever I may be weak, then I am powerful.

> # Grace is sufficient!

How different this is from the "name it and claim it" theology, or those purporting to have a miraculous healing ministry. Healings and miracles may have accompanied the proclamation of the kingdom evangel, for it pertained to earthly things; the kingdom to be restored upon the earth. But Paul's ministry pertains to the heavenly realm. The Body of Christ has no expectation upon this earth. Grace is sufficient; there is no need for miracles. God's power is perfected in man's weakness.

I have become imprudent; you compel me. For I ought to be commended by you, for I am not deficient in anything pertaining to the paramount apostles, even if I am nothing. The signs of an apostle are produced among you in all endurance, besides in signs and miracles and powerful deeds.

Even though God's power is perfected in man's weakness and grace is sufficient; Paul's ministry as an apostle was validated by signs and miracles, that none could doubt the validity of his apostleship.

All for your edification (12:14)

This third time I hold myself ready to come to you and I shall not be an encumbrance.

I will spend myself for your sakes. With the greatest relish shall I spend and be bankrupted for the sake of your souls, even if loving you more exceedingly diminishes your love for me; all for the sake of your edification.

I fear I may not find you as I want, and that I may be found by you as you do not want; lest there be strife, jealousy, fury, factions, vilifications, whisperings, puffing up, turbulences.

> Here is a list of behaviors presented by Paul as being unacceptable. Let us take note.

Not again at my coming will my God be humbling me toward you. I shall be mourning for many who have sinned before and are not repenting of the uncleanness and prostitution and wantonness which they commit.

CHAPTER 13

If I should be coming again I shall not spare those who have sinned before or the rest who are seeking a test of Christ speaking in me.

Need for an "adjustment" (13:4)

Even if He was crucified out of weakness, nevertheless He is living by the power of God. For we also are weak together with Him, but we shall be living together with Him by the power of God for you.

Try yourselves if you are in the faith; test yourselves. Or are you not recognizing that Christ Jesus is in you, except you are somewhat disqualified? Now I am expecting that you will know that we are not disqualified! Now we are wishing to God that you do not do anything evil; that you may be doing that which is ideal.

Now this we are wishing also: YOUR ADJUSTMENT. Therefore I am writing these things being absent that, being present I should not be using severity according to the authority which the Lord gives me for building up and not for pulling down.

Closing admonitions (13:11)

Furthermore, brethren, rejoice, adjust, be entreated, be mutually disposed, be at peace, and the God of love and of peace will be with you.

2 Corinthians
Questions & Issues concerning the evangel

God consoles us   1:4
- Enables us to console others
- Participants in the sufferings and consolation
- Confidence in God, not ourselves
- You assist by petition

Our example to the world   1:12
- Sincere behavior

Deal graciously with offenders   2:5
- Lest they be swallowed up by sorrow
- Lest we be overtaken by Satan
- Ratify your love to him

God MAKES us competent dispensers   2:17
- Who is competent?
- Not peddling God's word as the majority
- Do we need commendation letters?
- God MAKES us competent dispensers

The dispensation of righteousness (The Evangel)   3:7
- The evangel of righteousness exceeds law

Israel calloused ... truth veiled   3:12
- Israel's apprehensions veiled
- Veil will be lifted at turning back to the Lord

We are being transformed   3:17
- Spirit of the Lord brings freedom
- We are being transformed
- Not adulterating the word of God
- We are manifesting the truth
- Shown mercy ... we are not despondent

The evangel is covered   4:3
- Unbelievers blinded by god of this eon
- To the believer God illuminates

Treasure in earthen vessels 4:7
- That the power is of God and not of us
- As Jesus was roused, we will be roused
- The outward decays ... inward being renewed
- Taking note of what is not being observed

Groaning in these earthly tabernacles 5:1
- We have a building of God in the heavens
- We are also groaning
- We long to be at home with the Lord
- We seek to please God at home or away
- We have the earnest of the spirit

We will give an account to God 5:10
- Will appear before the dais of Christ

Any in Christ are a NEW CREATION 5:14
- If one died for all ... all died
- Now acquainted with no one according to flesh
- Even Christ not known according to flesh
- A new creation

God conciliated the world 5:18
- God conciliated the world to Himself
- We are ambassadors for Christ

Don't receive God's grace for naught 6:1
- "In a day of salvation I help you"
- Now is a day of salvation

Give no one cause to stumble 6:3

Be not yoked with unbelievers 6:24
- What partnership has righteousness/lawlessness
- Be severed
- You are God's temple

Be holy ... have joy in affliction 7:1
- Cleanse ourselves from every pollution
- God consoles us

Glad you were sorry to repentance   7:8
- Made sorry for repentance; according to God

Giving gleefully   8:1
- Macedonians gave of their own accord
- That you also may superabound in this grace
- Not an injunction ... genuineness
- Christ became poor because of you
- Doing the ideal before all men
- God loves the gleeful giver
- That you may superabound in every good work
- May He cause your righteousness to grow
- Bringing equality in the ecclesia

Subjection to the evangel   9:12
- This ministry not only to replenish wants
- Glorifying God at your subjection

Dealing with misunderstandings   10:1
- Not warring according to flesh
- Pulling down bulwarks of misunderstanding
- Some criticized Paul, they do not understand
- The Lord commends, not man
- Dealing with self confidence

Be not deluded   11:1
- I fear your being deluded
- Those heralding something different
- Paul defends his apostleship
- False apostles
- As they boast according to flesh, I will also
- Paul's apparitions and revelations

Grace is sufficient   12:7
- Sufficient is my grace
- Delighting in infirmities

All for your edification   12:14
- • I will not be an encumbrance
- • We speak all for your edification
- • I will spend myself for your sakes

Mourning for those who have sinned & not repented   12:21

The need for "adjustment"   13:4
- • Living by the power of God
- • Test yourselves
- • Doing that which is ideal
- • Writing for your "adjustment"

CLOSING THOUGHTS

As was the case with 1 Corinthians, this letter responds to questions and issues within the Corinthian ecclesia. In Romans, Paul presented the evangel entrusted to him. Despite man's inability to be righteous, God imparts His righteousness. The believer is justified and reckoned righteous. Doctrine was presented in Romans; the evangel revealed to Paul and entrusted to him. Paul's letters to the believers in Corinth dealt with issues they were facing.

The Companion Bible states that the Corinthian letters are about reproof of the practical failure to exhibit the teaching of Romans; through not seeing one's standing as having died and risen with Christ.

Galatians

An Overview of the Scriptures, by
BOB EVELY © *2018.*
An Independent Minister of Christ Jesus,
Of the church at Wilmore, Kentucky

"For freedom Christ frees us! Stand firm, and be not again enthralled with the yoke of slavery." (5:1)

1 Thessalonians	50-52 AD	During 2nd Journey
2 Thessalonians	52-53 AD	During 2nd Journey
Galatians (early theory)	54 AD	End of 2nd Journey
1 Corinthians	Spring 57 AD	During 3rd Journey
2 Corinthians	Fall 57 AD	During 3rd Journey
Galatians	**Winter 57 AD**	**During 3rd Journey**
Romans	Spring 58 AD	During 3rd Journey
Colossians	61-62 AD	During 1st Captivity
Ephesians	61-62 AD	During 1st Captivity
Philemon	62-63 AD	During 1st Captivity
Philippians	63 AD	During 1st Captivity
1 Timothy	67 AD	Between Captivities
Titus	67 AD	Between Captivities
2 Timothy	Spring 68 AD	During 2nd Captivity

CHAPTER 1

The address on the envelope (1:1)

Paul, an apostle; and all the brethren with me;
To the ecclesias of Galatia.

> Paul identifies himself as an *apostle*, from the Greek *apostello*. The same Greek word is translated "commission" when in verb form. An apostle is one who has been commissioned by God. But Paul is a new breed of apostle. Jesus chose only twelve. When Judas departed, the remaining eleven were careful to replace him with only one; bringing the number back to twelve. There were twelve tribes in Israel, and precisely twelve apostles when God was working thru Israel. But Paul is an additional apostle; not one of the Twelve.

The recipients of this letter are *the ecclesias of Galatia*. The word *ecclesias* is from the Greek *ekklesia;* literally out-called-ones. Often translated church the word simply means those who have been called out from a larger group. It does not always refer to the church. It is not always the same group that is called out. Modern Bible translators have done a disservice in translating ekklesia as church, because it could be that a different group of out-called-ones are being referred to in various instances. When we encounter the word, we must seek from the context to understand who the out-called-ones are.

To extricate us from the present wicked eon [(1:4)]

The Lord Jesus Christ gave Himself for our sins, so that He might extricate us out of the present wicked eon.

Eon comes from the Greek *aion* and refers to a period of time of indefinite length. We remember from our study of science that the word eon refers to a very long time period; but not endlessness.

We sometimes see aion (or eon) in Scripture in the singular, and sometimes in the plural. A careful study of Scripture reveals that there was a time before the eons (2 Timothy 1:9; Titus 1:2; 1 Corinthians 2:7) and there will be an end of the eons (1 Corinthians 10:11; Hebrews 9:26). There will be eons to come in the future (Matthew 12:32; Ephesians 1:21; Hebrews 6:5) and there will be an end to this present eon (Matthew 13:39; Matthew 24:3).

And there are a number of instances where Scripture refers to this present eon, as in this passage in Galatians 1.

Modern Bible translations confuse this distinction between the eons, using the word eternal where that word seems to fit, and using another word (like age or world) where eternal will not fit the context. But if we translate the Bible consistently we will see very clearly that there are different time periods being referred to (eons or ages), each with a beginning and an end.

This reference to being EXTRICATED OUT OF THE PRESENT WICKED EON appears to refer to the snatching away of the Body of Christ in 1 Thessalonians 4:13-18 (commonly referred to as the rapture), when Christ will descend and when the dead and the living will be snatched away to meet the Lord in the air.

Currently God is working thru the Body of Christ and not Israel. But after the snatching-away, when the Body is removed from the earth, the events described in the book of Revelation will take place upon the earth. And then once again God will be working thru Israel upon the earth, which explains the many references to Israel throughout the book of Revelation.

They were being led astray by a different evangel (1:6)

I am marveling that swiftly you are transferred from that which calls you in the grace of Christ to a DIFFERENT evangel, which is not another, except it be that some who are disturbing you want also to DISTORT the evangel of Christ (1:6).

> The Galatians were being led astray. The false message that is misleading them is not just another message of the same kind. It is a DIFFERENT message; a DISTORTION of the evangel of Christ. Paul warns that if anyone brings an evangel different from the one that he brings, it should be rejected.

If ever we also, or a messenger out of heaven, should be bringing an evangel to you beside that which we bring to you, let him be anathema!

> Even if Peter, for example, were to bring an evangel different from what Paul had brought, it should be rejected. As we read on, we will see that this is the problem. Peter and the Twelve were commissioned to proclaim an evangel to the Circumcision (Israel), while Paul has been called as a different kind of apostle (not one of the Twelve) and to declare a different evangel to the Body of Christ (thereby explaining the opposition Paul encounters). So Paul declares, "Listen only to the evangel that I bring."

But today most churches proclaim the evangel from Peter and the Twelve, ignoring Paul's admonition!

Most within the church today are being led astray to a different evangel; a distortion of the evangel; that mixes-in elements from the Circumcision evangel. Most denominations trace their pastoral authority to Peter as the rock upon whom the church was originated. But the ecclesia (called-out-ones) when Christ spoke those words to Peter was exclusively Jewish; and in Paul God is working in a different way, through the Body of Christ comprised of Gentiles and Jews alike with no distinction.

We who are within the Body of Christ today should heed the strong words Paul has for those who are presenting a different, distorted evangel; as he implores those in Galatia to accept only the evangel that he brings.

Paul's evangel came thru revelation (1:10)

If Paul was to proclaim the same message as the Twelve (but only to a different group of recipients; the Gentiles), it would have made sense to have Paul spend time being trained by the Twelve. After all, they were with Christ during the entire time of His ministry upon the earth. They witnessed His miracles, His crucifixion, His resurrection and His ascension into heaven. But Paul makes it clear that his evangel was not received from a man.

For I am making known to you, brethren, as to the evangel which is being brought by me, that it is not in accord with man. For neither did I accept it from a man, nor was I taught it, but it came through a revelation of Jesus Christ.

> # Paul received his evangel by revelation; not from men.

God severed Paul (1:15), or cut him apart from the others of his Jewish brethren. God called him through His grace, as opposed to judging him for his persecution of Christ. After his conversion, Paul did not seek guidance from Peter and the other apostles in Jerusalem. ...

I did not immediately submit it to flesh and blood, neither came I up to Jerusalem to those who were apostles before me, but I came away into Arabia, and I return again to Damascus.

> It is significant that Paul distanced himself in this way from the other apostles. The evangel he proclaimed was not taught to him by the others; it was revealed to Him by Jesus Christ. This should cause us to ask why this direct revelation was necessary. Could it be that the message Paul was to bear was different? Most Bible teachers today indiscriminately teach equally from Paul's writings and from the others as if there is no difference. But Paul goes out of his way to distance himself from the others here in Galatians. By blending together Paul's evangel with the evangel proclaimed by Peter and the others of the Twelve, are we guilty of distorting the evangel intended for us; and are we being led astray by a different evangel?

CHAPTER 2

Paul submits his evangel in Jerusalem (2:1)

> Three years lapsed after Paul's conversion before he went to Jerusalem, relating his story to Cephas (1:18). And after fourteen years he went again to Jerusalem to "submit" to them the evangel that he heralded. But was Paul REQUIRED by the apostles to go to Jerusalem?

Now I went up *in accord with a revelation* and submitted to them the evangel which I am heralding among the nations.

> Paul was not REQUIRED by the apostles to go to Jerusalem; he went in accord with a REVELATION.

> The fact that Paul submitted to the others the evangel he was heralding shows us that HIS EVANGEL WAS DIFFERENT from that which was being proclaimed by the others. Verse 3 shows us that the controversy that led to Paul's appearance in Jerusalem was concerning circumcision.

Not even Titus, who is with me, being a Greek, is compelled to be circumcised. Yet, it was because of the false brethren who were smuggled in, who came in by the way to spy out our freedom which we have in Christ Jesus, that they shall be enslaving us.

> Paul's evangel spoke of freedom in Christ Jesus, but those who had infiltrated the ecclesia were attempting to enslave them again to the law; promoting circumcision and other elements from the law.

When Paul went to Jerusalem he submitted his evangel to *those of repute* (2:2). But whatever the reasons for their being considered "of repute" was of no consequence to Paul.

Now from those reputed to be somewhat – what kind they once were is of no consequence to me (God is not taking up the human aspect) ...

Paul received his evangel directly from Christ Jesus thru a revelation, and he is not under the authority of Peter or the others who were of repute within the ecclesia in Jerusalem.

The evangel of the Uncircumcision (2:7)

I have been entrusted with the evangel of the Uncircumcision, according as Peter of the Circumcision.

Two different evangels!

There were two different evangels (gospels) to be proclaimed to two different people groups. The evangels were different. Paul did not simply bear the same evangel as Peter, but to the Uncircumcision. He was entrusted with "the evangel of the Uncircumcision." If Paul had consented to blending the two messages together, much controversy would have been eliminated. And when Paul returned to Jerusalem late in his ministry he would not have been opposed by the Jews who believed but who were zealous for the law (Acts 21:20).

But to blend the evangels together would have been a distortion and would have created a DIFFERENT evangel; and this is what Paul so vehemently defends against.

In Jerusalem, all agree that we, indeed, are to be for the nations, yet they for the Circumcision.

It seems clear that at this point in time there are two evangels; one proclaimed by Paul and Barnabas to the nations, and another by the Twelve to the Jews. Paul does not contend that Peter and the others needed to change the evangel they had been proclaiming to make it consistent with his. But they agreed to take the respective evangels entrusted to them to the groups God had placed under their care.

There appears, then, to be a Jewish ecclesia (church) hearing the evangel as proclaimed by Peter, and a Gentile ecclesia (church) hearing Paul's evangel. And if we study closely the writings of Paul as compared with the writings of Peter, James and John we will see many differences.

Evangel of Uncircumcision (Paul)	Evangel of Circumcision
The Body of Christ	The Bride of Christ
New creation	Born again
Expectation in the heavens	Expectation upon the earth
Awaiting Christ to snatch us away	Awaiting Christ to reign upon the earth
Justified by faith alone (Romans 4:1-3)	Justified by faith plus works (James 2:24)
No legal requirements (circumcision, sabbath, tithing, etc.)	Legal requirements observed

Peter's hypocrisy (2:11)

Despite the agreement in Jerusalem, when Cephas (Peter) comes to Antioch he severed himself from those of the nations, because he feared those of the Circumcision (2:13). Paul withstood Peter to his face, saying:

If you, being inherently a Jew, are living as the nations, and not as the Jews, how are you compelling the nations to be judaizing?

This, then, is the problem that Paul was contending with in this letter. The Jews were adding to Paul's evangel by requiring the Gentiles to observe elements of the law. There is conflict between Paul (and the message he brings to the Gentiles) and the Jewish believers. And the two groups (Circumcision believers and Uncircumcision believers) are largely severed from one another.

The message proclaimed by Paul to the Gentiles is freedom apart from any elements from the law, and the Circumcision believers have difficulty accepting that God is doing something so different apart from the Jews who had been His chosen instrument in the past.

The law cannot justify (2:15)

We, who by nature are Jews, and not sinners of the nations, having perceived that a man is not being justified by works of law, if it should not be through the faith of Christ Jesus, we also believe in Christ Jesus that we may be justified by the faith of Christ and not by works of law, seeing that by works of law shall no flesh at all be justified.

As Paul made clear in Romans, the law cannot justify (Romans 3:20). Even the Jewish ecclesia should understand this.

Crucified with Christ (2:19)

For I, through law, died to law, that I should be living to God. With Christ have I been crucified, yet I am living; no longer I, but living in me is Christ.

> Paul has died to law, just as Christ has died. With Christ he has been figuratively crucified, and that which now lives is not Paul but Christ living in Paul. And as Paul is living in flesh, he points out ...

I am living in faith that is of the Son of God.

> Justification is a gracious gift from God, provided on the basis of Jesus Christ's faith as he died for our sins. It is not "faith in Christ" that justifies us; it is the "faith OF Christ" (2:16). We come to a *recognition* of what God has accomplished when we believe and have faith "in" Christ. But justification is a gracious gift from God. One day all will believe; some thru faith and others by empirical evidence (sight). But when God's gracious gift is perceived by all, every knee will bow and proclaim Him Lord.

Do not repudiate grace (2:21)

> Adding legal requirements is rejecting grace. If righteousness can be gained thru works of law, then Christ would have died for no purpose. Expressing a freedom from the law, Paul is adamant ...

I am not repudiating the grace of God, for if righteousness is through law, consequently Christ died gratuitously.

> Paul's inference is that those wanting to add requirements from the law (like circumcision) to become righteous are repudiating God's grace and nullifying what Christ has accomplished thru His death. The Galatians had been deceived and were repudiating grace to fall back on the law once again.

CHAPTER 3

O foolish Galatians! Who bewitches you, before whose eyes Jesus Christ was graphically crucified?

> The believers had the spirit of Christ. Paul asks them to remember how they received that spirit.

Did you get the spirit by works of law or by the hearing of faith? So foolish are you? Undertaking in spirit, are you now being completed in flesh?

An example: Abraham [(3:5)]

Abraham believes God, and it is reckoned to him for righteousness. Those of faith are also sons of Abraham and are being blessed together with believing Abraham. Just as Abraham's fleshly descendants were sons of Abraham in the flesh, those of faith are sons of Abraham, irrespective of their fleshly heritage.

> So apart from any works of law, and strictly through God's grace; based upon the faith of Christ; man is justified. Those who believe God, as did Abraham, are reckoned righteous. God's gracious gift of justification will one day reconcile all mankind, at which point God will become All in all (1 Corinthians 15:28). Some will believe and be reckoned righteous in this present age, while others will doubt until they can see with their eyes, like Thomas (John 20:26-29).

> But do we *choose* to believe based on exercising our free will? Or does God select out of humanity a group to which He grants the *ability* to believe in this present age; to accomplish His purposes? Consider Philippians 1:29; *For to you it is graciously granted, for Christ's sake, not only to be believing on Him, but to be suffering for His sake also.* And consider 2 Corinthians 4:4; *In whom the god of this eon blinds the apprehensions of the unbelieving so that the illumination of the evangel of the glory of Christ, Who is the Image of the invisible God, does not irradiate them.* If all eyes are blinded, causing mankind to be unable to believe, could it be that God chooses a small group of humanity (the ecclesia; called-out-ones) who are given the gracious gift of belief; to be God's ambassadors in this present age, and to serve a specific purpose in the age to come as determined by God?

Shortcomings of the law [(3:10)]

For whoever are of works of law are under a curse, for it is written that, Accursed is everyone who is not remaining in all things written in the scroll of the law to do them.

> Those under the law must observe ALL of the law.

That in law no one is being justified with God is evident, for the just one by faith shall be living.

> Justification is thru faith, not law.

That we may be obtaining the promise of the spirit through faith.

> The promise of the spirit is through faith; not the law.

A human covenant having been ratified, no one is repudiating or modifying it. A covenant having been ratified by God, the law, having come four hundred and thirty years afterward, does not invalidate, so as to nullify the promise. For if the enjoyment of the allotment is of law it is no longer of promise. Yet God has graciously granted it to Abraham through the promise.

> The promises to Abraham pre-dated the law. No one can repudiate or modify a ratified covenant, and the promises were declared to Abraham 430 years prior to the law. The law cannot nullify the promise.

> The law served a temporary purpose ...

On behalf of transgressions was it added, until the Seed should come to Whom He has promised.

> The law was an "escort" ...

Now before the coming of faith we were garrisoned under law, being locked up together for the faith about to be revealed. So that the law has become our *escort* to Christ, that we may be justified by faith.

> The law was a guardian ...

For as much time as the enjoyer of an allotment is a minor, in nothing is he of more consequence than a slave, being master of all, but is under *guardians* and *administrators* until the time purposed by the father (4:1).

We are now sons of God (3:25)

Now, at the coming of faith, we are no longer under an escort, for you are all sons of God, through faith in Christ Jesus.

> Having considered the temporary purpose of the law, Paul now points out that we are now sons of God through faith.

There is no Jew nor yet Greek, there is no slave nor yet free, there is no male and female, for you all are one in Christ Jesus.

No Jew nor Greek? This is something new!

> There are no fleshly distinctions. Always in the past, preference had been given to the Jew first. Not so now thru Paul's evangel. The nations are now enjoyers of the allotment ...

Now if you are Christ's, consequently you are of Abraham's seed, enjoyers of the allotment according to the promise.

CHAPTER 4

Thus we also, when we were minors, were enslaved under the elements of the world.

> Once we were enslaved.

Now, when the full time came, God delegates His Son, come of a woman, come under law, that He should be reclaiming those under law, that we may be getting the place of a son.

> Christ reclaimed those under law.

Now, seeing that you are sons, God delegates the spirit of His Son into our hearts.

> The spirit of His Son is in our hearts. And as a result, Paul again states that ...

You are no longer a slave, but a son; and if a son, an enjoyer also of an allotment from God, through Christ.

Why turn back? (4:8)

Knowing God, yet rather being known by God, how are you turning back again to the infirm and poor elements for which you want to slave again anew? Days are you scrutinizing, and months and seasons and years.

> Paul seems to be referring to a dependence upon recognizing certain days as was required by the law, and which sons of God had been freed from; sabbaths and required feast days.

Where is your happiness?

Returning to the law has taken away their happiness. Paul had previously brought the evangel to the Galatians, and he was received as a messenger of God.

They are jealous over you, not ideally, but they want to debar you that you may be jealous over them.

In other words; they want to debar you from enjoying your freedom in Christ, making you jealous of their outward observance of the elemental things; their religiosity. The Galatians were giving up their freedom and placing themselves once again under the law. The motive of the false teachers was jealousy.

Allegory of Abraham's two sons (4:21)
Abraham had two sons; one out of the maid (Ishmael) and one out of the free woman (Isaac). One is begotten according to the flesh (Ishmael) and the other thru the promise (Isaac). This represents two covenants. One is from Mount Sinai, generating into slavery (the law). But you, brethren, as Isaac, are children of promise.

Even as then, the one generated according to flesh persecuted the one according to spirit; thus also it is now. But as the scripture says, Cast out this maid and her son, for by no means shall the son of the maid be enjoying the allotment with the son of the free woman.

CHAPTER 5

Christ frees us (5:1)
For freedom Christ frees us! Stand firm, then, and be not again enthralled with the yoke of slavery.

If you should be circumcising, Christ will benefit you nothing. Now I am attesting again to every man who is circumcising, that he is a debtor to do the whole law. Exempted from Christ were you who are being justified in law. You fall out of grace.

Faith, operating thru love (5:5)
We, in spirit, are awaiting the expectation of righteousness by faith.

While the believer is reckoned righteous, still we await the full experience of righteousness. As we believe God it is *reckoned* to us as righteousness, as was the case with Abraham. But here we see that righteousness is also an *expectation* and something we are awaiting. And

> as we await this expectation, we live by faith and are reckoned righteous as we believe God.

Circumcision or uncircumcision mean nothing. For in Christ Jesus neither circumcision is availing anything, nor uncircumcision.

> But if neither circumcision nor uncircumcision matter, what *does* matter?

Faith, operating through love.

> As we live by faith, love is in operation. It is love that guides us. It is love that will be manifest in us as we live by faith.

Why are you not persuaded? (5:7)

You raced ideally! Who hinders you not to be persuaded by the truth? This persuasion is not of Him Who is calling you. They are leaven, and they are leavening the entire loaf. They will bear their judgment.

> The Galatians were persuaded and led away from the truth by those who were not of God.

Paul is not heralding circumcision (5:11)

If I am still heralding circumcision, why am I still being persecuted? Consequently the snare of the cross of Christ has been nullified.

> Those disturbing the Galatians must have been announcing that Paul was including the requirement of circumcision in his evangel, but Paul makes it clear that there is no mixture of law in his evangel. If Paul was insisting upon circumcision, the snare of the cross would have been eliminated and Paul would not be persecuted.

> What is the "snare of the cross?" We may think it is simply the proclamation of Christ crucified; but Paul implies that if the law were simply added to the proclamation of Christ the snare would be removed. This, then, is the snare of the cross for believing Jews; the elimination of all requirements from the law. For Paul it is imperative that no law be mixed with the grace he proclaims in the evangel that had been revealed to him.

Freedom is not a license (5:13)

You were called for freedom, brethren, only use not the freedom for an incentive to the flesh, but through love be slaving for one another.

Some still think there is a need for legal requirements. Many today are afraid to remove legal requirements from the gospel (sabbath, tithing, Sermon on the Mount requirements, drinking, smoking; the list goes on) because they fear that believers will live however they please, guided only by satisfying their fleshly desires. But Paul does not respond to this challenge by adding legal requirements to his message of grace. The law has nothing to do with one's position with God.

But without adding legal requirements to his evangel, Paul does insist that OUR FREEDOM IS NOT TO BE ABUSED.

The entire law is fulfilled in one word, in this: You shall love your associate as yourself.

Love fulfills the law. Living to the flesh is to have selfish motivations. Living by love is to have selfless motivations; to be guided by a concern for one's associate. If we are guided by the flesh, biting and devouring one another we will be consumed by one another (5:15).

Walk in spirit (5:16)

So the believer has freedom and is not bound by the law, but Paul urges the Galatians ...

Walk in spirit, and you should under no circumstances be consummating the lust of the flesh.

Walking in the spirit (or not) has no bearing on our justification or our being reckoned righteous, which is dependent only upon belief (faith). But Paul admonishes the ecclesia to walk in spirit.

For the flesh is lusting against the spirit, yet the spirit against the flesh. Now these are opposing one another, lest you should be doing whatever you may want.

The flesh and spirit oppose one another.

Lest you should be doing whatever you may want.

If the believer is not under the law, what prevents him from doing whatever he wants; using his freedom as a license to sin? The holy spirit is given to the believer. When the believer allows himself to be led by the flesh, the opposition of the spirit is felt. If the spirit did not oppose the flesh through this inner struggle, we could be guided by the flesh

> with no reservations. But it is the struggle that holds us in check; the conscience.

Now, if you are led by spirit, you are not still under law.

> Those who walk in spirit fulfill the demands of the law without compulsion. The spirit of the law is fulfilled without any need for its form. They are LED by the spirit and are not under law.

> It is a FACT that the believer is led by spirit and is therefore not under law. In response, Paul prompts the ecclesia to walk in spirit.

The works of the flesh are apparent ... adultery, prostitution, uncleanness, wantonness, idolatry, enchantment, enmities, strife, jealousies, furies, factions, dissensions, sects, envies, murders, drunkenness, revelries, and the like. Those committing such things shall not be enjoying the allotment of the kingdom of God.

> Are good works needed, then, to gain the kingdom allotment? On the surface this seems to nullify the believer's salvation by faith. If one exhibits the works of the flesh they will not enjoy the allotment of the kingdom of God. This seems to imply works righteousness, and not faith.

> As Jesus proclaimed the kingdom evangel (Matthew, Mark, Luke, John) He called for repentance and living in accord with kingdom requirements (Sermon on the Mount). This was proclaimed to the sheep of Israel in preparation for the kingdom to be restored upon the earth. But Jesus was crucified. The Jews, who had been God's instrument were calloused and locked up in stubbornness (Romans 11:25-32). God is now working thru Paul's evangel of the Uncircumcision, where faith is the basis for righteousness; not legal requirements. And when the Body of Christ is snatched away (1 Thessalonians 4:13-18) and God once again turns to Israel to be His instrument upon the earth (Revelation), works will once again be the basis for God's judgment.

> Two possibilities exist for the present passage.

> First, since Paul is speaking to some extent to Jewish believers who are being enticed to return to the law, he may be pointing out that when the kingdom comes upon the earth God will be judging based upon the works of the flesh; and one would lose his allotment within the kingdom if committing such things. Not that those within the Body of Christ would lose their allotment (since that is determined by faith, and not by works);

but Paul may be simply pointing out God's expectations for those within the kingdom when it comes upon the earth, as he admonishes them to be guided by the spirit and not the flesh.

Second, Paul could be referring to the kingdom in the broader sense; not just the aspect of the kingdom to come upon the earth, but the larger kingdom of God which is over the entire universe, and already in place in the heavens. All believers will stand before the dais of Christ to receive payment for his works, whether good or bad (2 Corinthians 5:10; Romans 14:10). This payment has nothing to do with salvation, which is determined by belief (faith) alone. But there could be some loss of one's allotment within the kingdom.

Now the fruit of the spirit is love, joy, peace, patience, kindness, goodness, faithfulness, meekness, self-control: against such things there is no law.

How does the believer put away the works of the flesh, and exhibit the fruit of the spirit?

Those of Christ Jesus crucify the flesh together with its passions and lusts.

Observing the elements in spirit (5:25)

If we may be living in spirit, in spirit we may be observing the elements also. One who chooses to set aside certain days, even though not required to do so, may choose to do so as guided by the spirit.

One may CHOOSE to observe "the elements." Paul also spoke to this point in Romans. One, indeed, is deciding for one day rather than another day, yet one is deciding for every day. Let each one be fully assured in his own mind (Romans 14:5). The faith which you have, have for yourself in God's sight. Happy is he who is not judging himself in that which he is attesting. Now he who is doubting if he should be eating is condemned, seeing that it is not out of faith. Now everything which is not out of faith is sin (Romans 14:22).

But we must not challenge others as to their observation of the elemental things ...

We may not become vainglorious, challenging one another, envying one another.

Decisions as to the "elemental things" are to be made individually, for ourselves, based on the faith granted to us. We are not to judge others on these issues. And as for ourselves, we are guided by conscience.

Paul will conclude the Galatian letter with an additional note on this subject:

And whoever shall observe the elements by this rule, peace be on them, and mercy, also on the Israel of God (6:16).

CHAPTER 6

Bear one another's burdens (6:1)

Brethren, if a man should be precipitated in some offense, you, who are spiritual, be attuning such a one, in a spirit of meekness, noting yourself, that you, also, may not be tried.

If one stumbles and commits an offense, the spiritual one should "ADJUST" him in a spirit of meekness.

Bear one another's burdens, and thus fill up the law of Christ.

Exercising love, the believer must always seek the welfare of others.

For if anyone is supposing himself to be anything, being nothing, he is imposing on himself. Now let each one be testing his own work, and then he shall be having his boast for himself alone, and not for another, for each one shall be bearing his own load.

As for managing ourselves, we are to have a proper opinion of ourselves, and seek to bear our own load.

Now let him who is being instructed in the word be contributing to him who is instructing, in all good things.

We remember that despite this comment, Paul did not enlist support for himself, but gave up this right to proclaim the evangel for free.

Reaping what is sown (6:7)

Be not deceived, God is not to be sneered at, for whatsoever a man may be sowing, this shall he be reaping also. He who is sowing for his own flesh, from the flesh shall be reaping corruption, yet he who is sowing for the spirit, from the spirit shall be reaping life eonian.

This seems to reference our appearing before the dais of Christ (2 Corinthians 5:10; Romans 14:10) where we will receive payment for works, good or bad. Walking in the spirit and sowing for the spirit may not see reward in the present age. The reaping will occur at the dais of Christ; and the one sowing for his own flesh will reap corruption.

Working for the good of all (6:10)

Consequently, then, as we have occasion, we are working for the good of all, yet *specially* for the family of faith.

Believers may be under persecution and may be in need of works of goodness from others even more so than non-believers. But we work for the good of all, not just fellow believers.

"Specially"

Specially in this passage comes from the Greek *malista*. We see in this context that we are to work not exclusively for the good of believers. We are to work for the good of ALL; in a *special* way for believers, but for the good of all. The same Greek word is found in 1 Timothy 4:10 where we read that God is the Saviour of all mankind, *especially* of believers. Most within the church today would say that God will save only those who believe in this lifetime, but this passage tells us that God is the Saviour of *all*. Salvation pertains to the believer in a SPECIAL way, for he enjoys the expectation thru faith, and will have a special function in the age to come. But God is not the Saviour exclusively of believers; He is the Saviour of all.

Those compelling circumcision (6:11)

Whoever are wanting to put on a fair face in the flesh, they are compelling you to circumcise only that they may not be persecuted for the cross of Christ Jesus. They want you to be circumcised that they should be boasting in your flesh.

By adding the law to faith and distorting the evangel (1:7) those compelling circumcision seek to remove the sting from the message of the cross. And those compelling circumcision could claim "converts" for every believer circumcised and thus brought in line with the law. This is not much different from those evangelists of our own day boasting in the number they have "converted" to Christ.

A new creation (6:15)

In Christ Jesus neither circumcision nor uncircumcision is anything, but a new creation.

A New Creation!
Circumcision means nothing.

The fleshly, elemental things have no bearing on anything; because we have been crucified with Christ and are now figuratively a new creation.

Whoever shall observe the elements by this rule, peace be on them.

Some may voluntarily choose to observe the elements. The fleshly, elemental things have no bearing. And as new creations, those choosing to observe certain elemental things as led by the spirit, let each one be assured in his own mind; not judging others in this regard (Romans 14:5).

Galatians
Questions & Issues concerning the evangel

Being led astray by a different evangel   1:6
- Reject any evangel different from Paul's

Paul's evangel came through revelation   1:10
- Not received from a man
- Paul was "severed"
- Paul did not immediately go to the apostles

Paul submits his evangel in Jerusalem due to a "revelation" 2:1
- False brethren desiring to enslave
- Went to "those of repute"

Evangel of the Uncircumcision   2:7
- Paul entrusted with evangel of the Uncircumcision
- Peter entrusted with evangel of the Circumcision

Conflict between Circumcision & Uncircumcision   2:11
- Cephas came to Antioch & Paul opposed him
- Compelling the nations to be judaizing
- The law cannot justify
- Crucified with Christ (now Christ living in me)

Do not repudiate grace   2:21
- Who bewitched you?
- Did you receive the spirit of Christ thru Law?

Blessed as was Abraham   3:5
- Abraham believed God ... reckoned righteous
- Those of faith are also sons of Abraham

Shortcomings of the law   3:10
- Those under law must observe ALL of the law
- Justification is thru faith, not law
- Promise of the spirit is thru faith
- The promises to Abraham pre-dated the law
- The law served a temporary purpose (escort, guardian)

We are now sons of God 3:25
- Sons of God thru faith
- No fleshly distinctions
- Enjoyers of the allotment
- Once we were enslaved
- Christ reclaimed those under law
- The spirit of His Son in our hearts

Why turn back? 4:8
- Why return to the inform and poor elements?
- Has taken away your happiness
- Those leading you astray are jealous

Allegory of Abraham's two sons 4:21
- Children of slavery, or of promise?

Christ frees us 5:1
- Be not again enthralled with slavery
- Circumcising exempts you from Christ

Awaiting the expectation of righteousness by faith 5:5
- Circumcision or uncircumcision mean nothing
- Faith, operating thru love

Why are you not persuaded by the truth? 5:7
- Persuaded by those not of Him

Paul is not heralding circumcision 5:11
- If heralding circumcision, why persecuted?

Freedom is not a license 5:13
- Use not freedom for an incentive to the flesh
- Love fulfills the law

Walk in spirit 5:16
- Not consummating the lust of the flesh
- Flesh and spirit oppose one another
- "Lest you should be doing whatever you may want"
- Led by spirit ... not still under law
- Works of the flesh versus fruit of the spirit

- Those of Christ crucify the flesh
- Living in spirit, we may be observing the elements

Bear one another's burdens 6:1
- Spiritual one should "adjust" those stumbling in spirit of meekness
- Each shall be bearing his own load

Reaping what is sown (for the flesh, or for the spirit) 6:7

Working for the good of all 6:10
- "Specially" for the family of faith

Those compelling circumcision 6:11
- They seek to avoid persecution
- They do not keep the law themselves

A new creation 6:15
- The elemental things mean nothing
- Some may choose to observe the element "by this rule"

CLOSING THOUGHTS

Like the two Corinthian letters, Galatians was written to bring clarification and adjustment to the teachings presented in Paul's letter to the Romans. The primary issue is the desire of the Galatians to place themselves once again under the law, from which Christ had freed them.

Paul warns the Galatians against those who are distorting the evangel by adding legal requirements, such as circumcision. The Judaists were attempting to fuse together Paul's gospel and the law, but Paul insists that this fusion is not proper and actually results in a DIFFERENT; a DISTORTED gospel.

His evangel was not taught to him by men following his conversion; it came through a revelation of Jesus Christ (1:12). Whereas Peter was entrusted with the evangel of the Circumcision, Paul was entrusted with the evangel of the Uncircumcision (2:7). The differences in these evangels leads to misunderstandings, disagreements, and friction between the Jewish and Gentile believers.

The law cannot justify, yet the Galatians are being enticed by certain deceivers to return to the law; adding legal requirements to the grace given by God thru Christ. The law was given as an escort or guardian, until the promise made to Abraham had come. And now that God has delegated His Son to reclaim those under the law, making them sons and enjoyers of an allotment, why do they want to return to the law?

Christ frees us! (5:1) Yet we are not to use the freedom for an incentive to the flesh. The entire law is fulfilled in one word: You shall love your associate as yourself (5:14). Walk in the spirit, not consummating the lust of the flesh (5:16). Work for the good of all (6:10). Circumcision or uncircumcision have no bearing; you are a new creation (6:15).

Galatians is a very important letter, largely ignored by the church today! Many in the church indiscriminately mix the evangel of Paul with the evangel of Peter and the Twelve, which was intended for the Jewish ecclesia (called-out-ones) who looked for the restoration of the kingdom upon the earth. Many impose requirements upon the believer; water baptism, tithing, church attendance, church membership, consenting to a list of doctrinal beliefs based on the church's interpretation of Scripture. Paul vehemently opposed any additions to the justification and righteousness gratuitously given by God, through Christ Jesus. He warned against anyone preaching an evangel different from the one he preached; yet today's pulpits proclaim a different evangel (the Circumcision evangel) instead of Paul's evangel.

> # Observe the importance of correct doctrine!

When others attempt to teach the need for elements of the law to be added to the gospel, Paul does not dodge the issue. Nor does he compromise for the sake of unity and love. Love is the most important thing (1 Corinthians 14), but doctrine is also important. Whereas the two letters to the Corinthians were concerned more with practical matters, Galatians is focused on addressing doctrinal error.

"If ever we also, or a messenger out of heaven, should be bringing an evangel to you BESIDE THAT WHICH WE BRING TO YOU, let him be anathema!

𝕰𝖕𝖍𝖊𝖘𝖎𝖆𝖓𝖘

An Overview of the Scriptures, by
BOB EVELY © 2018.
An Independent Minister of Christ Jesus,
Of the church at Wilmore, Kentucky

"To me ... was granted this grace: to bring the evangel of the untraceable riches of Christ to the nations, and to enlighten all as to what is the administration of the secret, which has been concealed from the eons in God." (3:8-9)

"To make known the secret of the evangel" (6:20)

1 Thessalonians	50-52 AD	During 2nd Journey
2 Thessalonians	52-53 AD	During 2nd Journey
Galatians (early theory)	54 AD	End of 2nd Journey
1 Corinthians	Spring 57 AD	During 3rd Journey
2 Corinthians	Fall 57 AD	During 3rd Journey
Galatians	Winter 57 AD	During 3rd Journey
Romans	Spring 58 AD	During 3rd Journey
Colossians	61-62 AD	During 1st Captivity
Ephesians	**61-62 AD**	**During 1st Captivity**
Philemon	62-63 AD	During 1st Captivity
Philippians	63 AD	During 1st Captivity
1 Timothy	67 AD	Between Captivities
Titus	67 AD	Between Captivities
2 Timothy	Spring 68 AD	During 2nd Captivity

CHAPTER 1

The address on the envelope (1:1)

Paul, an apostle of Christ Jesus through the will of God;
To all the saints who are also believers in Christ Jesus.

> Saints is literally "holy ones;" those who have been made holy, or set apart for some purpose, by God.

Spiritual blessings (1:3)

Blessed be the God and Father of our Lord Jesus Christ, Who blesses us with every spiritual blessing among the celestials, in Christ.

> These are not, then, blessings realized in the flesh upon this earth as was the case with Israel, but spiritual blessings among the celestials, or heavenly realms.

Chosen before the disruption (1:4)

He chooses us in Him before the *disruption* of the world, we to be holy and flawless in His sight, in love designating us beforehand for the place of a son.

> *Disruption* (*katabole* in the Greek) is often translated "foundation," but it is clearly not a "building upon." It is instead a "casting down." This seems to refer to the event described in Genesis 1:1 which, when translated properly, tells us the earth BECAME a chaos and was then subsequently remolded by God in six days.

> *Us* (He chooses *us*) refers to those who Paul is associating himself with; the saints (holy ones; set apart ones) to whom he is writing. We do not *choose* to become saints but are chosen by God. Furthermore we were chosen long ago; before the disruption of the world. God does not develop His plan along the way. His plan was formulated long ago.

> But why were those within the ecclesia chosen?

Holy and flawless (1:5)

To be holy and flawless in His sight, in love designating us beforehand for the place of a son for Him through Christ Jesus; in accord with the delight of His will, for the laud of the glory of His grace.

> Certainly no man living in these mortal bodies of flesh can ever become truly flawless. But we are holy and flawless IN HIS SIGHT. Our sin and shortcomings have been addressed by Christ, God's solution to the sin problem. And as a result of this miraculous solution, out of all mankind we who have been chosen by God are seen as holy and flawless in His sight – because Christ was in reality holy and flawless and we have been made to become His body.

> Why would God do this? It is not for our own benefit, but because the plan He is unfolding is ...

In accord with the delight of His will, and it is for the laud of the glory of His grace, which graces us in the Beloved: in Whom we are having the deliverance through His blood, the forgiveness of offenses in accord with the riches of His grace, which He lavishes on us.

> This position we are granted is nothing we have earned or deserved, else we could boast. It is purely God's grace at work. We are chosen by Him, and He has graced us with sonship, deliverance and forgiveness. Why would God do this for a portion of humanity that He has chosen?

The secret (1:9)

Making known to us the secret of His will (in accord with His delight, which He purposed in Him) to have an administration of the complement of the eras, to head up all in the Christ – both that in the heavens and that on the earth.

> **God revealed to Paul a SECRET that had been concealed in the past. Therefore, Paul's evangel was most certainly different from the evangel proclaimed by Peter and the others of the Circumcision!**

> God chose us, a subset of humanity, to make known a secret. The Greek *musterion* is clearly not a "mystery" in the sense that it is something we can solve or figure out. It is a SECRET that was CONCEALED in the past and is now made known by God. And the secret is this. As a complement to the eras, the history of mankind that has preceded and that is a display of man's wickedness, sinfulness and imperfection, God now reveals His plan to head up all in Christ, not only that which is in the heavens but also that which is on the earth. Despite the chaos, wickedness and destruction we see all around us in this world, God's secret is that He is in the process of solving all of this. A COMPLEMENT is something that brings completion. There is one part, and by adding a complement that part is made whole, or complete. The chaos in the world today is in the process of being made whole or complete by the *complement* that God

has provided. All, not just some but all, will be headed up by Christ. (Turn to 1 Corinthians 15:20-28 to see this taking place.)

All in accord with the counsel of His will (1:12)

God is *operating all in accord with the counsel of His will,* that we should be for the laud of His glory, who are *pre-expectant in the Christ.*

> # All in accord with the counsel of His will. Think about this most important statement!

If this is so, what can possibly prevent Christ from heading up all that is in the heavens and upon the earth? Furthermore, if God is the Saviour of all mankind, especially (though not exclusively) of believers, (1 Timothy 4:10) and if it is God's will or desire that all mankind be saved and come into a realization of the truth, (1 Timothy 2:4) and if God is operating all in accord with the counsel of His will, (Ephesians 1:12) then what can possibly prevent these things from taking place?

Pre-expectant? This is an interesting phrase at the end of 1:12. *Pre-expectant* implies that what we, the saints, enjoy (sonship, forgiveness, grace) is just step one. All of humanity is expectant of these things, for God is in the process of heading up all in Christ. We who have been chosen beforehand, to serve God's purpose in some way, are *pre-expectant.*

Now we will see the process God is using to accomplish His will.

On *hearing* the word of truth, the evangel of your salvation – in Whom on *believing* also, you are *sealed* with the holy spirit of promise, which is an earnest of the enjoyment of our allotment.

First there is the word of truth that is brought forth by God, the evangel (gospel; good news) of your salvation. This good news is *heard* and then it is *believed,* and the believer is then *sealed* with the holy spirit of promise. The holy spirit is described as an *earnest* of (or a deposit toward) the enjoyment of our allotment. We see, then, that the

> deliverance that has been procured for us is not yet realized, and therefore we have been given an earnest deposit to assure us of what has been promised.

I do not cease giving thanks for you, making mention in my prayers.

> The emphasis Paul gives to prayer and giving thanks to God should be an example for us.

Coming to a realization of God (1:17)

That God may be giving you a spirit of wisdom and revelation in the *realization of Him,* the eyes of your heart having been enlightened, for you *to perceive what is the expectation of His calling,* and what the riches of the glory of the *enjoyment of His allotment* among the saints, and what the *transcendent greatness of His power* for us who are believing, which is operative in the Christ, raising Him from among the dead and seating Him at His right hand among the celestials, up over every sovereignty and authority and power and lordship.

> God had demonstrated His power in rousing Christ from among the dead and seating Him among the celestials (the heavens) with a position above all of creation. But the believers were not yet *enlightened,* they did not yet *realize* what they could expect in terms of their allotment, or the glory of what they could expect in the future. It is this failure to fully understand their expectation that would seem to give cause to Paul to write this letter. Whereas Romans provides basic doctrine, Ephesians goes beyond that (as a graduate course) and provides more advanced doctrine intended to further enlighten the believers.

Christ over all; in this eon and that which is impending (1:22)

God roused Christ from among the dead, seating Him at His right hand among the celestials, up over every sovereignty and authority and power and lordship, and every name that is named, not only in this eon, but also in that which is impending.

> Christ's seating among the celestials pertains not only in this eon, but also in that which is impending. So we see that *eon* (*aion* in the Greek), which is often translated "eternal" or "endless," is clearly a finite period of time. A close study of the Scriptures will show us there seems to be five eons, a period of time before the eons, and a conclusion to the eons (when timeless "eternity" would seem to begin). In this passage we see

mention made of two distinct eons; the current eon, and the eon which is impending.

Purpose of the ecclesia – the "complement" (1:22)

He subjects all under Christ's feet, and gives Him, as Head over all, to the ecclesia which is *His body*, the *complement* by which all in all is being completed.

> # The purpose of the ecclesia – to be Christ's "complement."

Eccelsia is often translated "church," but it would be better if this was not so. The word simply means "out-called-ones;" those who have been called out of humanity at large for some purpose. As God may have occasion to call out different subsets of humanity in different eras, each may be referred to as the ecclesia, but they should not be confused with each other if we want to correctly understand what God is revealing. At one time Israel was the ecclesia. In most of Acts Jewish believers were the ecclesia. When Paul introduces the Body of Christ (Jew and Gentile with no preference or distinction), the Body of Christ is the ecclesia. But we cannot look at ecclesia in every instance as the same group of "out-called-ones" as this is clearly not the case. We must correctly cut or rightly divide the Scriptures (2 Timothy 2:15) if we are to correctly understand the truth that God has revealed.

We also see in this passage that God subjects all under Christ (1:22) and Christ is the One completing the all in all (1:23). We see this process being completed in 1 Corinthians 28 when God does, in fact, become all in all.

But we also see in this passage an amazing fact that tells us, at least in part, why God has "out-called" the ecclesia, which is here referred to as Christ's *body*. The Body of Christ is the complement of the One completing the all in all (1:23). Remember that a "complement" is something that completes the whole. Christ is the One commissioned by God to bring all into subjection to Him so that He will ultimately become all in all, and the Body of Christ is the complement to Christ in this process.

How does the Body of Christ serve as Christ's complement? I think the best description is found in 2 Corinthians 5:18-21. Yet all is of God, Who conciliates us to Himself through Christ, and is giving us the dispensation of the conciliation, how that God was in Christ, conciliating the world to Himself, not reckoning their offenses to them, and placing in us the word of the conciliation. For Christ, then, are we ambassadors, as of God entreating through us. We are beseeching for Christ's sake, 'Be conciliated to God!'

We are charged, then, with announcing the fact that God has, through Christ, become conciliated to man. Despite man's wickedness and sin, because of Christ God is now conciliated to man and is not reckoning man's offenses to him. But all are not yet conciliated to God. Much of mankind is alienated from God. There is not yet reconciliation, but only a one-sided conciliation on God's part. We are charged, as ambassadors, to proclaim as if God were proclaiming through us, *Be conciliated to God!* This is the part we play as Christ's complement.

And when, in fact, all have become conciliated to God ... some by faith in this current era, and others by sight in an era to come ... there will be a total and complete reconciliation. All will be subjected to God through the work of Christ (the One completing the all in all) and His complement (the Body of Christ), and then we will see the triumphant conclusion to the eons when God becomes all in all (1 Corinthians 15:28).

CHAPTER 2

The Body seated among the celestials [2:1]

You, being dead to your offenses and sins, in which once you walked, in accord with the eon of this world, in accord with the chief of the jurisdiction of the air, the spirit now operating in the sons of stubbornness (among whom we also all behaved ourselves once in the lusts of our flesh, doing the will of the flesh and of the comprehension, and were, in our nature, children of indignation, even as the rest) ...

The eon of this world is under the influence of the Deceiver; Satan; the chief of the jurisdiction of the air, the spirit now operating in the sons of stubbornness. Those whom Paul now addresses (the Body of Christ) once walked in sin and offenses, behaving as the "sons of stubbornness,"

> doing the will of the flesh and following the lusts of the flesh. We were, in our nature, children of indignation, as the rest of humanity. YET ...

Yet God, being rich in mercy, because of His vast love with which He loves us (we also being dead to the offenses and the lusts), vivifies us together in Christ (in grace are you saved!) and rouses us together and seats us together among the celestials, in Christ Jesus, that, in the oncoming eons, He should be displaying the transcendent riches of His grace in His kindness to us in Christ Jesus.

> So despite the fact that we were just as the rest of humanity, walking in sin and the lusts of the flesh, children of indignation even in our very nature, God saves us and vivifies us (makes us alive) and seats us in the celestials. We are no better than the rest of humanity, yet God displays His grace and mercy in this way. Why would God do this?

> Remember that God desired to have a complement to Christ, the One completing the all in all. We also see another part of the reason why God chose a subset of humanity to be His ecclesia. That, in the oncoming eons, He will display the riches of His grace and kindness (2:7). While we serve as ambassadors in this present eon, Christ's complement; in the coming eon when God seats us in the celestials (the heavens), all of creation will come to see God's grace and mercy through this display.

> Our expectation in the eon to come is not here upon this earth. We do not await Christ to return to reign. We await His call to meet Him in the air (1 Thessalonians 4:13-18) and to serve our place in the celestials, where we will be a display of God's grace and mercy.

> As for now, Christ is already seated in the celestials, having been roused from among the dead. We in the Body of Christ have figuratively been roused and vivified and are seated in the celestials, but we have not yet fully realized this in a literal way. One day, though, we too will be roused from among the dead (just as Christ, the Firstfruit) and seated in the celestials.

We are His achievement (2:8)

For in grace, through faith, are you saved, and this is not out of you; it is God's approach present, not of works, lest anyone should be boasting. For His achievement are we, being created in Christ Jesus for good works, which God makes ready beforehand, that we should be walking in them.

It is all God at work here! Salvation is God's gift. We are God's achievement. We are created in Christ Jesus. We have nothing to boast about. Another purpose of the Body of Christ is noted here; being created in Christ Jesus for good works, which God makes ready beforehand, that we should be walking in them. We are not saved because of our works; but because we are saved we walk in the good works that God has intended for us.

A new humanity (2:11)

Remember that once you, the nations in flesh; termed Uncircumcision by those termed Circumcision; you were in that era, apart from Christ, being alienated from the citizenship of Israel, and guests of the promise covenants, having no expectation ...

In the past the nations had no expectation as did Israel, and at best were only guests of the promise covenants. But Paul now announces a new humanity.

Yet now, in Christ Jesus, you; once far off; are become near by the blood of Christ. For He is our Peace, Who makes both one, and razes the central wall of the barrier; nullifying the law of precepts in decrees, that He should be creating the two, in Himself, into one new humanity; reconciling both in one body.

The barrier between Israel and the nations has been razed, and the law of precepts in decrees (Israel's law) has been nullified. What had been two (Israel and the nations; the Circumcision and the Uncircumcision) has now been created into one new humanity; one body.

Consequently, then, no longer are you guests and sojourners, but are fellow-citizens of the saints and belong to God's family.

This is a new proclamation. Always in the past God has worked through Israel as His chosen people. Those of the nations could only enjoy the covenants by sojourning with Israel and observing the law that was given to Israel. In His earthly ministry Jesus came to the sheep of Israel. The ministry of the Twelve was to the sheep of Israel. Even the apostle Paul would always go first to Israel, and only after being rejected would he approach the Gentiles. Not so any longer. God now has a new creation; the Body of Christ, comprised of Jew and Gentile with no barrier, preference or distinction.

This is something new, not proclaimed in the past. We see this good news only in Paul's writings. It had not been revealed to others before Paul; not even by Christ Himself during His earthly ministry. This is why Paul found it necessary to note that his evangel was not something he learned from man; it was revealed to him by Christ (Galatians 1:12). This is why Paul refers to this as a secret. (3:1-5) And this is why Paul was so strongly opposed by Jews who believed but were zealous for the law (Acts 21:20).

> # Can we therefore understand why it is so crucial to "correctly cut" or "rightly divide" the Scriptures? (2 Timothy 2:15)

If we choose from the writings of the Twelve which were directed to Israel without distinguishing them from the writings of Paul which were directed to the Body of Christ, we would be mixing together two different things, and we would fail to understand this secret that Paul shares with us. We would be "stealing" truth that was intended only for Israel in a certain era, and we would fail to understand this precious secret concerning a new thing that God has created. God is moving beyond what He had established through Israel; which was the basis of the entire Old Testament, the four Gospels, most of the book of Acts, and the letters from the Circumcision apostles; and He has now proclaimed something new and far superior and advanced through Paul. Let us, therefore, look beyond the more elemental truths that were proclaimed in the majority of the Scriptures. Let us rightly divide the Scriptures so as to fully appreciate this new creation that Paul shares with us.

CHAPTER 3

Revealing the secret (3:1)
On this behalf I, Paul, the prisoner of Christ Jesus for you, the nations – since you surely hear of the administration of the grace of God that is given to me for you. For by revelation the secret is made known to me

(according as I write before, in brief, by which you who are reading are able to apprehend my understanding in the secret of the Christ, which, in other generations, is not made known to the sons of humanity as it was now revealed to His holy apostles and prophets). In spirit the nations are to be joint enjoyers of an allotment, and a joint body, and joint partakers of the promise in Christ Jesus, through the evangel of which I became the dispenser.

By REVELATION the secret is made known to me!

Again we see that Paul's gospel is not the same as the gospel that had been shared by the apostles before him. The gospel he shares was revealed to him; it was A SECRET NOT MADE KNOWN TO OTHERS BEFORE HIM. It was granted to Paul ...

... to bring the evangel of the untraceable riches of Christ to the nations, and to enlighten all as to what is the administration of the secret, which has been concealed from the eons in God, Who creates all, that now may be made known to the sovereignties and the authorities among the celestials, through the ecclesia, the multifarious wisdom of God, in accord with the purpose of the eons.

That which Paul now reveals concerning the Body of Christ is untraceable. It is not something that man could have discerned on his own from God's previous revelation, since it was a secret that had been concealed in the past and is only now revealed through Paul. Even those in the celestial (heavenly) realm did not see this coming. God's wisdom was not fully revealed until now. If what Paul writes here is true; if this is a secret that God had concealed in times past and that is now being revealed; how can we possibly think Paul is sharing the same gospel (good news) that others before him had shared (i.e. the Twelve)?

It may have seemed as though God's plan was failing. God chose Israel and provided the law to set His chosen people apart. But Israel could not keep the law. How could God save mankind from a final death when even the means provided to rescue man (the law, and Israel) had failed. But now we see an even greater wisdom that had not previously been made known; a multifarious wisdom in accord with the purpose of the eons. This, then, is the purpose of the eons; the purpose of the history of God's dealings with mankind; to bring us to this point where now we are ready to see the unveiling of this secret that is far superior to anything God has revealed before.

It is not just Israel that God has chosen, with dictates of law to be observed (which Israel found impossible to observe). The Body of Christ has now been revealed; those of all nations with no preference or distinction, for the purpose of serving as Christ's complement to bring about the total subjection of all mankind to God, that God may become All in all. Those of us who are within the Body of Christ find ourselves here only because of God's grace. We have done nothing to deserve this. We are no better than the balance of mankind. And we find ourselves in this position only to display God's grace to all of creation, both in the heavens and upon the earth, and to serve as Christ's ambassadors in proclaiming the evangel that is intended for this era, and in doing so we are acting as Christ's complement in bringing about God becoming all in all.

HIS faith (3:13)

Christ Jesus, our Lord, in Whom we have boldness and access with confidence, through His faith.

Think back to 2:8. For in grace, through faith, are you saved, and this is not out of you; it is God's approach present, not of works, lest anyone should be boasting. For His achievements are we.

But if all humanity is given a chance to believe, and if some believe and others do not, could we not say that we DO have reason to boast? We were smart enough to believe, while others were not!

It is His faith, not our faith, that gives us our position. Our English words *faith* and *belief* both come from the same Greek word, "*pistis*." We may, at times, try to make a distinction, but there is no distinction in the Greek.

Every kindred (3:14)

On this behalf am I bowing my knees to the Father of our Lord Jesus Christ, after Whom every kindred in the heavens and on earth is being named ...

> Is it only the believer that finds blessing? Here Paul notes that every kindred in the heavens and on earth (i.e. all of creation) is being named after the Lord Jesus Christ.

> And once again Paul shows us the importance of prayer. Here he prays that his audience (the Body of Christ) should be strong to ...

Grasp Christ's love (3:18)

Grasp the love of Christ which transcends knowledge, that you may be completed for the entire complement of God.

> Clearly, then, those within the ecclesia had not previously grasped the magnitude of God's grace or the love of Christ, but with these revelations being shared by Paul perhaps it will now be possible to do so. But again, if we fail to rightly divide the Scriptures and understand that Paul is revealing new truth, and if we continue to go back to the law and steal truths intended only for Israel in eras past, we will not grasp the magnitude of what God is doing.

Now to Him Who is able to do *superexcessively* above all that we are requesting or apprehending ...

> What an expression of the magnitude of what Paul is now sharing with us!

For the eon of the eons (3:21)

To Him be glory in the ecclesia and in Christ Jesus for all the generations *of the eon of the eons.*

"For the eon of the eons."

> Let us take a moment to consider this phrase. Eon (singular) and eons (plural) are often translated "endless" or "eternal." But if eon is intended to express endlessness, why is the plural form needed? And what would a phrase like eon of the eons mean? Clearly eon is a period of time that has

a beginning and an end, and since the plural is used we know there are multiple periods of time being referred to. In this present case reference is made to a single eon (the present eon in which we live) as compared with all of the eons.

When Bible translations fail to distinguish things like this, and when these distinct periods of time are simply mixed together into "eternity," how can we ever hope to fully understand all that God has revealed to us? We must go beyond the modern English versions and use study tools that are available to seek out truth. Young's Analytical Concordance, for example, will help us to search individual words as they appear in the Greek, not just as the words have been translated into English. The Concordant Literal New Testament with the Keyword Concordance will also let us go beyond the English translation and consider the precise distinctions made in the original Greek. If we are to understand truth and share the correct message with the world today as Christ's ambassadors, we cannot place our faith in Bible translators who clearly disagree with each other in many passages.

Endeavor to present yourself to God qualified, an unashamed worker, correctly cutting the word of truth (2 Timothy 2:15).

CHAPTER 4

Walk worthily (4:1)

I am entreating you; walk worthily of the calling with which you were called.

With chapter 4 we begin the second of two parts to this letter. Part one focused on doctrine. Now the focus changes to behavior; the practical application of doctrine. This is not a command or a legal requirement. As a response to God's grace that Paul has already proclaimed, he entreats the believers to walk worthily. This walk is described by Paul in specific ways ...

With patience, bearing with one another in love, endeavoring to keep the unity of the spirit with the tie of peace; one body and one spirit ... one Lord, one faith, one baptism.

The one baptism is clearly a spiritual baptism, not a water baptism that had been used in a previous era to model the forthcoming and superior spirit baptism.

Over all and through all and in all (4:6)

God is *over* all and *through* all and *in* all.

> There are no qualifications in this statement. God is over, through and in all, not just believers.

Grace in varying degrees (4:7)

Now to each one of us was given grace in accord with the measure of the gratuity of Christ.

Measures of grace.

> All have not been given, therefore, the same measure of grace. In terms of salvation, some have grace enough to believe in this present era, while others do not. Whatever grace we have to believe has been given to us by God as He chooses, toward the accomplishment of His purposes through us.

That He should be completing all (4:10)

He Who descends is the Same Who ascends also, up over all who are of the heavens, *that He should be completing [the] all.*

He is completing "the all."

> Christ descended to the earth, and he then ascended; something none other has ever done. And we see here the reason Christ ascended to the heavens first, as the firstfruit of what we will one day experience at the resurrection; that He should be completing all. We remember that Christ is the One completing the all in all (1:23); bringing all of creation into subjection to God the Father that He may become All in all (1 Corinthians 15:28).

Gifts are given in varying degrees (4:11)

And the same One gives these, indeed, as apostles, yet these are prophets, yet these as evangelists, yet these as pastors and teachers, toward the *adjusting* of the saints for the work of dispensing, for the upbuilding of the Body of Christ, unto the end that we should all attain to the unity of the faith and the realization of the son of God, to a mature man, to the measure of the stature of the complement of the Christ, that we may by no means still be minors, surging hither and thither and being carried about by every wind of teaching, by human caprice, by craftiness with a view to the systematizing of the deception.

> Not all parts of the Body of Christ are the same. There are different degrees of grace given, and different gifts; though all are given for the purpose of adjusting the saints for the work of dispensing (i.e. sharing the evangel in some way), and for upbuilding the body, for unity of the faith, for maturity and the realization of what it means to be a son of God.
>
> When Paul wrote to the Corinthians they were minors who were not ready for solid food (1 Corinthians 3:1-4). We could not therefore expect to see any deeper truths in that letter. But in Ephesians we do see deeper truths, for those who are mature within the Body of Christ.

The systematizing of the deception (4:14)

That we may by no means still be minors, surging hither and thither and being carried about by every wind of teaching, by human caprice, by craftiness with a view to *the systematizing of the deception.*

What is "the systematizing of the deception?"

> Paul refers here to those using human caprice and craftiness with the intent of deceiving in a systemic manner. What could this possibly refer to other than those within organized religion? Remember that by the end of Paul's lifetime he had been abandoned by nearly everyone (2 Timothy 1:15; 4:16; Acts 21:20). There were those who had been proclaiming a different evangel; a distortion of the evangel (Galatians 1:7). There were

those who followed Paul everywhere to distort his evangel of grace and freedom from the law, attempting to integrate the law into the evangel. The majority within "organized religion" were working against Paul, as they did not understand the evangel that God had revealed to him, which was different from the evangel that had been previously revealed and proclaimed by others.

Remember that Jesus, too, was opposed by "organized religion" during His earthly ministry. And the prophets of the Old Testament were often opposed by "organized religion" in their day.

We live in a day of apostasy, as both Peter and Paul warned of in their later letters; where the majority within "organized religion" do not understand that which God has revealed. They attempt to systematize (or "religion-ize") deception through organized structure and teachings. This is, in my opinion, the systematizing of the deception that Paul refers to in 4:14; and it is still alive today.

Making all grow into Him (4:15)

Now, being true, in love we should be making all grow into Him, Who is the Head – Christ – out of Whom the entire body, being articulated together and united through every assimilation of the supply, in accord with the operation in measure of each one's part, is making for the growth of the body, for the upbuilding of itself in love.

Here, then, is a part of our purpose as individual members of Christ's body; to cause all to grow into Him. Is this not our part in the process of serving as Christ's complement; He being the One completing the all in all? (1:23)

Each of us plays a part in accord with the measure of grace given us, and the goal is toward the upbuilding of the body; not the tearing down, condemning or criticizing of other members. Love is to be kept in mind (4:16). Love, after all, is the greatest thing (1 Corinthians 14).

Not continuing to walk as those of the nations (4:17)

By no means are you still to be walking according as those of the nations; in the vanity of their mind; their comprehension being darkened, being estranged from the life of God because of the ignorance that is in them, because of the callousness of their hearts, who, being past feeling, in greed give themselves up with wantonness to all uncleanness.

As Paul entreats the believer to walk worthily of the calling with which they were called (4:1) he reminds them not to continue walking as those of the nations (non-believers).

Instead, Paul calls on the believer to put off the old humanity which is corrupted, and instead put on the new humanity, rejuvenated in spirit (4:20-25). We are to speak the truth, and not falsehood, with our associates, because being a part of Christ's body we are members of one another (4:25).

Put off your former behavior [(4:20)]

By Christ you were taught to put off your former behavior, the old humanity which is corrupting in accord with its seductive desires, yet to be rejuvenated in the spirit of your mind, and to put on the new humanity. Put off the false, and speak the truth with your associate, for we are members of one another.

Don't be giving place to the Adversary. Those who steal must no longer steal; but rather be toiling; working with their hands; that they may have to share with one who has need. Instead of tainted words proceeding from your mouth, all should be toward edification; giving grace to those hearing.

Don't be causing sorrow to the holy spirit of God by which you are sealed for the day of deliverance. Let all bitterness and fury and anger and clamor and calumny be taken away from you. Become kind to one another, tenderly compassionate, dealing graciously among yourselves, according as God, in Christ, deals graciously with you.

This summarizes our goal as we live in response to God's grace. Our behavior is not commanded as a requirement for salvation or justification. It is, instead, encouraged as an appropriate response, because of the grace that has been shown to us by God when we did nothing to deserve it.

CHAPTER 5

Be imitators of God, walking in love [(5:1)]

Become, then, imitators of God; walking in love according as Christ also loves you and gives Himself up for us.

Again, this is not a command or requirement (as if we were under law) but is instead a call to respond to the grace given to us.

Once darkness; now light (5:3)

Let prostitution, uncleanness or greed not be named among you. Nor vileness, stupid speaking or insinuendo which are not proper; but rather thanksgiving. No paramour or unclean or greedy person, who is an idolater, has any enjoyment of the allotment in the kingdom of Christ and of God.

> Paul is not saying that salvation is dependent upon works, for he has countless times stressed that salvation and justification is by grace, not works. Remember that all mankind was destined to experience tribulation and judgment, in the day of God's indignation (Romans 1:18; 2:5). But the believer is conciliated to God and saved from indignation (Romans 5:9). What Paul is saying in 5:5 is a reminder that those of the nations who have not yet experienced God's grace in the form of salvation will not enjoy an allotment in the kingdom when it is established upon the earth. (Remember that the kingdom to come upon the earth, as proclaimed by Jesus in His earthly ministry, is extremely works-based.) So, since this behavior will keep those without salvation from having an allotment of the kingdom, Paul is entreating the believer to remember this, and to avoid such behavior. Again, Paul is not issuing a command upon which salvation is based. He continues to entreat the believer to live a life that is worthy of God's calling that they have experienced.

Let no one be seducing you with empty words, for because of these things the indignation of God is coming on the sons of stubbornness. Do not, then, become joint partakers with them, for you were once darkness, yet now you are light in the Lord.

Walk as children of light (5:9)

As children of light be walking (for the fruit of the light is in all goodness and righteousness and truth), testing what is well pleasing to the Lord. And be not joint participants in the unfruitful acts of darkness, yet rather be exposing them also, for it is a shame even to speak of the hidden things occurring, done by them.

> Again Paul encourages the children of light to be walking as such. Test what is pleasing to the Lord. Don't be joint participants in the unfruitful acts of darkness.

Be observing accurately, then, brethren, how you are walking, not as unwise, but as wise, reclaiming the era, for the days are wicked.

Therefore do not become imprudent, but understand what the will of the Lord is.

> Our walk must be a conscious walk, with an eye toward the will of the Lord.

Be not drunk with wine but filled with spirit; speaking to yourselves in psalms and hymns and spiritual songs, singing and playing music in your hearts to the Lord, giving thanks always for all things.

> It is not total abstinence from wine that is called for but avoiding an EXCESS of wine (i.e. drunkenness).

Be subject to one another (5:21)

Be subject to one another. Let wives be subject to their own husbands, as to the Lord, for the husband is head of the wife, even as Christ is Head of the ecclesia. As the ecclesia is subject to Christ, thus are the wives also to their husbands in everything.

> God has an established hierarchy. All things are to work together toward the purpose already stated; that all become subjected to God, and that He becomes all in all. Without order there is chaos.

> But beyond subjection, there is also to be love.

Husbands, be loving your wives according as Christ also loves the ecclesia. Christ gave Himself up for the sake of the ecclesia, to hallow it (i.e. set it apart from humanity at large) and to cleanse it, that it may be holy and flawless.

> Despite its imperfection, the ecclesia is deemed to be flawless because of Christ. This is stated as a FACT. And this is why Paul encourages the ecclesia to walk worthily. Parents will sometimes say to their children, "Act your age!" Paul says something similar to the ecclesia; "Act worthily!"

Thus husbands ought to love their wives as their own bodies, nurturing and cherishing them; just as Christ does so with the ecclesia; for we are members of His body. For this a man shall leave his father and mother and shall be joined to his wife, and the two shall be one flesh.

This secret is great: yet I am saying this as to Christ and as to the ecclesia.

> Is it not a great secret that Paul shares with us? Never before had this truth concerning the Body of Christ been revealed! Paul now proceeds to share other examples of subjection ...

CHAPTER 6

Children, obey your parents. Fathers, do not be vexing your children, but nurture them in the discipline and admonition of the Lord. Slaves, obey your masters according to the flesh, as slaves of Christ, doing the will of God from the soul, with good humor slaving as to the Lord and not to men. Be aware that whatever good each one should be doing, for this he will be requited [paid] by the Lord, whether slave or free.

And masters, be doing the same toward them [slaves], being lax in threatening, being aware that their Master as well as yours is in the heavens, and there is no partiality with Him.

> Here is the most important principle in the matter of subjection within the hierarchy God has established. Subjection is always within the broader context that we are all subjected to God. All must one day answer to the Lord Who is over all. All will one day be requited, or paid, for behavior, good or bad; the way, for example, that slaves serve their masters, and the manner in which masters treat their slaves; remembering that ALL are serving the Lord, whether slave or free.

> # God has established a hierarchy not to show preference to one versus another, but to create ORDER toward the end that all become subjected to Him!

> With the authority one may be granted over another (husbands over wives, masters over slaves) there is responsibility to love; and to serve the Lord.

Spiritual forces and spiritual armor (6:11)

Put on the panoply of God, to enable you to stand up to the stratagems of the Adversary, for it is not ours to wrestle with blood and flesh, but with the sovereignties, with the authorities, with the world-mights of this darkness, with the spiritual forces of wickedness among the celestials. Therefore take up the panoply of God that you may be enabled to withstand in the wicked day.

> # The struggles we face are not always driven by the visible. There is a spiritual realm at work, and spiritual armor is needed to equip us.

There is more to this universe than what is visible to our eyes of flesh. In the celestial realm there is a created order, and some of it is wicked. The struggles we face are not always driven by the obvious; the things that we can see. Therefore we must be on guard and equip ourselves with spiritual mechanisms that God has provided if we are to stand in the midst of these struggles. Paul goes on to describe some of what God provides for this purpose ...

Truth, righteousness, the evangel of peace, faith, salvation, and the declaration (or word) of God.

By way of example, when the wicked one attacks with his fiery arrows that challenge what we know to be truth as revealed by God, faith is our shield (6:16-17). If we allow our faith to go un-nurtured we will succumb to the challenges we are faced with (that are coming from spiritual forces). We will lose our faith and will be unable to stand and perform our role as Christ's complement. It is because of our role as Christ's complement that we receive challenges from the celestial realm; for the spiritual forces of wickedness among the celestials (6:12) are working against the plans of God. Since we play a part in those plans, we can expect challenges from the celestial realm that seek to prevent us from serving our role.

Prayer is needed [(6:18)]

During every prayer and petition be praying on every occasion (in spirit being vigilant also for it with all perseverance and petition concerning all the saints, and for me), that to me expression may be granted, in the opening of my mouth with boldness, to make known *the secret of the evangel,* for which I am conducting an embassy in a chain, that in it I should be speaking boldly, as I must speak.

The Adversary is opposing proclamation of THE SECRET OF THE EVANGEL!

Connected with the spiritual struggle Paul has just described, he calls for prayer on every occasion; with perseverance; for the secret of the evangel to be shared. Can we not see, then, that the forces which seek to prevent the secret of the evangel from being shared will seek to prevent the ecclesia from persevering in prayer? If we face struggles only with fleshly mechanisms (logic, philosophy, eloquence in public speaking, knowledge), how can we hope to succeed against the strategies of the Adversary?

Clearly from all of this we see that the Adversary seeks to prevent the secret of the evangel from being proclaimed. How can he accomplish this?

If God's Word is dumbed-down and inconsistently translated, thereby concealing and confusing truth that God has intended to reveal, is this not preventing the secret of the evangel that was revealed to Paul from being recognized? If the Deceiver can "systematize deception" (4:14) – deceiving in an organized fashion that appears to be legitimate and true – can he not prevent the secret of the evangel from being recognized? If the Deceiver can allow the evangel of grace to be distorted by adding elements of the law, even as was done among the Galatians in Paul's day, can he not hide the secret of the evangel that Paul is sharing in Ephesians? If the Deceiver can cause Peter's message to the Circumcision believers to be mixed with the different message that Paul proclaimed to the Body of Christ, can he not prevent the secret of the evangel from being proclaimed?

I personally believe that all of these things are accomplished by the Deceiver, in a systematized fashion, through the organized church today. Orthodox teachings that are passed from one generation to the next without challenge, contaminated Bible translations, churches, pastors, Bible teachers, mainstream Christian authors, seminaries and Bible colleges that simply pass "truth" along to every new generation of believers; all of these things have worked together to systematize deception; to prevent the Body of Christ from recognizing the secret of the evangel and from serving its role as the complement of Christ. I am convinced that to recognize the secret of the evangel and to fulfill our role as Christ's complement, we must escape the bonds of organized religion and its experts and authorities, turning to the Word of God in its purest form.

Have a pattern of sound words which you hear from me (2 Timothy 1:13).

Endeavor to present yourself to God qualified, an unashamed worker, correctly cutting the word of truth (2 Timothy 2:15).

If ever we also, or a messenger out of heaven, should be bringing an evangel to you beside that which we bring to you, let him be anathema! (Galatians 1:8)

Attain to the unity of the faith and of the realization of the son of God, to a mature man, to the measure of the stature of the complement of the Christ, that we may by no means still be minors, surging hither and thither and being carried about by every wind of teaching, by human caprice, by craftiness with a view to the systematizing of the deception (Ephesians 4:13-14).

> # Consider the difference between Paul's Ephesian ministry (as recorded in Acts) and his letter to the Ephesians which came much later!

In Paul's early ministry he describes his role as "competent dispensers of a new covenant" (2 Corinthians 3:6) and a "priest" (Romans 15:16), both related to Israel and not his later ministry to the Body of Christ. During this time Paul spoke to the sheep of Israel scattered among the nations, baptizing (Acts 19:5-6) and performing miracles (Acts 19:11). During this time he spoke only things that the prophets and Moses had previously shared (Acts 26:22).

But after the setting aside of Israel (Acts 28:28; Romans 11:25) and while imprisoned in Rome, Paul shared new truth that had been revealed to him by Christ Jesus; and we find this new truth in his letter to the Ephesians. In this letter he spoke of new things such as being blessed among the celestials (1:3; 1:20), secrets (1:9; 3:3; 3:4; 3:9), the Body (1:23; 2:16; 3:6), a new humanity (2:15), and no barrier between those of Israel and those of the nations (2:14).

With these stark contrasts we see the progressive revelation from God unfold. And we see the need to rightly divide the Word of God (2 Timothy 2:15) lest we attempt to apply truth from a previous era to a later era; thereby misunderstanding how God is working!

CLOSING THOUGHTS

Ephesians is the highest of revelations for the Body of Christ. It contains doctrine of a higher nature than has been seen in any previous letter. In Ephesians we hear details concerning a secret that had been concealed in the past and which is now being revealed. We would not expect, therefore, to read of things in Ephesians that have been introduced by others apart from Paul, or even that has been discussed by Paul in previous letters.

The letter is comprised of two primary parts:

✓ Part I: Doctrine (Chapters 1-3)
✓ Part II: Behavior (Chapters 4-6)

Let us consider the purpose of this letter, and the purpose of the Body of Christ, as has been presented by Paul.

Purpose of this letter

✓ To make known the secret of God's will; to have an administration of the complement of the eras, to head up all in the Christ – both that in the heavens and that on the earth (1:9-10).

✓ To enlighten believers as to their expectation, and to the transcendent greatness of God's power.

✓ To bring the evangel of the untraceable riches of Christ to the nations, and to enlighten all as to what is the administration of the secret, which has been concealed from the eons in God, Who creates all, that now may be made known to the sovereignties and the authorities among the celestials, through the ecclesia, the multifarious wisdom of God (3:8-11).

Purpose of the ecclesia (the Body of Christ)

✓ To make known the secret of His will; to head up all in the Christ (1:9-10).

✓ To serve as the complement of the One completing the all in all [Christ's complement] (1:23).

✓ To be Christ's ambassadors, as if God were entreating through us (2 Corinthians 5:18-21). To assist in bringing about God's becoming all in all, through the faithful proclamation of the evangel in the capacity of ambassadors.

- ✓ In the oncoming eons to be a display of the riches of God's grace and kindness (2:7).

- ✓ Created in Christ Jesus (as His body) for good works which God makes ready beforehand, that we should be walking in them (2:10).

- ✓ To make known to the sovereignties and the authorities among the celestials, the multifarious wisdom of God (3:8-11).

- ✓ To make all grow into Him, Who is the Head – Christ (4:15-16).

Philippians

An Overview of the Scriptures, by
BOB EVELY © *2018.*
An Independent Minister of Christ Jesus,
Of the church at Wilmore, Kentucky

To make known the secret of the evangel (6:20).

For our realm is inherent in the heavens, out of which we are awaiting a Saviour also, the Lord Jesus Christ, Who will transfigure the body of our humiliation, to conform it to the body of His glory, in accord with the operation which enables Him even to subject all to Himself (3:20-21).

1 Thessalonians	50-52 AD	During 2nd Journey
2 Thessalonians	52-53 AD	During 2nd Journey
Galatians (early theory)	54 AD	End of 2nd Journey
1 Corinthians	Spring 57 AD	During 3rd Journey
2 Corinthians	Fall 57 AD	During 3rd Journey
Galatians	Winter 57 AD	During 3rd Journey
Romans	Spring 58 AD	During 3rd Journey
Colossians	61-62 AD	During 1st Captivity
Ephesians	61-62 AD	During 1st Captivity
Philemon	62-63 AD	During 1st Captivity
Philippians	**63 AD**	**During 1st Captivity**
1 Timothy	67 AD	Between Captivities
Titus	67 AD	Between Captivities
2 Timothy	Spring 68 AD	During 2nd Captivity

CHAPTER 1

The address on the envelope (1:1)

Paul and Timothy, slaves of Christ Jesus,
To all the saints in Christ Jesus who are in Philippi,
Together with the supervisors and servants.

> The structure of the ecclesia (church) was much simpler in Paul's day, with very few titles and a rather informal structure; unlike what the man-made church has become in the present day. Here we see two titles used of those within the ecclesia; supervisors (from the Greek

"episkopos" and often translated bishop) and servants (often translated deacon).

Observe also that the letter is directed to all the saints in Philippi. Our traditional baggage may cause us to envision all these saints gathered together in one place where the bishop reads Paul's letter to them. But the saints in Philippi may not have gathered in one place at any time. The letter was simply addressed to them all; and probably circulated to them in their respective homes.

Paul's prayer (1:3)

I thank God for your contribution to the evangel. He Who undertakes a good work among you, will be performing it until the day of Jesus Christ. You all are joint participants with me of grace.

God is responsible for the good work being accomplished by the believers. It is not something the believers have simply elected to do on their own.

Love to superabound (1:9)

I pray that your love may be superabounding still more and more in realization and all sensibility.

While there may have been love among the believers, there is a need for it to grow and superabound.

Test the things of consequence (1:10)

Be testing what things are of consequence, that you may be sincere and no stumbling block.

This is as if to say, don't argue over lesser things, and in so doing become contentious and a stumbling block to those observing this behavior, but focus on the important things of consequence.

Be filled with the fruit of righteousness ... (1:11)

... for the glory and laud of God.

Paul's trials have advanced the evangel (1:12)

My affairs have rather come to be for the progress of the evangel, so that my bonds in Christ become apparent in the whole pretorium and to all the rest.

Never one to complain or to pray for escape from his frequent unpleasant situations, Paul instead rejoices that his bonds have resulted in the evangel being heard in the whole praetorium; where it would not have otherwise been heard. Additionally, because of Paul's situation other brethren are more exceedingly daring to speak the word of God fearlessly. What an attitude! Paul is so focused on that which will bring glory to God that he is unconcerned with his own trials and afflictions, and even sees benefit in going through those trials.

Some proclaim the evangel for lesser motives (1:18)

I am located for the defense of the evangel, yet those are announcing Christ out of faction, not purely, surmising to rouse affliction in my bonds.

Some who proclaim the evangel are seeking to cause Paul affliction in his bonds. They are perhaps finding fault with Paul and blaming his afflictions on his behavior or perhaps his teachings.

By every method, whether in pretense or in truth, Christ is being announced; I am rejoicing in this also.

Even though some proclaim for lesser motives, still Paul rejoices that the evangel is being proclaimed; by every method, whether in pretense or in truth.

Paul seeks every opportunity to proclaim the evangel (1:20)

With all boldness, as always, now also, Christ shall be magnified in my body, whether through life or through death. For to me to be living is Christ, and to be dying, gain. Now if it is to be living in flesh, this to me means fruit from work. Yet I have a yearning for *the solution* and to be together with Christ, for it, rather, is much better.

Paul's desire is that always Christ shall be magnified in his body.

The solution? Here Paul seems to be referring to the time when Christ will call believers heavenward to be with Him (1 Thessalonians 4:13). But despite this preference, Paul acknowledges that his time in the flesh is necessary for the benefit of the believers; for their progress and joy of faith (1:26).

Walk worthily; strive for unity (1:27)

Be citizens walking worthily of the evangel of Christ. Stand firm in one spirit, one soul, competing together in the faith of the evangel.

Paul does not threaten with punishment or issue a commandment to be observed. He instead *encourages* the believers to walk worthily. And he pleads for there to be unity among the believers; standing firm in one spirit, one soul.

Those opposing the evangel (1:28)

Don't be startled by those opposing in anything; which is a proof of their destruction and of your salvation. It is graciously granted, for Christ's sake, for you to be believing on Him; and suffering also.

The inference is that those who know and proclaim the evangel with Paul can do so because God has graciously *enabled* them; and those who oppose do not know the evangel because to them it has *not* been graciously granted. Had God not chosen some to understand and to proclaim the evangel, none would do so; for not one is seeking out God (Romans 3:11). So God's method, in the process of bringing all things into subjection to Himself, is to graciously grant SOME to understand and to proclaim the evangel; to be Christ's ambassadors. And therefore it should come as no surprise when others oppose the evangel.

CHAPTER 2

Some specifics in walking worthily (2:1)

Be mutually disposed (i.e. subjected) to one another.
Have mutual love.
Let there be no faction among you.
Have no vanity.
Deem others as being superior to one's self.

The example of Christ (2:5)

Follow the example of Christ, Who was in the form of God; but Who emptied Himself and took the form of a slave, and the likeness of humanity, and Who humbled Himself and was obedient even unto death. And as a result, God exalted Christ and gave Him a name above all names, that in the name of Jesus EVERY KNEE SHOULD BOW AND EVERY TONGUE ACCLAIM THAT HE IS LORD.

Carry your own salvation into effect (2:12)

With fear and trembling, be carrying your own salvation into effect, for it is God Who is operating in you to will as well as to work for the sake of his delight.

It is not that salvation is somehow earned by works. As a matter of fact it is made clear here that when one desires to work for God, it is because God is operating in that person; not because the person has decided independently to work for God. Salvation has been graciously given by God as a gift, lest any should boast. And as a result of that salvation, Paul now encourages the believer to manifest the effects of God's work, through works for the glorification of God instead of self.

If it is God working in me that causes me to desire good works, and if these works are not of me, why does Paul encourage good works at all? Is God not simply causing these desires and works that flow from me, without any personal desire or work on my part? Here is my understanding on this matter. Without God's work within the believer, none would desire God, or seek Him, or have any inclination toward working for Him. We would simply carry out our own selfish flesh-driven desires. God has graciously chosen to reveal the evangel to the believer, and He has graciously granted to us a desire for the things of God. But there is a tension within us as we live within these bodies of flesh. While God is working within us, we still have our fleshly will at work too. Paul is encouraging the believer to set aside our fleshly will, considering ourselves as figuratively dead (as Christ literally died) and now alive in Christ; concerned with the will and the work of God. This is Paul's encouragement to the believer; Set aside the desires of the flesh and focus on the desires of God as He enables you to do.

More specifics concerning walking worthily (2:14)

Don't murmur.
Become blameless.
Become children of God.
Be flawless in the midst of a crooked and perverse generation.
Be luminaries (lights) in the world.

Plans to come to Philippi (2:19)

I am expecting, in the Lord Jesus, to send Timothy to you quickly. I have no one equally sensitive who will be genuinely solicitous of your concerns; for all are seeking their own; not that which is Christ Jesus. He slaves with me for the evangel. And I have confidence in the Lord that I myself shall be coming to you quickly.

> Here we see a glimpse of the apostasy that had already taken root in the ecclesia. Only Timothy could be sent. All other are seeking their own; and not the Lord's.

For now I deem it necessary to send to you Epaphroditus, my brother and fellow worker and fellow soldier, yet your apostle and minister. He is infirm, and very near death, but God is merciful to him.

> Infirm and near death? Why not have faith and claim healing? What was true in that previous era, during Jesus' earthly ministry, is no longer the case. Now grace is sufficient.

CHAPTER 3

Rejoice, and beware of evil workers ^(3:1)

Rejoice in the Lord. Beware of evil workers and the *maimcision*.

> Here Paul interjects a play on words. There are those that are circumcised as to the flesh, but they are not the true Circumcision; and Paul refers to them as the *maimcision* instead of the circumcision.

We are the circumcision who are offering divine service in the spirit of God, and are glorying in Christ Jesus, and have no confidence in flesh.

> Here, then, is what the evil workers are guilty of, and what Paul is warning of; confidence in the flesh instead of confidence in God.

Confidence in the flesh? ^(3:4)

If any presume to have confidence in flesh, I rather. I was circumcised, an Israelite of the tribe of Benjamin, a Hebrew of Hebrews, a Pharisee, zealous, and a keeper of the law. But all of this I forfeit and consider refuse because of Christ. Not having my righteousness out of law; but that which is through the faith of Christ, the righteousness which is from God, FOR faith. Conforming to His death, if somehow I should be attaining to the resurrection that is out from among the dead. Not that I already obtained or am already perfected. Yet I am pursuing.

Forgetting those things which are behind, yet stretching out to those in front, toward the goal am I pursuing for the prize of God's calling above in Christ Jesus.

Whoever are mature may be disposed to this. And if in anything you are differently disposed, this also shall God reveal to you. And in what we outstrip others there is to be a mutual disposition to be observing the elements by the same rule.

- 202 -

And in what we outstrip others (i.e. we have an understanding that others do not yet have) there is to be a mutual disposition to be observing the elements by the same rule. That is to say, it is possible to live amongst those that lack a full understanding while agreeing on the "elements" or basics. We faithfully proclaim the evangel as we are called to do, without lauding it over those that do not yet understand.

Has the Body of Christ replaced Israel as the Circumcision?

If Paul is saying that those who are confident in their fleshly circumcision are really the maimcision, and we (Paul's audience in Philippi) are the true Circumcision, does this mean that everything promised to Israel in the past now belongs to the Body of Christ?

Callousness, in part, on Israel has come, until the complement of the nations may be entering. And thus all Israel shall be saved, according as it is written, Arriving out of Zion shall be the Rescuer. He will be turning away irreverence from Jacob. And this is My covenant with them whenever I should be eliminating their sins (Romans 11:25-27).

So Israel's turning away, or callousness, is only temporary. And while those of Israel that have confidence in their fleshly circumcision are deemed to be the maimcision, this is not a permanent condition. Ultimately Israel as a people will be restored as the prophets have said; they will not be rejected forever with another people-group taking their place.

In the Philippian context Paul is not saying that Israel (the Circumcision) has been replaced by the Uncircumcision. He is obviously speaking figuratively in terms of the Body of Christ being the Circumcision. If Paul was saying that the Circumcision was literally being replaced by the Body of Christ, this would be contrary to his statement in Romans 11, and it would be contrary to the words of the Prophets when they speak of Israel's restoration (not replacement).

Become imitators (3:17)

Become imitators together of me, and be noting those who are walking thus, according as you have us for a model.

> It is one thing to be told how we are to live, but much easier to grasp when we have a model; like Paul and others who serve as examples.

Enemies of the cross (3:18)

Many are walking as enemies of the cross, whose end is destruction, whose god is their bowels (or their self-absorbed will) and who are disposed to things terrestrial as opposed to things spiritual.

> *Destruction.* A study of the word *apolleia* in the Greek (destruction) reveals that the meaning is a loss of life, either in this age or in the age to come. Destruction is not a permanent condition; it is a "save-able" condition, as demonstrated in Luke 19:10 where we read that the Son of Mankind came to seek and to save the *lost* (same Greek as *destroyed*).
>
> *god.* Note the word god in this passage. God (theos in the Greek) means "subjector." God the Father is the ultimate Subjector, for one day all things will be brought into subjection to Him (2 Corinthians 15:28). In this present era, and in Paul's era, all things have not yet been brought into subjection to God the Father, and there are other gods operative that many are subjected to. Satan is described as the god of this eon (2 Corinthians 4:4). In this Philippians passage we see that some are subjected to their own flesh, which subjects them through the dominance of fleshly desire. There are many "subjectors" at work, but God calls for all to be subjected to Him. And through the work of Christ (the One completing the all in all – Ephesians 1:23 and 1 Corinthians 15:25-28), and through the faithful ambassadorship of the Body of Christ (the complement of the One completing the all in all – Ephesians 1:23), one day there will be but *one* Subjector operative; when all things are subjected to God the Father, that He becomes all in all (1 Corinthians 15:28).

Our realm is not terrestrial, but in the heavens (3:20)

Our realm is inherent in the heavens, out of which we are awaiting a Saviour also, the Lord, Jesus Christ, Who will transfigure the body of our humiliation to conform it to the body of His glory, in accord with the operation which enables Him to subject all to Himself.

We are reminded of Christ's "transfiguration" during His earthly ministry, which was a demonstration of His glorified condition that was to come. Likewise we, too, will one day be "transfigured" from these fleshly bodies of humiliation to a glorified body (1 Corinthians 15:42-55).

And in this passage we also see God's intent to bring all things into subjection to Himself. We see this being realized at the end of the eons (1 Corinthians 15:20-28).

CHAPTER 4

Being mutually disposed ^(4:1)

Stand firm in the Lord. I entreat Euodia and Syntyche to be mutually disposed in the Lord. I am asking you to be aiding them.

Mutually disposed in the Lord is to be mutually subjected and in unity. Always Paul calls for unity, and for believers to be subjected to God and to the things of God, and to be subjected to one another (see Ephesians 5:21-6:9 where Paul talks much of this mutual subjection and provides examples from various kinds of relationships).

Rejoice, pray, and give thanks always ^(4:4)

Be rejoicing in the Lord always! Let your lenience be known to all men. The Lord is near. Let nothing worry you, but in everything, by prayer and petition, with thanksgiving, let your requests be made known to God. And the peace of God, that is superior to every frame of mind, shall be garrisoning your hearts and your apprehensions in Christ Jesus.

The believer's focus ^(4:8)

Whatever is true, grave, just, pure, agreeable, renowned; if there is any virtue or applause be taking these into account. Put into practice that which you learned and accepted and have seen in me.

Contentment ^(4:10)

I learned to be content in that in which I am. I know what it is to be humbled and to be superabounding. In everything I am satisfied. For all am I strong in Him Who is invigorating me – Christ!.

Contributions ^(4:14)

You do ideally in your joint contribution in my affliction. When I came from Macedonia not one ecclesia participated with me in the matter of giving, except you only. In Thessalonica also you sent twice to my need. I have been filled full, receiving from Epaphroditus the things from you; a fragrant odor, and acceptable sacrifice, well pleasing to God.

Greetings (4:21)

Greet every saint in Christ Jesus. Greeting you are the brethren with me. Greeting you are all the saints, especially those of Caesar's house.

Caesar's house is where Paul is imprisoned.

CLOSING THOUGHTS

Philippians focuses primarily upon behavior within the Body of Christ. In light of opposition and affliction Paul encourages the believer to:

- ✓ Be walking worthily
- ✓ Have mutual love that superabounds
- ✓ Seek unity
- ✓ Seek for the advancement of the evangel
- ✓ Be luminaries in the world
- ✓ Be mutually disposed (subjected) to one another
- ✓ Give thanks and pray always, in all circumstances
- ✓ Focus on the things of God, and not the things of this world
- ✓ Be content

Colossians

An Overview of the Scriptures, by
BOB EVELY © 2018.
An Independent Minister of Christ Jesus,
Of the church at Wilmore, Kentucky

"... in accord with the administration of God, which is granted to me for you, to complete the word of God – the secret which has been concealed from the eons and from the generations, yet now was made manifest to His saints, to whom God wills to make known what are the glorious riches of this secret among the nations, which is: Christ among you, the expectation of glory ..." (1:25-27)

1 Thessalonians	50-52 AD	During 2nd Journey
2 Thessalonians	52-53 AD	During 2nd Journey
Galatians (early theory)	54 AD	End of 2nd Journey
1 Corinthians	Spring 57 AD	During 3rd Journey
2 Corinthians	Fall 57 AD	During 3rd Journey
Galatians	Winter 57 AD	During 3rd Journey
Romans	Spring 58 AD	During 3rd Journey
Colossians	61-62 AD	During 1st Captivity
Ephesians	61-62 AD	During 1st Captivity
Philemon	62-63 AD	During 1st Captivity
Philippians	63 AD	During 1st Captivity
1 Timothy	67 AD	Between Captivities
Titus	67 AD	Between Captivities
2 Timothy	Spring 68 AD	During 2nd Captivity

CHAPTER 1

The address on the envelope (1:1)

Paul, an apostle of Christ Jesus, and brother Timothy;
To the saints and believing brethren in Christ in Colossae.

> Saints (hagios in the Greek) means "holy ones;" literally "set-apart-ones."

Always praying (1:3)

We are thanking the God and Father of our Lord Jesus Christ, always praying concerning you; hearing of your faith in Christ Jesus, and the love you have for all the saints.

> Observe the nature of Paul's prayer; not self-centered but centered on Christ Jesus and love for others.

The expectation (1:5)

Because of the expectation reserved for you in the heavens, which you heard in the word of truth of the evangel. It is bearing fruit and growing, from the day you heard and realized God's grace as you learned it from Epaphras, a faithful dispenser of Christ.

Paul's desire; that the believers fully realize God's will (1:9)

... requesting that you may be filled full with the realization of His will, in all wisdom and spiritual understanding ...

And that this full realization would lead to ... (1:10)

... you to WALK WORTHILY of the Lord for all pleasing, bearing fruit in every good work, and growing in the realization of God; for all endurance and patience with joy. And give thanks to the Father.

> It is possible, then, to have a realization of God and His grace; but not a FULL realization. Paul's prayer is for the believers to grow into a FULL realization, and to walk worthily.

Consider what God has done; making you competent (1:12)

The Father makes you competent for a part of the allotment of the saints. He rescues you out of the jurisdiction of darkness. He transports us into the kingdom of His Son.

In the Son we have deliverance; the pardon of sins. The Son is the *image* of the invisible God. He is Firstborn of every creature.

> # The Son is the IMAGE of God.

> This passage does not say that Christ Jesus (the Son) is God; but that He is the Image of God. He is the Firstborn of every creature. Could it

be that the revered "Trinity" doctrine is incorrect? Could it be that Christ was the very first of God's creation, high above all else that was subsequently created, and even the agent of that subsequent creation?

But consider this. The Scriptures do not tell us to proclaim a correct doctrine as to the personhood of God the Father as compared with the personhood of Christ Jesus the Son. Certainly we are to seek an understanding of what the Scriptures reveal, and we are to praise and glorify God the Father and Christ Jesus the Son. But as to the message we are to convey as Christ's Ambassadors, and as the complement of Christ, we are instructed to proclaim the effects of what God the Father and Christ Jesus the Son have accomplished. Be conciliated to God! That is to be the focus of our proclamation. Yet much effort is expended, and much dissention is created, by arguments between those that have varying understandings of the personhood of God the Father and Christ Jesus the Son. Let us all seek a growing understanding of what the Scriptures convey, but let us show patience and tolerance toward those having a different understanding than our own relative to the personhood issue (i.e. Trinitarians, Unitarians, Modalists).

In Him is ALL created (1:16)

In Him is all created; that in the heavens and earth; visible and invisible; whether thrones, lordships, sovereignties or authorities. All is created through Him and for Him, and He is before all, and all has its cohesion in Him.

As it pertains to believers ... (1:18)

Christ is the Head of the body, the ecclesia. Sovereign, Firstborn from among the dead, that in all He may be becoming first. For in Him the entire complement delights to dwell.

Through Him ALL is reconciled (1:20)

Through Him to reconcile all to Him; whether those on the earth or those in the heavens; making peace through the blood of His cross.

> # In Him ALL is created.
> # Through Him ALL is reconciled!

Remember the ALL in this context, from 1:14, refers to all of creation. Believers (the Body, or ecclesia) are noted in a special way, but *all* refers to all of creation. The reconciliation in 1:20 is a parallel to the creation in 1:14. All are created; and through Christ all are to be reconciled. This is the CLIMAX of God's reconciliation with His entire creation!

Believers were once estranged (1:21)

And you, being once estranged and enemies in comprehension, by wicked acts, yet now He reconciles by His body of flesh.

Enemies in comprehension, as they had an incorrect understanding.

Yet now He reconciles, through His death, to present you holy and flawless and unimpeachable in His sight, since surely you are persisting in the faith, grounded and settled and are not being removed from the expectation of the evangel.

Not perfect; but flawless *in His sight.*

When we look at 1:20, we see that all creation will ultimately be reconciled. At present the ecclesia (Body of Christ) is reconciled. Remember the differentiation as seen in 2 Corinthians 5:18-21 between conciliation (one-sided) and reconciliation (two-sided). The 2 Corinthians passage tells us that in Christ, God was conciliating the world to Himself. But the world is not yet conciliated to God. The world is estranged from God. Our proclamation, as Christ's ambassadors, is: "Be conciliated to God!" Those heeding that call, and who become conciliated to God, would then be reconciled. And, as we see in Colossians 1:20, through Christ will ALL be reconciled.

His Body; the ecclesia (1:23)

The evangel is being heralded in the entire creation which is under heaven of which I, Paul, became the dispenser ... for His Body, which is the ecclesia of which I became a dispenser.

Paul became the dispenser of the evangel, through which the expectation is proclaimed. It is for His Body, the ecclesia, of which he became a dispenser.

The word "ecclesia" is translated "church" in most Bible versions (except in those cases where the notion of "church" does not fit), causing us to lose valuable insights provided by God. "Ecclesia" means called-out-ones;

those whom God has called out of the larger group of humanity for some specific purpose. But just as there are different presidential administrations enforcing different policies in our political realm, so also there are different administrations in God's workings in the world. Paul references here the specific administration of God that was granted to him, in which he proclaims that the Body of Christ is the specific ecclesia, or group of called-out-ones, for which he became a dispenser of good news.

The Body of Christ was not introduced by any other person in the Scriptures, either before or after Paul. It was Paul's specific commission. Peter and others within the Twelve addressed the believers among Israel; that was the called-out-group (ecclesia) they addressed. Paul had a different commission, in a different administration, and the Body of Christ was the called-out-group that he addressed.

TO COMPLETE THE WORD OF GOD (1:25)

I became a dispenser, in accord with the administration of God, which is granted to me for you, to *complete* the word of God; the *secret* which has been concealed from the eons and from the generations, yet now was made manifest to His saints, to whom God wills to make known that are the glorious riches of this secret among the nations ...

> # To COMPLETE the Word of God.
> # This is a major point, not
> # to be overlooked!

In the past God spoke through certain individuals he had chosen; Moses, Abraham, Isaac, Jacob. He spoke through the prophets of the Old Testament. He spoke most directly through His Son, Jesus Christ. And after the crucifixion and resurrection God spoke through prophets in the early ecclesia. Now comes Paul, who informs us that he has come to COMPLETE the word of God. After this point there would no longer be the need for prophecy or prophets, for the word of God would now be complete. The Scriptures preserved by the apostles (including Paul) say it all! There would be nothing to add to what had already been revealed. Did Paul not tell us that prophesies, at some point, would be discarded and languages (tongues) would cease? (1 Corinthians 13:8)

Note also that as Paul completes the word of God, he reveals a SECRET. This is proof that Paul's message was different, and not the same as that of the Twelve; else it would not be a secret that had been concealed in the past.

Paul's secret (1:27)

Christ among you, the expectation of glory, Whom we are announcing, admonishing every man and teaching every man in all wisdom that we should be presenting every man mature in Christ Jesus.

There are other mentions in Paul's writings of a secret, and to gain a complete understanding of the secret(s) revealed by Paul we should study all passages where this is noted. As for what we are told concerning the secret in this current passage ... There is a need for growth and maturity in the Body of Christ (unlike the immaturity and fleshliness that Paul confronted in 1 Corinthians).

Turning once again to 1 Corinthians 13:8, where Paul tells us of a time when prophecies will be discarded and languages will cease, we note that this would happen when maturity comes (1 Corinthians 13:10). And now in Colossians, as Paul announces his charge to complete the word of God, we see his additional charge to present every man mature in Christ Jesus. As maturity comes, and as the word of God is completed, there is no longer a need for the inferior devices (prophecy, languages) to guide believers.

CHAPTER 2

Paul wants the believers to FULLY understand the secret (2:1)

I want you to perceive what the struggle amounts to; to all the riches of the assurance of understanding, unto a realization of the secret of the God and Father, of Christ, in Whom all the treasures of wisdom and knowledge are concealed.

Be walking in Him (2:6)

As you accepted Christ Jesus, the Lord, be walking in Him, having been rooted and being built up in Him; being confirmed in the faith according as you were taught; superabounding in it with thanksgiving.

Beware of philosophy and human tradition [(2:8)]

Beware that no one shall be despoiling you through philosophy and empty seduction, in accord with human tradition, in accord with the elements of the world, and not in accord with Christ. And you are *complete* in Him.

Beware of philosophy and human tradition.

Believers are complete in Christ. Nothing is to be added to God's grace. No law, rules or regulations are needed. Paul introduces maturity and completion; the believer is complete in Christ.

"Religion" in all ages has incorporated much philosophy and human tradition. Beware of religion. Cling simply to the truth as revealed by God in His completed Word.

You were circumcised; baptized [(2:11)]

In Him you were circumcised with a circumcision not made by hands, in the stripping off of the body of flesh in the circumcision of Christ. Being entombed together with Him in baptism; roused together with Him also through faith in the operation of God, Who rouses Him from among the dead. You also being dead to offenses. He vivifies us together with Him, dealing graciously with all our offenses.

Paul speaks of circumcision and baptism in a figurative way in this passage. Just as the law was a requirement that served as a shadow of what was to come, so also the physical acts of circumcision and baptism had served the same purpose; and here we see that the believer is circumcised, entombed, baptized, and roused in a figurative sense.

Food, drink, festivals, sabbaths [(2:16)]

Let no one, then, be judging you in food or in drink or in the particulars of a festival, or of a new moon, or of sabbaths, which are a shadow of those things which are impending – yet the body is the Christ's.

In short; all of these outward and visible "do's and don'ts" served their purpose but are not to be enforced upon the Body of Christ.

If, then, you died together with Christ from the elements of the world, why, as living in the world, are you subject to decrees: "You should not be touching, nor yet tasting, nor yet coming into contact," ... in accord with the directions and teachings of men?

> Religious circles today are filled with requirements and rituals. Churchgoers are convinced that they must celebrate "the sabbath" by attending worship services, abstaining from work, etc. Many are convinced they must be water baptized. Is it not clear from what Paul is saying here that these things do not matter? Christ has surpassed these things, yet religious leaders continue to impose elements of the law upon believers. Observe once again verse 8; BEWARE of human tradition!

CHAPTER 3

Seek that which is above (3:1)

If, then, you were roused together with Christ, be seeking that which is above, where Christ is, sitting at the right hand of God. Be disposed to that which is above, not to that on the earth, for you died.

> Since we figuratively died with Christ and were roused with Him, there is no longer a need or requirement for us to be disposed to earthly things; like the law, feasts and festivals, sabbaths, dietary restrictions. And we are also to set aside other earth-bound characteristics:

Deaden, then, your members that are on the earth: prostitution, uncleanness, passion, evil desire and greed, which is idolatry, because of which the indignation of God is coming on the sons of stubbornness – among whom you also once walked when you lived in these things.

> Those within the world will one day face the indignation of God (Romans 2:9) on the day of indignation (Romans 2:5) because of these behaviors. Paul is not saying that believers will also face God's indignation if they persist in these behaviors. Salvation is not based upon works, but God's grace. God has called the Body of Christ for special work that will ultimately contribute toward reconciling the entire world to God; and we are spared from this coming indignation (Romans 5:9). What Paul is saying in this passage is: "Since these behaviors will result in God's indignation upon those of the world, and since we have been spared from the day of indignation by God's grace, let us not walk in these same behaviors."

Specific behaviors to "put away" and to "put on" (3:8)

Be putting away anger, fury, malice, calumny, obscenity, and lying.

> Why is this important if we have been saved by grace, and not works? ...

To accord with the Image of the One Who creates it, wherein there is no Greek and Jew, Circumcision and Uncircumcision, barbarian, Scythian, slave, freeman, but all and in all is Christ.

Alternatively, put on, then, as God's chosen ones; pitiful compassions, kindness, humility, meekness, and patience (bearing with one another and dealing graciously among yourselves as the Lord deals graciously with you).

And above all these put on love, which is the tie of maturity. Let the peace of Christ be arbitrating in your hearts. Become thankful. Let the word of Christ be making its home in you richly, in all wisdom, teaching and admonishing yourselves. Everything you do, in word or act, do all in the name of the Lord Jesus Christ, giving thanks to God.

> Observe that it is the word of Christ that teaches and admonishes us, not a priest, pastor or minister. In times past, before maturity, these fleshly designates were needed to teach and admonish. But Paul's words in Colossians are of a higher nature, and it is the word of Christ that now teaches and admonishes without the need for a mediator.

> # Observe a key difference in Paul's writings.

There is no Greek and Jew, Circumcision and Uncircumcision, barbarian, Scythian, slave, freeman, but all and in all is Christ (3:11).

> ALWAYS before this time Israel had been primary. The Gentile could only be blessed through Israel. During Jesus' earthly ministry He came only to the sheep of Israel. Even in Paul's early ministry he would go first to the synagogues, and only to the Gentile when Israel rejected his message.

But now, clearly, there is a difference. Paul, and only Paul, revealed the Body of Christ; God's chosen ones (3:12) within which there is no longer a superiority granted to Israel. This is clearly different from the teachings of the entire Old Testament, the four Gospel accounts, and the ministry and epistles of the Twelve. Paul is the apostle to the Gentiles, and his message is clearly different from all that preceded him.

Subjection and love (3:18)

Wives, be subject to your husbands. Husbands, love your own wives. Children, obey your parents. Fathers, do not vex your children. Slaves, obey in all things your masters according to the flesh. All, whatever you do, work from the soul, as to the Lord and not to men.

Ultimately all will be subjected to God. In this temporal world in which we live, God has designed an organized system of subjection in order that His purposes can be accomplished. But wherever there is subjection, there is also love and compassion. And while, as to the flesh, there is a system of subjection; all (subjectors and subjectees alike) serve a single master; the Lord. Subjectors in this world must keep in mind: He who is injuring shall be requited for that which he injures, and there is no partiality (v 25).

The bottom line ...

CHAPTER 4

Masters, tender that which is just and equitable to your slaves, being aware that you also have a Master in the heavens.

Regardless of our station in this world, we are all servants of the Master!

Persevere in prayer (4:2)

Persevere in prayer, with thanksgiving, that God should be opening for us a door of the word, to speak the secret of Christ.

It is always interesting to examine the subject matter of Paul's prayers. Here is a most unselfish prayer; centered solely on the glorification of God.

Walk in wisdom toward those outside (4:5)

Walk in wisdom toward those outside, reclaiming the era, your word being always with grace; perceiving how you must answer each one.

The Body of Christ was chosen to proclaim the message of reconciliation to the world. How we live before the world is important if we are to be effective ambassadors. And as we share the evangel (good news) it is not just WHAT we say but HOW we say it; our words "being always with grace."

Paul's fellow servants [(4:7)]

Tychicus and Onesimus shall make known to you all things here. Aristarchus (my fellow captive), Mark (cousin of Barnabas), and Jesus (termed Justice); who are of the Circumcision.

Paul mentions a number of his fellow servants, some of whom are acting as his messengers as he is imprisoned.

That you may stand mature [(4:12)]

Epaphras is always struggling for you in prayers, that you may stand mature and fully assured in all the will of God.

Again we see the desire of God that those within the Body of Christ grow in maturity and completeness in an understanding of God's will.

Greetings [(4:14)]

Greeting you is Luke and Demas. Greet the brethren in Laodicea, and Nympha, and *the ecclesia at her house*. Cause that the epistle should also be read in the Laodicean ecclesia, and that you also may be reading that [epistle] out of Laodicea.

It is always interesting to note church organization as it is described in Paul's writings. Far from the denominational and even independent church structures we see today, is the simplicity and informal nature of *the church at her house.* Mention is also made of the Laodicean ecclesia; simply the believers the reside collectively in Laodicea; not some formal group that meets together every Sunday in a structure that is owned by the church organization. Food for thought!

CLOSING THOUGHTS

Colossians stresses maturity and completion. Following are some key points made by Paul in this letter.

- ✓ Paul prays that the believers come to fully realize God's will (1:9)
- ✓ Walk worthily (1:10)
- ✓ Continued growth in the realization of God (1:10)
- ✓ Paul granted the administration to *complete* the word of God (1:25)
- ✓ Paul tasked with presenting every man mature in Christ Jesus (1:28)
- ✓ That the believers fully realize and understand the secret (2:1-2)
- ✓ Beware of philosophy and human tradition (2:8)
- ✓ Seek that which is above; set aside undesirable earthly behaviors (3:1)
- ✓ That you may stand mature (4:12)

1 Thessalonians

An Overview of the Scriptures, by
BOB EVELY © 2018.
An Independent Minister of Christ Jesus,
Of the church at Wilmore, Kentucky

"... for the Lord Himself will be descending from heaven with a shout of command, with the voice of the Chief Messenger, and with the trumpet of God, and the dead in Christ shall be rising first. Thereupon we, the living who are surviving, shall at the same time be snatched away together with them in clouds, to meet the Lord in the air ..." (4:13-18)

1 Thessalonians	50-52 AD	During 2nd Journey
2 Thessalonians	52-53 AD	During 2nd Journey
Galatians (early theory)	54 AD	End of 2nd Journey
1 Corinthians	Spring 57 AD	During 3rd Journey
2 Corinthians	Fall 57 AD	During 3rd Journey
Galatians	Winter 57 AD	During 3rd Journey
Romans	Spring 58 AD	During 3rd Journey
Colossians	61-62 AD	During 1st Captivity
Ephesians	61-62 AD	During 1st Captivity
Philemon	62-63 AD	During 1st Captivity
Philippians	63 AD	During 1st Captivity
1 Timothy	67 AD	Between Captivities
Titus	67 AD	Between Captivities
2 Timothy	Spring 68 AD	During 2nd Captivity

CHAPTER 1

The address on the envelope (1:1)

From Paul and Silvanus and Timothy,
To the ecclesia of the Thessalonians.

Paul's unintermittent prayers (1:2)

We are thanking God always concerning you all, making mention of you in our prayers, unintermittingly remembering your work of faith and toil of love and endurance of expectation of our Lord Jesus Christ.

> This is not a selfish petition, but strictly God-centered.

The evangel (1:5)

The evangel of our God did not come to you in word only, but in power, and in holy spirit, and much assurance. And you became imitators of us and of the Lord, *receiving* the word in much affliction with joy; and you became *models* to all the believers in Macedonia and Achaia. It is reported how you turn back from idols, slaving for the living and true God, waiting for His Son out of the heavens; our Rescuer out of the coming indignation.

> Observe the context for all of this. The Thessalonians were in the midst of affliction. And what were they expecting? They were waiting for the Son out of the heavens; their Rescuer out of the coming indignation.

Rescued out of the coming indignation!

> So there is a coming indignation, but the ecclesia is saved from indignation. Remember that indignation was coming upon the world (Romans 2:9) on the day of indignation that is set by God (Romans 2:5). But the believer is saved from this coming indignation (Romans 5:9) by our Rescuer out of the coming indignation (1 Thessalonians 1:10). We within the Body of Christ are saved from the coming indignation not because we are better than others of humanity; but because God has elected to choose a subset of humanity; giving them the ability to believe and perceive that which He has revealed; and enabling them to serve as a complement of Christ in this age and in the ages to come; toward the end that God's will for mankind be accomplished; that all mankind be saved and come to a realization of the truth (1 Timothy 2:4).

CHAPTER 2

Entrusted to share the evangel faithfully (2:1)

We are bold in our God to speak the evangel of God to you with a vast struggle. Our entreaty is not out of deception, or uncleanness, or with guile. We have been tested by God to be *entrusted* with the evangel. We speak not to please men, but God. We do not flatter in expression, or with a pretense for greed. We do not seek glory from men. We became gentle in your midst; delighting to share with you the evangel of God, and our souls also.

Working so as not to be a burden (2:9)
Remember our toil and labor. Working night and day so as not to be burdensome to any of you we herald to you the evangel of God. You are witnesses how benignly and justly and blamelessly we became to you who are believing. We were as a father to you, consoling and comforting you.

> In other words, Paul worked to support himself, and did not derive his income from preaching the evangel; thereby allowing complete freedom to proclaim the evangel with pure motive, seeking only to please God.

Walk worthily (2:12)
Be walking worthily of God, Who calls you into His own kingdom and glory.

> Far from threatening the believers if they failed to have faith, Paul simply *encourages* them to be walking worthily of God.

Paul's word is the word of God (2:13)
In accepting the word heard from us, from God you receive not the word of men but the word of God, as it truly is; *operating* in you who are believing.

> We note here a distinction between the believer and unbeliever. While the word of God may be *heard* by those who are not believing, it is *operating* in the believer. This must be so, in order to equip the believer for the task to which he is called by God.

Suffering among the believers (2:14)
You suffered by your own fellow-tribesmen, according as they also by the Jews; forbidding us to speak to the nations that they may be saved.

> The Thessalonian believers were not, then, persecuted by unbelieving Jews; but by believers who were forbidding them to speak to the nations.

Paul's desire to come (2:17)
We yearn to see your face, but Satan hinders us.

CHAPTER 3

Remaining alone in Athens we send Timothy, our brother and God's servant in the evangel of Christ, to establish and to console you for the sake of your faith. I send to know of your faith, lest the trier tries you and our toil may be coming to be for naught.

> Paul tried more than once to come to the Thessalonians, but Satan hindered him. The Deceiver plays a part in events that take place upon the earth, but never to the extent that God's plans are thwarted.

But Timothy returns to us, bringing the evangel of your faith and your love, so we are consoled. We beseech God to see your face, and to adjust the deficiencies of your faith.

> *Evangel,* often translated "gospel;" means *good news.* Here the good news is simply a message received by Paul concerning the faith of the believers in Thessalonica. Each time we encounter the word *evangel* we must ask; what is the good news in this context?

> While Paul was encouraged by the steadfastness of their faith, there were still deficiencies that needed to be corrected and strengthened. At least one of the deficiencies is referred to …

May our Lord cause you to increase and superabound in love for one another and for all; to establish your hearts unblamable in holiness in front of our God and Father.

> It is not just for fellow believers that love should superabound, but for all. And it is this superabounding love that will cause the believers' hearts to be unblamable in holiness (set-apart-ness) before God.

CHAPTER 4

Behavior within the ecclesia (4:1)

As you accepted from us how to be walking and pleasing God, be superabounding yet more. For this is the will of God; your holiness.

> Some of the specific behaviors Paul considers …

Be abstaining from all prostitution. Be aware of your own vessel; acquiring it in holiness and honor, NOT LUSTFUL PASSION as the nations who are not acquainted with God. God call us for HOLINESS; not uncleanness. Whoever repudiates this is not repudiating man, but God; who is giving His holy spirit to you.

LOVE one another. You are already doing this, but we entreat you to be superabounding yet more.

Be ambitious to be QUIET; be engaged in your own affairs. BE WORKING with your own hands, that you may be walking respectably toward those outside and that you may have need of nothing.

The expectation of the ecclesia (4:13)

We do not want you to be ignorant, brethren, concerning those who are reposing, lest you may sorrow according as the rest, also, who have no expectation.

> It is not that the believer does not sorrow. He sorrows in a different way than those outside the ecclesia because he possesses an expectation that those outside do not recognize. The believer knows with *certainty* what will take place in the ages to come. This, then, is one of the distinctives in believing.

For, if we are believing that Jesus died and rose, thus also, those who are put to repose, will God, through Jesus, lead forth together with Him. For this we are saying to you by the word of the Lord, that we, the living, who are surviving to the presence of the Lord, should by no means outstrip those who are put to repose, for the Lord Himself will be descending from heaven with a shout of command, with the voice of the Chief Messenger, and with the trumpet of God, and the dead in Christ shall be rising first.

The expectation of the Body of Christ is the "snatching away" to meet the Lord in the air.

> There will come a day when the trumpet sounds and the believers who had previously died will be resurrected.

Thereupon we, the living who are surviving, shall at the same time be SNATCHED AWAY together with them in clouds, to meet the Lord in the air. And thus shall we always be together with the Lord.

> Commonly known as "the rapture," here is the moment when Christ calls the Body of Christ to be with Him. Those still living at this time do not

> die but are snatched away into the clouds to be with the Lord; reunited with those who had previously died who are resurrected and also snatched away.

So that, console one another with these words.

> Knowing this day is coming is our expectation and it enables us to mourn our losses differently than those outside the ecclesia that do not share this expectation. This is not to say that those outside the ecclesia will not also be resurrected. This will occur at a subsequent time. But because the Body of Christ has been called, in part, to serve God's purposes in the heavenly realm in the ages to come, we are called first on this day described to the Thessalonians.

CHAPTER 5

The Day of the Lord [(5:1)]

The Day of the Lord is as a thief in the night. They may say that all is peaceful and secure, yet extermination will come. But you are not in darkness about these events so as to be overtaken as a thief. Consequently; be watching and sober; and not drowsing.

> So while others may be ignorant about what will take place when the Day of the Lord comes, the believer is not.

We, being of the day, may be sober, putting on the cuirass of faith and love, and the helmet, the expectation of salvation, for God did not appoint us to indignation but to the procuring of salvation through our Lord Jesus Christ, Who died for our sakes, that, whether we may be watching or drowsing, we should be living at the same time together with Him.

The Day of the Lord is different from the day of "the snatching away."

> From this description we see that the Day of the Lord is not the same event as the Snatching Away (or Rapture). It is a time when there will be

> extermination (death) and indignation. But the believer can have faith and love because God did not appoint us to indignation. First will come the snatching away of the ecclesia, whereupon we will be with the Lord; and then will come the Day of The Lord upon the earth.

And with this knowledge; this expectation of what lies ahead; whether we may be watching or drowsing, we should be living at the same time together with Him.

> Our salvation and rescue from indignation is not dependent on our being watchful. We are called to be watchful and sober (not drowsing and drunk), but even if we fail to be watchful we are living with Him; both figuratively in the present age, and literally once we are snatched away to be with Him.

Church organization (5:12)

Now we are asking you, brethren, to perceive those who are toiling among you and presiding over you in the Lord and admonishing you, and to deem them exceedingly distinguished in love, because of their work.

> Here is a glimpse at the structure within the ecclesia in Paul's day. There were those presiding over others, whose task included admonishing the believers as appropriate. But while we see glimpses like this of "church organization," it is far from what the modern-day church has become with its bureaucratic structure and the power vested in its leaders. The ecclesia of Paul's day was very informal and loosely structured.

Behavior within the ecclesia (5:13)

✓ Be at peace among yourselves.
✓ Admonish the disorderly.
✓ Comfort the faint-hearted.
✓ Uphold the infirm.
✓ Be patient toward all.
✓ See that no one may be rendering evil for evil.
✓ Always pursue that which is good for one another as well as for all.
✓ Be rejoicing always.
✓ Be praying unintermittingly.
✓ In everything be giving thanks.
✓ Quench not the spirit.
✓ Scorn not prophecies.
✓ Be testing all, retaining the ideal.

✓ Abstain from everything wicked to the perception.

> Relative to Paul's statement concerning prophecies, this is an indication that the letter to the Thessalonians was an earlier letter than Colossians, where Paul indicates that he was charged with completing the word of God. Once Paul completed that commission, could it be that prophecy was no longer required, since the word from God had been completed?

Closing (5:23)

Now may the God of peace Himself be hallowing you wholly; and may your unimpaired spirit and soul and body be kept blameless in the presence of our Lord Jesus Christ! Faithful is He Who is calling you, Who will be doing it also.

> It is not by human effort that the believer lives a holy life. It is God Who will be doing it. Remember, *holy* simply means set-apart, distinct or different. But it is God that deems something or someone set-apart. He has deemed the Body of Christ set-apart, and those within the body remain set-apart regardless of their behavior. It is God that has declared certain things or certain ones to be set-apart, and He will be wholly setting us apart through His works, not our own. Among Paul's other closing remarks ...

Pray concerning us. Read this epistle to all the holy brethren.

CLOSING THOUGHTS

This letter is primarily concerned with doctrine and instruction, centered in large part on the Lord's coming. Paul had "planted" the ecclesia at Thessalonica (Acts 17:1-9) and it was comprised primarily of Gentiles, though there were also some Jews that believed.

The letter finds the ecclesia in the midst of affliction. Paul writes to encourage them to stand firm in the faith. He reminds them of their expectation (or "hope"). And he encourages proper behavior among the ecclesia.

But why has God chosen a certain, select group from mankind (the Body of Christ in this present age)? What makes this group different from the rest of mankind?

✓ All mankind may hear the word of God, but the word of God is *operating* in the believer. (2:13)

✓ The believer has *expectation*; a knowledge with certainty as to what will occur in the ages to come; the resurrection. (4:13)

2 Thessalonians

An Overview of the Scriptures, by
BOB EVELY © 2018.
An Independent Minister of Christ Jesus,
Of the church at Wilmore, Kentucky

"Yet faithful is the Lord, Who will be establishing you and guarding you from the wicked one." (3:3)

1 Thessalonians	50-52 AD	During 2nd Journey
2 Thessalonians	**52-53 AD**	**During 2nd Journey**
Galatians (early theory)	54 AD	End of 2nd Journey
1 Corinthians	Spring 57 AD	During 3rd Journey
2 Corinthians	Fall 57 AD	During 3rd Journey
Galatians	Winter 57 AD	During 3rd Journey
Romans	Spring 58 AD	During 3rd Journey
Colossians	61-62 AD	During 1st Captivity
Ephesians	61-62 AD	During 1st Captivity
Philemon	62-63 AD	During 1st Captivity
Philippians	63 AD	During 1st Captivity
1 Timothy	67 AD	Between Captivities
Titus	67 AD	Between Captivities
2 Timothy	Spring 68 AD	During 2nd Captivity

CHAPTER 1

The address on the envelope (1:1)

From Paul, Silvanus, and Timothy,
To the ecclesia of the Thessalonians.

Endurance and faith in affliction (1:3)

Your faith is flourishing and your love for one another is increasing. We glory in your endurance and faith in all your persecutions and afflictions, a display of the just judging of God to deem you worthy of the kingdom of God for which you are suffering.

It is just of God to repay affliction to those afflicting you; and ease for us at *the unveiling* of the Lord Jesus from heaven; dealing our vengeance to those not acquainted with God and those not obeying the evangel of our Lord Jesus Christ – who shall incur the justice of eonian extermination from the face of God when He comes to be glorified in His saints.

> The unveiling: Consider the opening words of the last book in the Bible, commonly called Revelation: *The unveiling of Jesus Christ.* The words are similar, as Paul here references the same event.
>
> Eonian extermination means death for an eon or eons to come. It is eonian (for an eon, or multiple eons) extermination (death); not everlasting destruction as some translations erroneously report. It is not a final condition, but a step in the process of God's dealings with mankind.

We pray that our God should be counting you worthy of the calling and should be fulfilling every delight of goodness and work of faith in power, SO THAT the name of our Lord Jesus may be glorified in you, and you in Him.

> Always Paul's desire is that the Lord is glorified. Should this not be the goal of every believer?

CHAPTER 2

The Day of the Lord is not yet here [(2:1)]

Don't be shaken in your mind or alarmed through spirit or word or an epistle; that the Day of the Lord is present. No one should be deluding you.

> # The Day of the Lord is not yet here.

> Some in their midst were declaring that the Day of the Lord was already present, but Paul warns them not to be deluded. The Day of the Lord is that time, following the removal of the Body of Christ unto the heavens (1 Thessalonians 4:13ff), when the events immediately preceding and culminating with the return of Christ to the earth will take place.
>
> Could this same warning be valid today? Some today are claiming that the Day of the Lord has already come, just as some were saying in Paul's day.

> Did the Day of the Lord commence since the time of Paul's writing to the Thessalonians? I think not, based on what Paul says next …

The apostasy will come first, and the man of lawlessness will be revealed; the son of destruction who is opposing and lifting himself up over everyone called a god, so that he is seated in the temple of God demonstrating that he is God.

> Certain things must occur prior to the Day of the Lord. The apostasy must come first, and the man of lawlessness must be unveiled; seated in the temple of God, demonstrating that he is God.

He will be unveiled in his own era. The secret of lawlessness is already operating, but only when the present *detainer* may be coming out of the midst, then the lawless one will be unveiled – the one whom the Lord Jesus will discard by the advent of His presence.

The lawless one's presence is in accord with the operation of Satan, with all power and signs and false miracles, and with every seduction of injustice among those who are perishing, because they do not receive the love of the truth for their salvation. So God will send them a deception, for them to believe the falsehood, that all may be judged who do not believe the truth but delight in injustice.

Something is detaining the man of lawlessness.

> While the secret of lawlessness is already operating, THE MAN OF LAWLESSNESS HAS NOT YET BEEN UNVEILED. He will be unveiled in his own era, but only when the present detainer may be coming to be out of the midst. And then the man of lawlessness will be unveiled and will exhibit power and signs and false miracles. We read of this all taking place in the book of Revelation, when the Day of the Lord comes.

> From this description and coupled with Paul's mention of the Body of Christ's removal from the earth in 1 Thessalonians 4:13ff, it seems that the detainer that Paul mentions here is the Body of Christ, or more probably the holy spirit that is operating within the Body of Christ. Once

this is removed from the earth, the man of lawlessness will be unveiled, and the Day of the Lord will commence.

Preferred from the beginning (2:13)

God prefers you from the beginning for salvation, in holiness of the spirit and faith in the truth, into which He calls us through the evangel for the procuring of the glory of our Lord Jesus Christ.

> Since none are righteous or even seeking God, why would God prefer and select SOME; in this case those within the Body of Christ? Note the purpose; to procure the glory of our Lord Jesus Christ. We demonstrate to the world Christ's glory!
>
> So while the Day of the Lord will one day come upon the earth, God has called a subset of humanity (the Body of Christ) to be set apart (i.e. holy; differentiated). God's method of calling these set-apart-ones is through Paul's evangel.

Stand firm (2:15)

Consequently; stand firm and hold to the traditions you were taught by us. May our Lord Jesus Christ, and God our Father, Who loves us and gives us an eonian consolation and a good expectation in grace, be consoling your hearts and establish you in every good work and word.

> Paul is encouraging those who are facing affliction and persecution to stand firm in their faith, strengthened and consoled by the expectation that is theirs.

CHAPTER 3

Pray for us (3:1)

Pray concerning us that the word of the Lord may race and be glorified, as it is with you, and that we should be rescued from abnormal and wicked men.

> Paul's frequent use of prayer displays its importance, and the nature of Paul's prayers is always enlightening. Far from self-centered, Paul's concern is always with the glory of God and the success of the evangel.

The Lord will establish you (3:3)

The Lord will establish you and guard you from the wicked one. We have confidence in you in the Lord that what we are charging, you are doing also and will be doing. Now may the Lord be directing your hearts into the love of God and into the endurance of Christ.

> Paul's confidence is not in the Thessalonians; but in the Lord. And Paul does not direct the believers to *strive* toward love and endurance in their own strength; he asks the Lord to direct their hearts toward those ends.

Admonish the disorderly (3:6)

Avoid those walking disorderly, and not in accord with the tradition which they accepted from us. Imitate us; for we are not disorderly among you.

Work (3:8)

We did not eat bread gratuitously from anyone, but with toil and labor, we are working night and day, so as not to be burdensome to any of you. Not that we have not the right, but that we might be giving you ourselves as a model to be imitating. Even when we were with you we charged: *IF ANYONE IS NOT WILLING TO WORK, NEITHER LET HIM EAT.*

> Paul had the right to ask for their support, but he voluntarily forfeited that right and instead became a model to be imitated.

We are hearing that some among you are walking disorderly, working at nothing, but meddling. We are charging and entreating you to work with quietness, eating your own bread.

Don't commingle with the disorderly (3:13)

Don't be despondent in ideal doing. If anyone is not obeying our word through this epistle, don't commingle with him. Don't deem him as an enemy but admonish him as a brother.

> While the disorderly are to be admonished, they are to be admonished as a brother; not deemed as an enemy. The one who is not heeding Paul's words has not lost his salvation and is not excommunicated as a "member of the church;" but he is to be cast out of fellowship of the brethren.

CLOSING THOUGHTS

This letter is a sequel to Paul's first letter to the Thessalonians. The continual persecution and trial had led the believers to think that God was against them, and that the day of indignation and judgment had begun. Paul assures them that while lawlessness had taken root, its fullness would not come until the Body of Christ had been removed; for the Body was God's means to keep things in check until the appointed time.

We see that false teachers were influencing the ecclesia, leading to this belief that the Day of the Lord had already begun. This led to Paul's focus on things to come, and he includes details on the Lord's coming. But first must come the falling away; not the conversion of the world as some believe must first take place.

1 Timothy

An Overview of the Scriptures, by
BOB EVELY © 2018.
An Independent Minister of Christ Jesus,
Of the church at Wilmore, Kentucky

"God, Who is the Saviour of all mankind, especially of believers." (4:10)

1 Thessalonians	50-52 AD	During 2nd Journey
2 Thessalonians	52-53 AD	During 2nd Journey
Galatians (early theory)	54 AD	End of 2nd Journey
1 Corinthians	Spring 57 AD	During 3rd Journey
2 Corinthians	Fall 57 AD	During 3rd Journey
Galatians	Winter 57 AD	During 3rd Journey
Romans	Spring 58 AD	During 3rd Journey
Colossians	61-62 AD	During 1st Captivity
Ephesians	61-62 AD	During 1st Captivity
Philemon	62-63 AD	During 1st Captivity
Philippians	63 AD	During 1st Captivity
1 Timothy	**67 AD**	**Between Captivities**
Titus	67 AD	Between Captivities
2 Timothy	Spring 68 AD	During 2nd Captivity

CHAPTER 1

The address on the envelope (1:1)

From Paul
To Timothy.

> This is a personal letter to one man, Timothy. Thus it differs from Paul's letters to this point that were directed to the ecclesia in various places. We must take care to distinguish between general truths for the ecclesia, and those things intended for one man (Timothy) in his unique position.

False teachings (1:3)

Charge some not to be teaching differently, nor to heed myths and endless genealogies, which are affording exactions rather than God's administration which is in faith.

Some were teaching differently (from Paul's evangel). Some were heeding myths. Some were heeding endless genealogies (which seems to imply an emphasis on the flesh).

Some want to teach the law (1:5)

The consummation of our charge is love out of a clean heart, a good conscience, and unfeigned faith, from which some are swerving and exhibit vain prating, wanting to be teachers of the law. The law is ideal if it is used lawfully. The law is not laid down for the just, but for the lawless, the insubordinate, the irreverent, sinners, the malign and profane, thrashers of mothers and fathers, homicides, paramours, sodomites, kidnapers, liars, perjurers, and all others that oppose sound teaching in accord with the evangel of the glory of the happy God, with which I am entrusted.

The law is not laid down for the just. We recall that the believer is justified (Romans 3:28, Romans 5:1, Galatians 2:16, Galatians 3:23-25), and is dead to the law and to sin (Romans 7:1-6, Galatians 2:19), so the use of the law among believers is not proper.

While some of the behaviors noted by Paul unfortunately exist among believers, his point is that the purpose of the law was to address these issues among the unrighteous. Later came the implementation of God's grace in a more powerful way; justifying the believer, freeing him from the law, and reckoning him as dead to sin and alive in Christ.

In short, there is no place for the law in the midst of this grace. Paul fought the commingling of law and grace in Galatians, and he continues to fight it here.

Paul's case is a "pattern" (1:12)

I am grateful to Christ Jesus our Lord who invigorates me and deems me faithful, assigning me a service. I was formerly a calumniator, a persecutor, and an outrager. But I was shown mercy, seeing that I do it in ignorance and unbelief. But the Lord's grace *overwhelms* with faith and love.

Christ Jesus came into the world to save sinners, foremost of whom am I. But therefore I was shown mercy, that in me, the foremost, Jesus Christ should be displaying all His patience, for a *pattern* of those who are about to be believing on Him for life eonian.

Paul is a "pattern."

Did you catch this? Under the "old rules" Paul's opposition and persecution of Christ would have warranted rejection and wrath. This is often preached today; rejection and wrath upon those that fail to believe. Yet Paul who deserved rejection and wrath was instead shown mercy, and his case became a PATTERN for others who would be led to believe. Will any escape this mercy? Remember Paul's words; the grace of our Lord *overwhelms*.

The King of the eons (1:17)

Not to the King of the eons, the incorruptible, invisible, only, and wise God, be honor and glory for the eons of the eons!

In verses 16-17 the Greek AION is used in a variety of interesting forms. Those believing will find life eonian. To translate this eternal life would be an incorrect manipulation of the Greek. The point here is that believers will experience life in the eons to come. This does not mean that life will cease once the eons have concluded. The believer will put on immortality (1 Corinthians 15:54) and will therefore continue to live at the conclusion of the eons. But the point of this present passage is that the believer will have life in the eons to come. Let us not alter the Greek by injecting our theological understandings. Let us instead seek to render the Greek accurately, lest we fail to correctly handle the Scriptures and hinder our ability to understand God's revelation to us.

In verse 17 Paul uses the phrase *King of the eons*. Some say this proves that eons (plural) must mean forever, since Christ is immortal. Again; let us not inject our theological understandings into the translation effort. I have five children; Cris, Dusty, Chad, Kari and Scott. When I find myself among Chad's friends I may say, "I am the father of Chad." Does this mean I am not also the father of my other four children? No; it is simply that in that context of Chad's friends I seek to identify myself as his father. So also in the context of the eons; these finite periods of time in which man's history is recorded in the Scriptures; Christ is the King of the eons.

Lastly, in verse 17 we see the phrase *for the eons of the eons.* If eon (singular) or eons (plural) means eternity, then what purpose would there be in saying eons of the eons? If we fail to notice the distinctions in the various forms of aion as used in the Greek, and if we simply inject our theological understandings regardless of the form; saying eternal when that seems to fit and age when eternal clearly does not fit the context; then we will fail to grasp the rich meaning of God's revelation to us.

A close study of the Scriptures seems to tell us of five distinct eons or ages in the history of mankind. Eon (singular) is speaking of one of these periods of time. Eons (plural) speaks of more than one of these periods of time. Eons of the eons is like saying "two or more ages in particular, in the context of all five ages" (if five is the correct number; that is simply my observation). The last two eons are those following the return of Christ to the earth. Paul is emphasizing these two glorious eons in his benediction; Now to the King of the eons, the incorruptible, invisible, only, and wise God, be honor and glory for the eons of the eons! Amen!

Timothy's charge – the "ideal warfare" (1:18)

Be warring the ideal warfare, having faith and a good conscience. Some, thrusting it away, have made shipwreck as to the faith; of whom are Hymeneus and Alexander, whom I give up to Satan, that they may be trained not to calumniate.

Paul gives up Hymeneus and Alexander to Satan that they may be *trained* not to calumniate. Those who believe and who reject the faith are not, then, lost forever. Paul gives them up to Satan (the Deceiver) for constructive purposes; so they are trained not to calumniate, or speak evil of the truth.

CHAPTER 2

To live a quiet life (2:1)

I entreat that petitions, prayers, pleadings, thanksgiving be made for all mankind, for kings and all those being in a superior station, that we may be leading a mild and quiet life in all devoutness and gravity, for this is ideal and welcome in the sight of our Saviour.

Observe the behaviors that are ideal and welcome in the sight of our Saviour; a mild and quiet life, and devoutness. Remember that the government in Paul's day did not adhere to Christian principles, and it probably condoned many behaviors and lifestyles that were unacceptable to Christians. Yet Paul did not advocate reform, criticism or overthrow of that government. Instead he recognized that despite its flaws it served a purpose; to maintain peaceful conditions so that believers could live a quiet life.

God's will; the salvation of all mankind (2:4)

God, *Who wills that all mankind be saved and come into a realization of the truth.* For there is one God, and one Mediator of God and mankind, a Man, Christ Jesus, Who is giving Himself *a correspondent Ransom* for all *(the testimony in its own eras)*, for which I was appointed a herald and an apostle; a teacher of the nations.

> # God's will is that ALL mankind are saved.

Consider closely these words, for they are clearly contrary to the common orthodox belief in eternal torment.

It is God's will that ALL MANKIND be saved. Remember also that God is operating all things in accord with His will (Ephesians 1:11). That being the case, what can prevent the salvation of all from happening? Some say it is man's stubborn, free will that stands in the way; but are we saying that the Creator is unable to lead every last one of mankind into a realization of the truth, if that is His will? Remember that Paul refers to the Lord's grace as overwhelming, and Paul himself was most certainly led in a very overwhelming way to the truth on the road to Damascus.

> # Christ is a "correspondent ransom."

Some say that if all are saved then Christ's death upon the Cross becomes unnecessary. Far from that! It is not only necessary, but far more effectual than orthodoxy would claim. For Christ gave Himself as a correspondent Ransom for all (not just for some). Just as death came to all mankind through Adam, so life comes to all mankind through Christ, the correspondent, one-for-one Ransom for all. Correspondent ransom differs from the simple notion of ransom. The thought expressed in the Greek is the idea of equivalence. It is a one-for-one (i.e. "correspondent") ransom of all mankind.

Testimony in its own eras!

What is meant by the testimony in its own eras? (1:6) I believe this means that the *realization* of the truth by all mankind is a progressive thing. Some of us have been gifted with faith in this present age, but others do not yet see. But they will see in a future era. As Christ's Ambassadors we are to proclaim the correct evangel; pleading with mankind to be reconciled to God (2 Corinthians 5:18-21). But many within Christianity today spend all of their time preaching Old Testament wrath, warnings of eternal torment, observance of the law, and multitudes of teachings that are not intended for this present era. We mix the law and grace and distort the truth. Thousands of different churches teach thousands of different and contrary things, breeding confusion.

Satan, the Deceiver, has done a good job of hiding the truth that is so clear in the Scriptures. Orthodoxy is often his instrument for hiding the truth and breeding confusion. But rejoice; for IT IS GOD'S WILL THAT ALL MANKIND BE SAVED AND COME TO A REALIZATION OF THE TRUTH, AND NOTHING CAN PREVENT THAT FROM HAPPENING.

Men to pray; women in subjection (2:8)

I am intending that men pray in every place. Women are to adorn themselves in modesty and sanity; that which is becoming to a woman professing a reverence for God; with good works. Let a woman be learning in quietness, with all subjection. I am not permitting a woman to be teaching, nor to be domineering over a man, but to be in quietness. For Adam was first molded, thereafter Eve. And Adam was not seduced, but the woman was deluded and came to be in the transgression. But she shall be saved through *the child bearing*, if ever they should be remaining in faith and love and holiness with sanity.

> Is all of this a rule to be observed in all eras and in all situations, or is it pertinent to the specific situation Paul was then dealing with in the ecclesia? Before we quickly cast this off as "situational" let us not simply do so out of convenience so we can feel good about condoning women teachers and preachers in our current day. If we are quick to do so, we can simply cast off any Scriptures we do not like as situational.
>
> One thing that seems to imply these passages are situational is the fact that there were woman teachers within the ecclesia that were condoned by Paul. Priscilla (wife of Aquilla) is an example.
>
> Remember this is a personal letter to one man; Timothy. Could it be that women in this specific ecclesia had gotten out of hand, and were creating discord and falsehoods that needed to be addressed? I think this was the case, but there is also a hierarchy designated by God that must be considered; for the sake of peace and unity within the ecclesia. Note Paul's reasoning which goes beyond the current situation he faced. For Adam was first molded, thereafter Eve, and Adam was not seduced, yet the woman, being deluded, has come to be in the transgression.
>
> One last point in this section before we move on. What is meant by the words, *Yet she [woman] shall be saved through the child bearing?* Despite the fact that the woman was deceived and introduced the transgression upon mankind, woman will also give birth to the Man who will bring salvation from sin. The definite article "the" that precedes "child bearing" seems to be speaking of a single, specific child bearing; not child bearing in general.

CHAPTER 3

Qualifications for supervisors (3:1)

The supervisor must be:
- ✓ Irreprehensible
- ✓ The husband of one wife
- ✓ Sober
- ✓ Sane
- ✓ Decorous (of good behavior)
- ✓ Hospitable
- ✓ Apt to teach

✓ No toper (given to wine)
✓ Not quarrelsome, but lenient
✓ Pacific
✓ Not fond of money
✓ Controlling his own household ideally
✓ Having his children in subjection with all gravity
✓ No novice (which would make the person more prone to conceit)
✓ Having an ideal testimony

Servants are to be:
✓ Grave
✓ Not double-tongued
✓ Not addicted to much wine
✓ Not avaricious (greedy)
✓ Having faith with a clear conscience
✓ Tested
✓ Their wives also to be grave, not adversaries, sober, faithful
✓ Husbands of one wife
✓ Controlling children and their own households ideally

> The organized church in our present day has built an intricate system of bureaucracy which seems quite different from the ecclesia's simplicity as found in the Scriptures. While there is certainly some structure to the ecclesia, leadership seems to be far less formal than the present-day world of bishops, archbishops and popes. And even within most Protestant denominations or independent churches, great power is often vested in the clergy. But in Paul's day we see a loosely bound ecclesia that simply recognized elders (those more mature in the faith), supervisors (from the Greek episkopos, and often translated bishop in English translations today), and servants (from the Greek diakonos, and often translated deacon). Those in Paul's day that did assume a leadership role had certain qualifications.

Behavior in the ecclesia [3:14]

These things I write to you that you may perceive how one must behave in God's house, which is the ecclesia of the living God. Great is the secret of devoutness, which was manifested in flesh, justified in spirit, seen by messengers, heralded among the nations, believed in the world, taken up in glory.

After outlining these qualifications for those supervising and serving within the ecclesia, Paul speaks to how one must behave in God's house, which is the ecclesia of the living God, the pillar and base of the truth. So while the qualifications were stated for supervisors and servants, they are also an expression of proper behavior for all within the ecclesia.

Observe the basis for this behavior. The secret of devoutness, which was manifested in flesh is Christ! Let Him be our example.

Note that "God's house" is not a building as some understand it to be. God's house is the ecclesia; the people comprising the Body of Christ.

CHAPTER 4

In future eras some will fall away (4:1)

In subsequent eras some will be withdrawing from the faith, giving heed to deceiving spirits and the teachings of demons, in the hypocrisy of false expressions, ...

Paul warns of a future day when there would be a falling away from the faith; a deception that grows to the point where there are false expressions (incorrect understandings) and legal requirements added to faith (forbidding marriage, rejection of certain foods).

... their own conscience having been cauterized; forbidding to marry, abstaining from foods, which God creates to be partaken of with thanksgiving by those who believe and realize the truth, seeing that every creature of God is ideal and nothing is to be cast away, being taken with thanksgiving, for it is hallowed through the word of God and pleading.

Their conscience having been cauterized. Here we are reminded that the conscience is given to man as a means for knowing good versus evil; truth versus falsehood. But it is possible for one's conscience to be cauterized, where is can no longer see distinctions between good and evil, truth and falsehood.

Responding to the falling away (4:6)

By suggesting these things to the brethren, you should be an ideal servant of Christ Jesus, fostering with the words of faith and of the ideal teaching which you have fully followed. Profane and old womanish myths refuse.

In short, Timothy is to speak of the true faith, with true teachings, in the midst of this falling away. No promise is made for success in reversing the apostasy, but in suggesting these things to the brethren Timothy will be acting as an ideal servant of Christ Jesus.

Think about this for a moment. We tend to think that Paul planted churches and they grew in number through the years to become the churches of today. But here Paul talks of a setback; a falling away among believers. We do not hear of this apostasy being reversed in Paul's day, so when exactly do we think this happened in the history of the church? When, following the death of the apostles, did believers finally make doctrinal correction?

I would suggest that the majority of the church is still in apostasy today, having set aside Paul's teachings while continuing to add law to grace, just as in Paul's day. The truth was never found in the majority; not in the days of the prophets, in Jesus' day, in the days of the apostles, or even today. Seek truth from the Scriptures, not in the church fathers, the creeds, orthodoxy, or the organized churches of today; all of which are steeped in the traditions of men.

Note that there are profane and old womanish myths in the midst of the ecclesia; perhaps one of the reasons Paul forbid women to speak or lead in that context.

Exercise in devoutness (4:8)

Exercise yourself in devoutness. Bodily exercise is beneficial for a few things, yet devoutness is beneficial for all; having promise for the life which is now, and that which is impending.

Again we see Paul stressing the need for devoutness; and devoutness requires exercise, just as we might exercise the body.

The Saviour of all mankind (4:10)

God, Who is the Saviour of all mankind, especially of believers.

> # The Saviour of ALL mankind!

Many Bible teachers claim that God is the Saviour of all mankind, but this is only effectual for those who believe in this lifetime. But the word here is ESPECIALLY, not exclusively. God is the Saviour of all mankind, and in a SPECIAL way this affects believers. We who believe can realize and enjoy the expectation we have for things to come once this life has ended, while those who do not believe do not enjoy that assurance. We who believe know that we will live in the eons to come, after the resurrection and snatching away of believers into heaven as promised in 1 Thessalonians 4:13 and following. Some will not experience life in the eons to come. But nothing will prevent God from ultimately becoming the Saviour of all mankind at the end of the eons, as expressed in 1 Corinthians 15:20-28. Remember, it is God's will that ALL mankind be saved and come to a realization of the truth (2:4). Nothing can prevent that from happening.

While the Saviour of all mankind is truth, Paul was experiencing reproach for speaking the truth (4:9). Remember that many among Israel objected to Paul taking his evangel to the Gentiles, and to proclaim that God is the Saviour of all mankind would have been extremely objectionable to the believers among Israel in his day.

But this truth is also objectionable to many Christians in our present day.

These things be charging and teaching.

But if Timothy were alive today, and if he were to teach these things in most traditional churches, he would be reproached as Paul was. There is among believers today very limited reception of the truth that God is the Saviour of all mankind; where most prefer the distorted message of eternal torment which is in actuality an affront to and a blasphemy of God.

Timothy is to be an example (4:12)

Become a model for the believers, in word, in behavior, in love, in faith, in purity. Give heed to reading, to entreaty, and to teaching. Let your progress be apparent to all.

Attend to yourself and to the teaching. Be persisting in them, for in doing this you will save yourself as well as those hearing you.

This seems odd. Can one save himself? We have a tendency from our church upbringing to think that *saved* always means the same thing. But the meaning of saved can vary from one instance to the next, depending on the context. In some Old Testament examples, saved might simply mean saved from being killed by enemy soldiers. In this present context Timothy would be saving himself, as well as those hearing him, from withdrawing from the faith; since that is the context of Paul's letter.

But while an individual might waver in his faith, the faith of Christ does not waver, and a believer chosen by God is a believer still, despite the wavering.

CHAPTER 5

Treat those in the ecclesia as family (5:1)

Do not upbraid an elderly man but entreat him as a father. Treat the younger men as brethren, the elder women as mothers, the younger as sisters.

Widows (5:3)

Honor widows who are really widows. If a widow has children or descendants, let them learn to be devoted to their own household first. One who is really a widow, and alone, relies on God. But she who is a prodigal, though living, is dead. If anyone is not providing for his own, and especially his family, he has disowned the faith and is worse than an unbeliever.

Let no widow be listed of less than 60 years, having been the wife of one man, attested by ideal acts; hospitable, nourishing children, washing the feet of the saints, relieving the afflicted. But refuse the younger widow; for they are wanting to marry and will become idle, gossips, and meddlers. Younger widows are to marry, bear children, manage the household; giving an opposer nothing to revile. Let not the ecclesia be burdened, that it should be relieving those who are really widows.

Pauls' extensive comments demonstrate that the care of widows was a problem in the ecclesia of his day. Widows were to be honored; those who are really widows.

"Listing" seems to imply a formal system to determine which were truly widows and deserving of support from the ecclesia. And if supported by the ecclesia they were to serve; nourishing children, being hospitable, washing feet and relieving the afflicted.

Respect for elders ^(5:17)

Let elders who have presided ideally be counted worthy of double honor, especially those who are toiling in word and teaching. Worthy is the worker of his wages.

Do not assent to an accusation against an elder except before two or three witnesses. But those who are sinning are to be exposed in the sight of all, that the rest may have fear.

Instructions to Timothy ^(5:21)

Do nothing from bias. On no one place hands too quickly.

> In other words, don't be hasty in recognizing leaders within the ecclesia.

Keep yourself pure. Don't drink only water but use a sip of wine for your stomach and your frequent infirmities.

> What happened to prayers for healing? It seems that God's administration has changed, and grace is now sufficient.

CHAPTER 6

Slaves ^(6:1)

Slaves; deem your owners worthy of all honor, lest the name of God and the teaching may be blasphemed. Don't despise believing owners, seeing they are brethren. Slave for them, as they are believing and beloved.

> Observe the reason; lest the name of God and the teaching may be blasphemed. Far from an individual's rights; all is done toward the glorifying of God. That is the motive.

False teaching ^(6:3)

If anyone is teaching differently and is not approaching with sound words, <u>even those of our Lord Jesus Christ</u>, and the teaching in accord with devoutness, he is conceited, versed in nothing, but morbid about questionings and controversies, out of which is coming envy, strife, calumnies, wicked suspicions, altercations of men of a decadent mind and deprived of the truth

> Here is a caution for those who are teaching. Are we seeing controversies? Envy? Strife? Let us check ourselves to be sure our teachings are correct.

And note that it is possible to use even the words of our Lord incorrectly. This would seem to imply that the words of Jesus from His earthly ministry may not always apply in all situations in all eras. I believe this is what is meant by correctly cut or rightly divide the Word of God (2 Timothy 2:15). Always consider the context and what group of people are being addressed by the words of Scripture. We cannot assume, for example, that which was spoken to Israel in a particular era applies to believers in our present era.

Devoutness and contentment [(6:6)]

Devoutness with contentment is great capital; for nothing do we carry into the world, and it is evident that neither can we carry anything out. Having sustenance and shelter, with these we shall be sufficed. Those intending to be rich are falling into a trial and a trap and the many foolish and harmful desires which are swamping men in extermination and destruction. For the root of all evils is the fondness for money, which some, craving, were led astray from the faith and try themselves on all sides with much pain.

Contentment!

How much more we crave beyond sustenance and shelter. But the goal Paul sets here is CONTENTMENT. And the danger of having a fondness for money is that it can lead us away from the faith.

Devoutness!

Observe how often Paul uses the word devoutness in this epistle. Devoutness seems to carry the meaning "well-reverence," or the revering of right things. In Paul's context the word seems to denote the revering of God and the things of God, as contrasted with the revering of worldly pursuits such as money.

Correct behavior for believers ^(6:11)

Pursue righteousness, devoutness, faith, and love ... with endurance, suffering and meekness. Contend the ideal contest of the faith; avow the ideal avowal in the sight of many witnesses.

> In the subsequent verse we see our example; Jesus Christ as He testified the ideal avowal before Pontius Pilate.

God is vivifying all ^(6:13)

God, *Who is vivifying all ...*

> To vivify is to make alive.

Keep this precept unspotted, irreprehensible, unto the advent of our Lord, Christ Jesus, which, *to its own eras,* the happy and only Potentate *will be showing.*

> God is vivifying all. He will be showing this plan to each "in its own era."

> All are not vivified at the same time, nor is the knowledge of this precept (vivification of all) made known to all at the same time; but in its own eras.

He alone has immortality ^(6:16)

He is King of kings and Lord of lords, Who alone has immortality.

> He alone has immortality!

> The common belief that the human soul is immortal comes from Greek philosophy. Here we see the Scriptures clearly teaching that only Christ has immortality. It will only be at the resurrection that we put on immortality (1 Corinthians 15:54). When we die we will cease to have any

form of life and will lie in the grave totally dependent upon God to resurrect us, as Christ Himself laid in the grave totally dependent upon God to do so. Yet we die with the assurance that God promises to do just that; to resurrect us at some future point when we will put on immortality, thereby rid of the enemy (death) forever.

Do not rely upon riches; be rich in ideal acts (6:17)

Charge those who are rich in the current eon not to be haughty, nor to rely on the dubiousness of riches; but on God. Be rich in ideal acts; liberal contributors, treasuring up an ideal foundation for that which is impending that you may get hold of life really.

The focus for the believer should not be in the present eon, but in that which is impending. That is where the real life exists.

Guard the truth (6:20)

Timothy, guard that which is committed to you, turning aside from the profane prattling and antipathies of falsely named knowledge, which some are professing. As to the faith, they swerve.

Clearly some professed to teach knowledge, when really it was profane (unimportant or useless) prattling. Timothy's charge was to guard truth against such things.

CLOSING THOUGHTS

1 Timothy is primarily concerned with conduct. It sets forth rules for organized assemblies, and for the selection of elders (to act as supervisors) and servants. There is to be an orderly arrangement in the ecclesia; but not to the extent of becoming hierarchical. There is no warrant given for the widespread bureaucratic organization we see in the church today.

There are increasing heresies. Some had swerved and even turned away from the truth. Some denied truth and were turning others away from the faith.

Proper behavior within the ecclesia is outlined by Paul, *For this is ideal and welcome in the sight of our Saviour* (2:3). What are some behaviors we find noted in 1 Timothy that are ideal and welcome in our Lord's sight?

- ✓ Love, from a clean heart, a good conscience and unfeigned faith (1:5, 6:11)
- ✓ Faith and a good conscience (1:18-19, 6:11)
- ✓ To lead a quiet life (2:2)
- ✓ Devoutness (2:2, 3:16, 4:8, 6:5-6, 6:11)
- ✓ Gravity (2:2)
- ✓ Irreprehensible (3:2)
- ✓ Husband of one wife (3:2)
- ✓ Sober (3:3)
- ✓ Sane (3:3)
- ✓ Decorous (3:3)
- ✓ Hospitable (3:3)
- ✓ No toper (3:3)
- ✓ Not quarrelsome (3:3)
- ✓ Pacific (3:3)
- ✓ Not fond of money (3:3)
- ✓ Controlling one's own household ideally (3:4)
- ✓ Having an ideal testimony (3:7)
- ✓ Grave (3:8)
- ✓ Not double-tongued (3:8)
- ✓ Not addicted to much wine (3:9)
- ✓ Not avaricious (3:9)
- ✓ Contentment (6:6)
- ✓ Pursue righteousness (6:11)
- ✓ Meekness (6:11)
- ✓ Be rich in ideal acts (6:18)
- ✓ Be liberal contributors/givers (6:18)

2 Timothy

An Overview of the Scriptures, by
BOB EVELY © 2018.
An Independent Minister of Christ Jesus,
Of the church at Wilmore, Kentucky

"Endeavor to present yourself to God qualified, an unashamed worker, correctly cutting the word of truth." (2:15)

1 Thessalonians	50-52 AD	During 2nd Journey
2 Thessalonians	52-53 AD	During 2nd Journey
Galatians (early theory)	54 AD	End of 2nd Journey
1 Corinthians	Spring 57 AD	During 3rd Journey
2 Corinthians	Fall 57 AD	During 3rd Journey
Galatians	Winter 57 AD	During 3rd Journey
Romans	Spring 58 AD	During 3rd Journey
Colossians	61-62 AD	During 1st Captivity
Ephesians	61-62 AD	During 1st Captivity
Philemon	62-63 AD	During 1st Captivity
Philippians	63 AD	During 1st Captivity
1 Timothy	67 AD	Between Captivities
Titus	67 AD	Between Captivities
2 Timothy	Spring 68 AD	During 2nd Captivity

CHAPTER 1

The address on the envelope (1:1)

From Paul, an apostle of Christ Jesus, through the will of God;
To Timothy, a child beloved.

> This is a personal letter to one man (Timothy). Thus it differs from Paul's letters that were directed to the ecclesia in various places. We must take care to distinguish between general truths for the ecclesia, and those things intended specifically for Timothy in his unique position.

Introductory remarks to Timothy (1:3)

Be rekindling the gracious gift of God which is in you. God gives us not a spirit of timidity, but of power and of love and of sanity. You may not be ashamed, then, of the testimony of our Lord.

God gave the gift. It is Timothy's responsibility to keep it kindled.

Called in accord with God's purpose before times eonian (1:9)

[God] saves us and calls us with a holy calling, not in accord with our acts, but *in accord with His own purpose* and the grace which is given to us in Christ Jesus *before times eonian, yet now is being manifested* through the advent of our Saviour, Christ Jesus, Who, indeed, abolishes death, yet illuminates life and incorruption through the evangel of which I was appointed a herald and an apostle and a teacher of the nations. For which cause I am suffering; but I am not ashamed. For I am aware Whom I have believed, and I am persuaded that He is able to guard what is committed to me, for that day.

Observe three things from this passage.

First; our position in the Body of Christ, and even our salvation (the fact that we are in the Body of Christ at all) is an appointment of God that has nothing to do with our acts or behavior. It is a selection made by God in accord with His purposes and His grace. Whatever gifts we may have, they come from God and we have nothing to boast about.

Second; God's purposes were formulated before the eonian times we read about in the Scriptures; before the dawn of mankind. God is not developing His plan along the way.

Third; God's calling of the Body of Christ, while purposed before times eonian, was not revealed or manifested until Paul's day, through the advent of Christ Jesus and the proclamation of Paul's evangel. This, then, is the purpose of proclaiming the evangel (at least in part); to make manifest the calling of the ecclesia; the Body of Christ.

Have a pattern of sound words (1:13)

Have a pattern of sound words, which you hear from me.

Have a pattern of sound words!

It is one thing to quote from or teach from the Scriptures. It is quite another to have a pattern of soundness when handling the Scriptures. We must take care in our handling of the Scriptures so as not to incorporate pre-conceived biases that might influence our understanding. Even orthodoxy and the organized church may be wrong in its understanding, so we must escape those biases and seek truth directly from a sound handling of the Scriptures.

Perhaps Miles Coverdale said it best in the Preface to the 16th Century version of the Bible; "It shall greatly help ye to understand Scripture if thou mark not only what is spoken or written but: To whom, and by whom; With what words, and at what time; Where, and to what intent; With what circumstance; Considering what goeth before and what followeth."

Guard the truth (1:14)

The ideal thing committed to you, guard through the holy spirit which is making its home in us.

Timothy's charge is to guard the truth in the face of false teachings. And we see that the holy spirit; God's spirit; is making its home in "us."

All were turned away (1:15)

Of this you are aware, that all those in the province of Asia were turned from me, of whom are Phygellus and Hermogenes.

> # All were turned away!

This passage should shock us! Is not Paul considered the missionary apostle, who took Christianity to the nations; planting and nurturing churches? Is it not the understanding of modern-day Christianity that Paul's work continued to flourish and grow into the churches of our day? Yet we see here that Paul's work took a huge step back near the end of his life and ministry. There was an apostasy; a falling away. All in Asia had turned from him and from the truth he taught. Looking again at 1:13, when Paul said: *Have a pattern of sound words, which you hear from me;* we see that as the majority turned away from Paul they were turning away from the sound words proclaimed by Paul.

At what point did the organized church recover from this setback? At what point following Paul's life did the majority of believers finally get it right and stand for the truth. In Paul's day truth is apparently in the hands of the minority, like Timothy and a select few; with the majority having turned from the truth. I would contend that since Paul's day the organized church has continued in apostasy from the truth. Yes, there are believers that can be found in the pews of churches around the world; but the preachers, teachers, scholars, authors and other leaders within the organized church cannot be trusted for understanding and teaching the truth. Brothers and sisters, we are on our own. We cannot trust the organized church that is in apostasy from the truth, regardless of the denomination. *All those in the province of Asia were turned from me.* We must seek truth from the Scriptures, properly and carefully handled, with a focus on having a pattern of sound words.

Paul is imprisoned in Rome (1:16)

Onesiphorus often refreshes me and was not ashamed of my chain, but, coming to be in Rome, he seeks me diligently and found me.

CHAPTER 2

Commit teachings to faithful men (2:1)

What things you hear from me through many witnesses, these commit to faithful men, who shall be competent to teach others also.

Those within most of the ecclesias (churches) had turned away from Paul. How, then, can the truth be preserved?

Here, late in Paul's ministry, we do not see an organized church structure comprised of elders and deacons, or the bishops and pastors of our present day. Truth was to be preserved by *faithful men* identified by Timothy who could then teach the truth to others.

Please the one who enlists you (2:3)

No one who is warring is involved in the business of a livelihood, that he should be pleasing the one who enlists him.

Timothy is advised to focus on his spiritual responsibilities, without being distracted by the business of a livelihood. Obviously, then, Timothy had the means to support himself. Still, we must remember that Paul himself was a tentmaker, and did not rely upon support for his ministry to survive. So this present passage cannot be taken as a carte blanche mandate for all in the ministry to fully support themselves by the ministry as a vocation. And whatever the means of Timothy's support, the point Paul is making is to avoid distractions from the world while focusing on the important spiritual work at hand.

Proclaiming the evangel (2:8)

Remember Jesus Christ, Who has been roused from among the dead, is of the seed of David ...

While Paul's evangel (good news) contains a variety of components, here we see the oft repeated heart of the evangel. And as Paul suffers evil to proclaim the evangel ...

I am enduring all because of those who are chosen, that they also may be happening upon the salvation which is in Christ Jesus with glory eonian.

Paul has been commissioned by Christ and is Christ's instrument in proclaiming the good news to those gifted with faith (belief) in this present life.

Salvation and rewards (2:11)

For if we died together, we shall be living together also;
If we are enduring, we shall be reigning together also;
If we are disowning, He also will be disowning us;
If we are disbelieving, He is remaining faithful –
He cannot disown Himself.

Salvation and rewards are two different things. The believer has died with Christ (Romans 6:2-11). This is a fact apart from works. So it follows that the believer will live in the eons to come. This is also a fact. Salvation cannot be earned; it is a free gift. Yet enduring will lead to reigning. There will be differing rewards that are based upon works (Romans 14:10; 2 Corinthians 5:10).

Avoid controversy (2:14)

Of these things be reminding them; not to engage in controversy for nothing useful, to the upsetting of those who are hearing.

Finding ones-self in the midst of controversy may be unavoidable at times for the sake of the truth. Even Paul found this to be the case. But let us be sure these occasions are not for *nothing useful* (i.e. insignificant issues).

Correctly cut the word of truth (2:15)

Endeavor to present yourself to God qualified, an unashamed worker, correctly cutting the word of truth.

> This goes beyond memorizing Scripture and applying it in superficial ways, ignoring the context. It is to know in which situations a Scriptural reference applies, and when it does not. As an example, to correctly cut the word of truth means we cannot take a Scripture directed to Israel and assume that it applies to the Body of Christ. It may have been a word intended for a particular group of people at a particular point in time.

"Correctly cut" or "rightly divide" the word of truth. This is Paul's directive to Timothy in his final letter.

> This is Paul's last letter. He knew of the danger of carrying over things from a past dispensation which did not belong in the new dispensation. There were those clinging to the Law, and to the primacy of Israel. But these were things from a past era. God was doing a new thing; Israel having been set aside for a season. Israel is no longer in a seat of preference. The Body of Christ, as revealed by God thru Paul, was comprised of Jew and Gentile with no barrier or preference. To reach into the past and to carry over truths from that previous era would contaminate or confuse the truth that God now wanted to reveal. Paul knew the danger of this as his life neared its end, and here in his last letter he saw the need to warn Timothy. The truth as found in all of God's revelation must be RIGHTLY DIVIDED!

Avoid profane prattling (2:16)

Yet from profane prattling stand aloof, for they will be progressing to more irreverence, and their word will spread as gangrene.

> Profane prattling, or a centering of discussions on common things, will lead to irreverence; a focus away from God. And this can lead to a distortion of truth, as the example provided displays.

Hymeneus and Philetus, who swerve as to truth, saying the resurrection has already occurred, and are subverting the faith of some.

> A focus away from the truth and profane prattling has led these two believers to a misunderstanding, and they now lead others astray. When we hear speculation instead of a focus on what the Scriptures are actually saying, we should take heed of this warning.
>
> Consider for a moment the specific error of Hymeneus and Philetus. They had reached the conclusion that the resurrection had already occurred. Has not much of the organized church fallen into the same error? The common teaching is that at the time of death the believer is immediately alive in the presence of the Lord. How, then, will that person (already living) be resurrected at some future time? Is this not the same as those in Paul's day who taught that the resurrection had already come?

Let everyone who is naming the name of the Lord withdraw from injustice.

Purge yourself from dishonorable things (2:20)
In a house there are not only gold and silver utensils, but also wooden and earthenware; some for honor yet some for dishonor. If one should purge himself of all dishonor he will be a utensil for honor, hallowed and useful to the Owner; ready for every good act.

Become mature (2:22)
Youthful desires flee: yet pursue righteousness, faith, love, peace.

Refuse stupid and crude questionings (2:23)
Now stupid and crude questionings refuse, being aware that they are generating fighting.

> Akin to the destructive profane prattling, we are to avoid stupid and crude questionings; speculations on unimportant matters; as they will lead to fighting.

Be gentle and meek; even with those antagonizing (2:24)

Now a slave of the Lord must not be fighting, but be gentle toward all, apt to teach, bearing with evil, with meekness training those who are antagonizing, seeing whether God may be giving them repentance to come into a realization of the truth, and they will be sobering up out of the trap of the Adversary.

> Timothy is charged, then, to teach with gentleness and meekness those who are antagonizing, to see if God will give them repentance. Timothy is God's instrument, but it is God who will give them repentance.

CHAPTER 3

Wickedness will grow in the last days (3:1)

Now this know, that in the last days perilous periods will be present, for men will be selfish, fond of money, ostentatious, proud, calumniators, stubborn to parents, ungrateful, malign, without natural affection, implacable, adversaries, uncontrollable, fierce, averse to the good, traitors, rash, conceited, fond of their own gratification rather than fond of God ...

> Are we in the last days today? This seems to be an apt description of our current society. But read on ...

Having a form of devoutness yet denying its power.

> This, then, speaks not of society; but of organized religion. There is a form of devoutness (reverence of God), but it is only form and not substance. It is the organized church (religion) that will grow in wickedness in the "last days" described by Paul.

Shun false teachers (3:6)

Shun these. They slip into homes. They are led by lusts and gratifications. They are always learning but never come into a realization of the truth. They are like Jannes and Jambres who opposed Moses, withstanding the truth; men of a depraved mind, disqualified as to the faith. But they shall not be progressing more, for their folly shall be obvious to all.

> Just as Jannes and Jambres were exposed and thwarted, so also will every false teacher, as God is in control.

Follow me ^(3:10)

Fully follow me in my:
- ✓ Teaching
- ✓ Motive
- ✓ Purpose
- ✓ Faith
- ✓ Patience
- ✓ Love
- ✓ Endurance
- ✓ Persecutions
- ✓ Sufferings

> But Paul warns ...

All who are wanting to live devoutly in Christ Jesus shall be persecuted.

> There is little persecution of church-going Christians today in the USA. The organized church has become a comfortable part of society. Considering Paul's words, does the absence of persecution point to a major problem within the church today? Is spiritual truth to be found within the organized church?

Wickedness will grow ^(3:13)

Wicked men and swindlers shall wax worse and worse, deceiving and being deceived.

The sacred scriptures ^(3:14)

The sacred scriptures are able to make you wise for salvation through faith which is in Christ Jesus. All scripture is inspired by God, and is beneficial for teaching, for exposure, for correction, for discipline in righteousness, that the man of God may be equipped, fitted out for every good act.

> While all Scripture is inspired by God and beneficial for these purposes, this does not mean that all Scripture can be applied to all situations in all eras. We remember Pauls' words elsewhere in this same letter. Have a pattern of sound words (1:13). Endeavor to present yourself to God qualified, an unashamed worker, correctly cutting the word of truth (2:15).

CHAPTER 4

Christ will be judging [(4:1)]

Christ Jesus, Who is about to be judging the living and the dead, in accord with His advent and His kingdom.

> *About to be* tells us that Paul saw Christ's advent, or coming, as imminent. This verse seems to speak not of the snatching away of the Body of Christ (1 Thessalonians 4:13ff) but Christ's return to the earth when the great throne judgment will take place. We will see shortly that Paul knew his death was imminent, and he knows Christ will call the Body of Christ heavenward (1 Thessalonians 4:13ff), and at some point after that Christ will return to the earth to establish His kingdom and judge. It appears that Paul saw the sequence of these events to be quite swift; or at least he recognized the possibility that they could be swift. Paul's words here give urgency to Timothy in heralding the word.

Herald the word [(4:2)]

Herald the word. Stand by it opportunely, inopportunely, expose, rebuke, entreat, with all patience and teaching.

They will turn away from sound teaching [(4:3)]

For the era will be when they will not tolerate sound teaching, but, their hearing being tickled, they will heap up for themselves teachers in accord with their own desires, and, indeed, they will be turning their hearing away from the truth yet will be turned aside to myths.

> Could this be a description of Christianity today, with so many flocking to dumbed-down, easy-to-read Bible translations and popular authors and Bible teachers; to have their hearing tickled?

Do the work of an evangelist [(4:5)]

Be sober in all things. Suffer evil as an ideal soldier of Christ Jesus. Do the work of an evangelist. Fully discharge your service.

> Paul charges Timothy with proclaiming the evangel. Since many will turn from the truth and not tolerate sound teaching, it is important for Timothy to carry on Paul's work; to be the voice of truth at a time when they (the majority) will be turning from the truth.

Paul's death is imminent [(4:6)]

For I am already a libation, and the period of my dissolution is imminent. I have contended the ideal contest. I have finished my career. I have kept the faith.

Here we see the reason Paul is preparing Timothy to carry on his work. His death is imminent. Note that at the end of Paul's life the "church" is turning away from the truth; seeking teachers who teach in accord with their own desires. Does this not describe the organized church today? If one hears a word he does not like, he simply moves on to a different church preaching a message that is more appealing. Can we not see that many different churches preaching conflicting messages breeds confusion? How can one find the truth? Only through a study of the Scriptures, and not through the teachings and doctrines of the majority (i.e. the organized church).

Future rewards (4:8)

Furthermore, there is reserved for me the wreath of righteousness, which the Lord, the just Judge, will be paying to me in that day; yet not to me only, but also to all who love His advent.

The believer will be rewarded for good works at the dais (platform) of Christ (Romans 14:10; 2 Corinthians 5:10). Good works do not play a part in salvation, but they do play a part in rewards or loss of rewards at the dais, effectual in the eons to come.

Come quickly (4:9)

Endeavor to come to me quickly, for Demas, *loving the current eon,* forsook me and went to Thessalonica, Crescens to Galatia, Titus to Dalmatia. Luke only is with me. Lead Mark back with you, for he is useful to me for service. When you come, bring the traveling cloak which I left in Troas with Carpus, and the scrolls, especially the vellums. Alexander the coppersmith displayed to me much evil: the Lord will be paying him in accord with his acts. Very much he withstood our words.

Those forsaking Paul were loving the current eon more than the evangel and the things of God.

Timothy is asked to bring with him Mark, and to bring the travelling cloak which Paul left in Troas with Carpus, and the scrolls, especially the vellums. Travelling cloak (*phelanes* in the Greek, or *bark*) could be a reference to a covering for the scrolls and vellums; writings Paul wished to preserve knowing his death was imminent and knowing that the majority were already turning away from correct doctrine. How could truth be preserved after Paul's death? (This is the only time *phelanes* is used and is translated *valise* in the Syriac version.)

Ernest Martin, in his book, *The Original Bible Restored*, argues that when Paul wrote to Timothy his primary goal was that sound doctrine be preserved after his death. Therefore it was necessary for the apostles to leave behind an official documentation of truth. It would not make sense that the apostles would simply die and allow "church leaders" to set Scriptural standards. If they couldn't trust the doctrines of many in their midst while they still lived, how could they depend on them to preserve correct doctrine in the future?

We know that many in Paul's day were writing "gospels" (Luke 1:1 and note the many publications in our present day that purport to be "lost scriptures"). There was a danger of losing the truth altogether if the apostles did not act to leave behind some official documentation.

Martin notes that Paul wanted John Mark, the author of the Gospel of Mark, to come with Timothy to perform a "service." John Mark was at times an associate of Paul, but he was more closely tied to Peter who refers to him as "my son" (1 Peter 5:13). When asking Timothy to bring Mark, he also asks him to bring the traveling cloak which I left in Troas with Carpus, and the scrolls, especially the vellums (4:13). Cloak could refer to a receptacle for the scrolls and vellums (or parchments), much like the cover for a book, or a case. Martin hypothesizes that knowing his death was approaching, Paul asks Timothy and Mark to come to Rome with certain specific writings (the scrolls and vellums), and the "service" Paul intended for Mark was perhaps to take Paul's inspired writings to Peter for inclusion in the Scriptural canon.

In light of the apostasy growing within the ecclesia, Paul's impending death, and his concern for the preservation of truth, Martin's hypothesis seems to make great sense. And while we cannot be sure that Martin is correct on all counts, one thing is certain; Paul sees the preservation of correct doctrine as essential.

All forsook me (4:16)

At my first defense no one came along with me, but all forsook me.

All forsook me!

> Again we see that near the end of Paul's life the majority had turned from him. This should cause us to question the "truth" being taught by the majority (i.e. the organized church in its variety of denominations and sects). At what point in history, following Paul's death, did the majority suddenly reverse its apostasy and error and find the truth?

Yet the Lord stood beside me, and He invigorates me, that through me the heralding may be fully discharged, and all the nations should hear.

> The apostasy will not be reversed. But the success of Paul's ministry is that all the nations would hear the evangel, even if they turned away from it.

His celestial kingdom (4:18)

The Lord will be rescuing me from every wicked work and will be saving me for His celestial kingdom.

> It is not that Paul's life will be spared, for he has already indicated his dissolution (or death) is imminent. But instead Paul looks to the coming eons. No enemy in the present life can rob Paul of his life in the eons to come. His celestial kingdom refers to that aspect of the kingdom that is already in full force in the celestials (the heavens), even as the earth awaits the return of Christ to physically establish the kingdom here.

Final greetings (4:19)

Greet Prisca, Aquila and the household of Onesiphorus. Endeavor to come before winter. Greeting you is Eubulus, Pudens, Linus, Claudia and all the brethren.

> While many were abandoning Paul, he does have a small following.

No greetings to the ecclesias?

It is interesting that here, near the end of Paul's life, he no longer sends greeting to or from the ecclesia at various places. Instead his greetings refer to individuals. This shows the growing informality of the ecclesia, or church, and the fact that the truth is in the hands of individuals who had not turned away.

Charles Welch (Christian theologian and writer 1888-1967) observed that 2 Timothy reveals a church in ruins, and the discipline that was possible when the church was intact was no longer effective. So Timothy is instructed to exercise discipline upon himself, not upon others (2:19; 3:5). Beware of the organized church. Seeks truth from the Scriptures, questioning doctrine being taught by the majority. Remember that even in Paul's day, near the end of his life, the majority had rejected the truth and were in apostasy.

CLOSING THOUGHTS

This is perhaps Paul's final letter. His career was finished (4:7). The ecclesia had become filled with evil. And Paul's basic instruction is to separate from evil.

Consider the change that had taken place since Paul's first letter to Timothy. In 1 Timothy there were false teachers in the ecclesia (1:3-7) but Paul still emphasized the leadership to be provided by supervisors and servants; "bishops" and "deacons" in the Authorized Version. Paul warned that in latter times some would depart from the faith (4:1). But elders that ruled well were to be honored (5:17).

But in 2 Timothy we hear that all in Asia had turned away (1:15). Orderly rule is now succeeded by ruin. Instead of mentioning supervisors, servants or elders within the ecclesia, Timothy is instructed to commit the truth to "faithful men" (2:2). Paul's instruction is simply to preach the truth, and to commit truth to faithful men who would be able to teach others. There is no longer any talk of organization within the ecclesia; for the ecclesia is now in ruin. And worse things were to come in the last days.

The ecclesia had departed from truth. Leaders such as Hymenaeus and Philetus were leading some astray, teaching that the resurrection had already occurred (2:18). Whereas 1 Timothy provided characteristics to be found within supervisor and servants who would lead the ecclesia, in

2 Timothy we simply read that a servant of the Lord was to be gentle and meek (2:24). Deceit and apostasy within the ecclesia were growing. In the last days, perilous times were to come (3:1). There would be a form of godliness that denied the power (3:5). Evil men would grow worse; and this referred to men within the ecclesia who would be deceiving and being deceived (3:13). The time would come when *they* (those within the ecclesia) would not endure sound doctrine (4:3). Demas, Crescens and Titus forsook Paul, preferring the present world (4:10).

And so we note the transition between a somewhat organized structure within the ecclesia in 1 Timothy; with an emphasis on supervisors and servants (bishops and deacons); and the absence of structure in 2 Timothy where we see an emphasis on the individual servant of the Lord, and committing the truth to faithful men. And in the midst of this growing apostasy within the ecclesia; even within the leadership of the ecclesia; Paul knew his death was drawing near (4:6). So he makes provision for Timothy and Mark to gather his writings and to bring them to him, where he would make arrangements for these writings to be preserved after his death, in order that the truth might be preserved in the midst of growing apostasy (4:12).

With all of this in mind, does it not cause us to question the teachings propagated by the leaders within the organized church today? At what point following Paul's death did the apostasy cease? At what point was spiritual truth, as proclaimed by Paul, finally recognized and taught by the majority within the church?

Titus

An Overview of the Scriptures, by
BOB EVELY © *2018.*
An Independent Minister of Christ Jesus,
Of the church at Wilmore, Kentucky

"For the saving grace of God made its advent to all humanity, training us that, disowning irreverence and worldly desires, we should be living sanely and justly and devoutly in the current eon ..." (2:11)

1 Thessalonians	50-52 AD	During 2nd Journey
2 Thessalonians	52-53 AD	During 2nd Journey
Galatians (early theory)	54 AD	End of 2nd Journey
1 Corinthians	Spring 57 AD	During 3rd Journey
2 Corinthians	Fall 57 AD	During 3rd Journey
Galatians	Winter 57 AD	During 3rd Journey
Romans	Spring 58 AD	During 3rd Journey
Colossians	61-62 AD	During 1st Captivity
Ephesians	61-62 AD	During 1st Captivity
Philemon	62-63 AD	During 1st Captivity
Philippians	63 AD	During 1st Captivity
1 Timothy	67 AD	Between Captivities
Titus	**67 AD**	**Between Captivities**
2 Timothy	Spring 68 AD	During 2nd Captivity

CHAPTER 1

The address on the envelope (1:1)

Paul, a slave of God, yet an apostle of Jesus Christ,
To Titus, a genuine child according to the common faith.

> This is a personal letter from Paul to Titus. It differs from Paul's letters that were directed to the ecclesia in various places. We must take care to distinguish between general truths for the ecclesia, and those things intended specifically for Titus in his unique position.

God's progressive revelation [(1:1)]

... a realization of the truth, which accords with devoutness, in expectation of life eonian, yet manifests His word *in its own eras* by heralding, with which I was entrusted.

> # God's revelation is progressive.

The realization of eonian life (life in the eons to come) is made known by proclaiming the evangel, and it is manifested *in its own eras,* or progressively. To Israel the prophets had foretold an eventual restoration of the kingdom and a resurrection for life upon the earth. But it was not until the revelation given to Paul that we learn of the Body of Christ and its destiny in the heavens in the ages to come. God's truth is manifested progressively, in its own eras.

If God's revelation is progressive, we see the great importance of "rightly dividing" the Word; else we run the risk of applying statements and situations to our current situation when they were, in fact, intended for a previous era.

Find elders and supervisors [(1:5)]

This is why I left you in Crete, that you should amend what is lacking and constitute elders, city by city.

There was a "lacking" within the ecclesia that needed to be addressed, and Titus is instructed to find elders city by city. Here we see some semblance of structure within the ecclesia, but far from the formal religion that has been created throughout the present day organized church.

And just as Paul instructed Timothy, note the qualifications needed for one to be considered as an elder.

If anyone is unimpeachable, the husband of one wife, having believing children, not under the accusation of profligacy or insubordinate – for the supervisor must be unimpeachable as an administrator of God, not given to self-gratification, not irritable, no toper, not quarrelsome, not avaricious, but hospitable, fond of that which is good, sane, just, benign, self-controlled; upholding the faithful word according to the teaching, that he may be *able to entreat with sound teaching* as well as to *expose those who contradict.*

> These behaviors give us information as to what is good in God's eyes, and what is not. Salvation is a free gift from God apart from works, but in this life there are behaviors that are good in God's eyes and behaviors that are not. In response to the graciousness of God, let us respond by displaying those behaviors that God has deemed as proper.

Expose false teachers; preserve sound faith (1:10)

Many are insubordinate, vain praters and imposters, especially those of the Circumcision, who must be gagged, who are subverting whole households, teaching what they must not, on behalf of sordid gain.

Be exposing them severely, *that they may be sound in the faith,* not heeding Jewish myths and precepts of men who are turning them from the truth.

All is clean to the clean, but to the defiled and unbelieving nothing is clean, but their mind as well as conscience is defiled. They are avowing an acquaintance with God, yet by their acts are denying it, being abominable and stubborn, and disqualified for every good act.

> There were problems to be addressed at Crete, especially among the Circumcision.

CHAPTER 2

The aged are to teach and set an example (2:1)

Now you be speaking what is becoming to sound teaching. The aged men are to be sober, grave, sane, sound in the faith, in love, in endurance.

Similarly the aged women, in demeanor, are to behave as becomes the sacred; not adversaries, not enslaved by much wine, teachers of the ideal, that they may bring the young wives to a sense of their duty to be fond of their husbands, fond of their children, sane, chaste, domestic, good, subject to their own husbands, that the word of God may not be blasphemed.

Entreat the younger men to be sane as to all things.

Tender yourself a model of ideal acts, in teaching with uncorruptness, gravity, with sound words, uncensurable, that the contrary one may be abashed, having nothing bad to say concerning us.

> Why is "holy" (set-apart) behavior important? That the word of God may not be blasphemed (2:5). To blaspheme is to talk negatively. *Blasphemos* in the Greek is translated *blaspheme* when referring to God or His Word and *calumniate* when referring to others.

> All of these behavioral instructions have the central purpose, that no one has cause to say anything bad concerning the ecclesia or the word of God.

> While salvation is not based upon works, there are most certainly behaviors that are condoned by God, and those that are not. And if one is a leader within the ecclesia he is to exhibit acceptable behaviors and lead by example.

Slaves (2:9)

Slaves are to be subject to their owners, to be well-pleasing in all things, not contradicting; not embezzling, but displaying all good faithfulness, that they may be adorning the teaching that is of God, our Saviour, in all things.

> Paul declared himself to be a slave of God (1:1). To follow his example is to declare that we, ourselves are slaves of God, subject to our Owner. It is interesting that Paul does not condemn slavery and seek to reform the culture or government of his day. He has more important matters to be concerned with, and simply advises slaves to act in a manner befitting their station within the Body of Christ.

Saving grace to all humanity (2:11)

For the saving grace of God made its advent to all humanity ...

> Consistent with so many other passages in the Scriptures that are often limited and restricted to SOME, Paul here notes to Timothy that God's saving grace has come to ALL humanity.

Therefore let us respond with ideal acts (2:12)

God's saving grace is training us that, disowning irreverence and worldly desires, we should be *living sanely* and *justly* and *devoutly* in the current eon, *anticipating that happy expectation,* the advent of the glory of the great God and our Saviour, Jesus Christ, Who gives Himself for us, that He should be redeeming us from all lawlessness and be cleansing for Himself a people to be about Him, zealous of ideal acts.

> God's glory is not yet evident in this present eon, but we know it is coming and can therefore "expect" it and bask in that happy expectation.
>
> As for this call to be zealous of ideal acts; salvation is not dependent upon acts as it is entirely a gracious gift from God. But in response to that gift we should exhibit ideal acts.

Entreat and expose (2:15)

Speak of these things and entreat and expose with every injunction.

> We cannot remain silent when false teaching takes place within the ecclesia. We must speak the truth and expose any false teachings. It seems there are those within the Body of Christ that emphasize behavior at the expense of sound doctrine, and there are those that emphasize sound doctrine at the expense of courteous behavior motivated by love. But to Paul, BOTH are important.

CHAPTER 3

Remind them of proper behavior (3:1)

Remind them ...

- ✓ To be subject to sovereignties and authorities
- ✓ To be yielding
- ✓ To be ready for every good work
- ✓ To be calumniating (speaking badly of) no one
- ✓ To be pacific
- ✓ To be lenient
- ✓ To display meekness toward all humanity

> Why?

Because we also were once foolish, stubborn, deceived, slaves of various desires and gratifications, malicious, envious, detestable and hateful. But when our Saviour's kindness and fondness for humanity made its advent, not according to works but according to His mercy, He saves and renews us, justifies us in His grace, and makes us enjoyers in expectation of the allotment of *life eonian*.

Insist that believers exhibit ideal acts (3:8)

Insist that those who have believed God may be concerned to preside for ideal acts, for this is ideal and beneficial for humanity. Stand aloof from stupid questionings, genealogies, strifes and fightings about law; as they are of no benefit.

> Again; salvation is not dependent on works, or ideal acts. But Paul continually stresses the importance of works within the ecclesia.

Turn out the sectarian man [(3:10)]
After warning a sectarian man a second time, refuse him. He has turned himself out and is sinning and self-condemned.

Come to me [(3:12)]
Endeavor to come to me in Nicopolis where I will be wintering. Send Zenas the lawyer and Apollos, that nothing may be lacking in them. And those who are ours should be learning to preside over ideal acts. Greet our friends in faith.

CLOSING THOUGHTS

Paul writes to Titus to insist upon sound teaching and ideal acts within the ecclesia in response to God's saving grace. Acts or behavior are not conditions of salvation, but they are the appropriate response. It is important that believers display appropriate behavior so that God's word is not blasphemed (2:5).

Paul also speaks of organized assemblies as in 1 Timothy, including the appointment of elders who would supervise within the ecclesia. The elders, the aged and even slaves were to exhibit proper behavior, and Titus is instructed to insist that believers exhibit ideal acts (3:8).

Philemon

An Overview of the Scriptures, by
BOB EVELY © *2018.*
An Independent Minister of Christ Jesus,
Of the church at Wilmore, Kentucky

"Yet apart from your opinion I want to do nothing, that your good may not be as of compulsion but voluntary." (:14)

1 Thessalonians	50-52 AD	During 2nd Journey
2 Thessalonians	52-53 AD	During 2nd Journey
Galatians (early theory)	54 AD	End of 2nd Journey
1 Corinthians	Spring 57 AD	During 3rd Journey
2 Corinthians	Fall 57 AD	During 3rd Journey
Galatians	Winter 57 AD	During 3rd Journey
Romans	Spring 58 AD	During 3rd Journey
Colossians	61-62 AD	During 1st Captivity
Ephesians	61-62 AD	During 1st Captivity
Philemon	**62-63 AD**	**During 1st Captivity**
Philippians	63 AD	During 1st Captivity
1 Timothy	67 AD	Between Captivities
Titus	67 AD	Between Captivities
2 Timothy	Spring 68 AD	During 2nd Captivity

CHAPTER 1

The address on the envelope (1:1)

Paul, a prisoner of Christ Jesus, and brother Timothy,
To Philemon, the beloved, and our fellow worker,
And to sister Apphia, and to Archippus, our fellow soldier,
And to the ecclesia at your house.

> This is a personal letter from Paul to Philemon. We must take care to distinguish between general truths for the ecclesia, and those things intended specifically for Philemon in his unique position. While he includes Timothy in his "signature" it is clear that the letter is from Paul alone; *I am rather entreating, being such a one as Paul the aged* (:9). And while the address seems to direct the letter to Philemon, Apphia, Archippus and the ecclesia at your house (:2), in reality he is addressing Philemon

who would be the owner of the slave Onesimus. Clearly Timothy is with Paul and the others mentioned are with Philemon, but the content of the letter is from Paul to Philemon.

The ecclesia at your house (1:2)

Observe the simplicity of church structure in the statement, *The ecclesia at your house*. Unlike the "First Church of XYZ" of our day or the multitudes of denominations and organizational hierarchies, here we see the simplicity of a church, or ecclesia (called-out-ones) at the house of a believer. And let us not make the assumption that there is a regular, weekly assembly at this house. Paul seems to be simply greeting those who are a part of the ecclesia (the called-out-ones) that reside at this house.

Paul commends Philemon (1:4)

I thank God, hearing of your love, and the faith you have toward the Lord Jesus and for all the saints, and seeing that the compassions of the saints are soothed through you.

Entreaty for Onesimus (1:8)

I entreat you concerning Onesimus, whom I sent back to you. I had intended to keep him for myself, to serve me in the bonds of the evangel. But apart from your opinion I want to do nothing, that your good may not be as of compulsion but voluntary.

Paul would like Philemon to give Onesimus his release from slavery, allowing him to serve Paul in the bonds of the evangel. Yet Paul is sending back Onesimus (who had obviously fled) to Philemon, hoping he will be released voluntarily. Paul notes that the release of Onesiumus would be proper, but because of love he *entreats* rather than compels.

Perhaps he is separated for an hour, that you may be collecting him as an eonian repayment, no longer as a slave but a brother; beloved, especially to me.

Perhaps Onesimus was separated from Philemon for a purpose. For now he returns not as a slave but as a beloved brother.

Take him to yourself as me. If in anything he injures you or is owing you, be charging this to my account. Not that I may say to you that you are owing me. But may I be "profiting" from you in the Lord. Soothe my compassions in Christ.

> He asks that Onesimus be received as if he were Paul himself, and if
> Philemon experienced loss of any kind Paul asks that it be charged to his
> own account. (Although Paul does include a subtle reminder that Philemon
> owes Paul.)

Having confidence in your obedience I write to you, being aware that
you will do even above what I say.

> Paul expresses confidence that Philemon will do above what is asked, and
> he asks Philemon to prepare a place for him to stay as he expects to be
> able to come.

Greetings (1:23)

Greeting you are Epaphras, my fellow captive in Christ Jesus, Mark,
Aristarchus, Demas, Luke, my fellow workers.

CLOSING THOUGHTS

This is a private, personal letter from Paul to Philemon. What would a
personal letter contribute to the Word of God, making it worthy of
inclusion in the Scriptures? This is a wonderful picture of God's grace;
and a practical exhibition of how an individual is to walk in light of God's
grace.

Interestingly we do not see Paul advocating the end of slavery in total.
He does not comment on slavery as being good or bad, consistent with
his practice of allowing the government to function in the worldly realm
without criticism. Paul's concern is faith and behavior within the
ecclesia, not in society, government or the world.

What the letter reveals is a model for relationships that are based on
love, employing entreaty rather than compulsion when asking another to
do what is right. This becomes a larger picture of God's dealings with
humanity, as He *leads* rather than forces all to salvation through
Christ's work. And just as Paul is confident in Philemon's obedience,
knowing he will do even more than what is asked (:21), so also God is
quite capable of leading all mankind to ultimate salvation and
reconciliation, to the end that He becomes All in all (1 Corinthians
15:28).

𝕿𝖍𝖊 𝕻𝖆𝖚𝖘𝖊 (𝕾𝖚𝖒𝖒𝖆𝖗𝖞)

An Overview of the Scriptures, by
BOB EVELY © *2018.*
An Independent Minister of Christ Jesus,
Of the church at Wilmore, Kentucky

As we conclude our journey through Paul's life and letters, and as we prepare to look at Revelation, let's recap a few things.

First; Paul is the only voice found in the New Testament that is directed to the nations ... those who are outside of the people of Israel. On the road to Damascus he received a dual commission: *He is a choice instrument of Mine, to bear My name before both the nations and kings, besides the sons of Israel* (Acts 9:15-16). Peter, John, James and other New Testament writers had a commission to Israel *only*. Paul *alone* was commissioned to go to the Gentiles.

As Paul went to the Gentiles his message was not the same as the message proclaimed to the believers of Israel by the others. Paul stressed that the gospel he proclaimed was not received from man, but it came through a revelation of Jesus Christ (Galatians 1:11-12). If he preached the same gospel, why would he not have studied under the Twelve who had heard and observed Christ during His earthly ministry? And why would Paul refer to his proclamation as "my evangel" instead of "the evangel" (Romans 2:16; 16:25-26)?

Paul had been entrusted with the evangel of the Uncircumcision, and Peter had been trusted with the evangel of the Circumcision (Galatians 2:7). He did not say that his was the evangel *to* the Uncircumcision; but *of* the Uncircumcision. It was a *different* message.

Paul tells us that at some point Israel had been temporarily set aside: *Callousness, in part, on Israel has come UNTIL the complement of the nations may be entering* (Romans 11:25). So Israel, which had long been God's chosen instrument through which He worked, was set aside. But this setting aside is not permanent, but only UNTIL!

Now as Paul proclaimed God's grace and freedom from the law, he noted there will come a day of indignation. But *God did not appoint us* [the Body of Christ] *to indignation* (1 Thessalonians 5:8). We will read of this "day of indignation;" the Day of the Lord; in Revelation. But since the Body of Christ was not appointed to indignation, how will God bring this about upon the earth?

There will come a day when the Body of Christ is "snatched away" (1 Thessalonians 4:13) to serve Christ in the celestials (Ephesians 2:6). This must occur so that the day of indignation (Romans 2:5) can come upon the earth, without subjecting the Body of Christ to this indignation. And this removal is necessary, since the man of lawlessness (the antichrist) cannot be revealed until "the detainer" (2 Thessalonians 2:6) is removed.

And so we will notice when studying Revelation that the Body of Christ is not to be found, for the Body has been "snatched away" from the earth before the events of Revelation (God's indignation) unfold. With this in mind let us now turn to the final book in God's Word; Revelation.

Index

Abraham as example	153
Abraham's two sons	156
Adam & Christ, parallel	63, 113
Adjustment	140
All, completing the	183
All condemned-All justified	64
All created-all reconciled	209
All, for all and on all	59
All, God's will all be saved	239
All humanity, saving grace to	272
All in accord with the counsel of	172
All in all	113
All mankind to be blessed	73
All, over all, thru all, in all	183
All, Savior of	52, 244
All things to all men	103
All together for good	71
All vivified	249
Ambassadors	131
Apollos corrected by Priscilla &	22
Apostasy, all turned away	28, 255, 265
Apostasy in future eras	243, 260, 261, 262
Apostle, Paul a different	48
Apostleship, Paul defends his	137
Areopagus (Athens)	19
Assembling not for the better	106
Authorities, subject to	78
Bear one another's burdens	161
Bear with those of weaker faith	79
Behavior	78

Behavior, judging immoral	97
Behavior, put off the former	186
Behavior, let us respond w ideal acts	272
Behavior, remind them of	273
Behavior within the ecclesia	222, 225, 242, 248
Behaviors, to put away & put on	215
Belief, the evangel is covered	127
Belief reckoned as righteousness	61
Believing, our choice?	51, 60
Bereans	19
Boasting	97
Body of Christ	107
Body, the ecclesia	210
Body, one	77
Body, one with no barrier	177
Celestial kingdom	265
Celestials, our realm	204
Celestials, seated among	175
Come quickly	263
Commission, our great	93, 132
Complete the word of God	211
Conciliated	63
Conciliating the world	131
Contentment	135, 205, 248
Controversy, avoid	257, 259
Conversion, Paul's	5
Cornelius	7
Correctly cut the word of God	258
Created, in Him is all	209
Crucified with Christ	152
Dais, all will give account	80, 130
Day of the Lord	224

Day of the Lord not yet here	230
Death, what happens?	129, 249
Detaining man of lawlessness	231
Devoutness	244, 248
Disorderly, admonish, don't commingle	233
Disposed above what is written	97
Disputes, settling	99
Disruption, chosen before	170
Ecclesia at your house	82, 217, 275-6
Ecclesia, the body	210
Ecclesia, the complement	174
Ecclesia, elders & supervisors	27, 270
Ecclesia, a mob	25
Ecclesia, qualification of leaders	241-42
Ecclesia, two?	28
Elements, observing	160
Elymas blinded until	10
Eon of the eons	181
Eon, present wicked	146
Eon, this eon and the impending	173
Eons, King of the	237
Eonian, called before times	254
Ephesians, Acts vs. Paul's letter	193
Ephesus elders	27
Era, unveiled in his own	231
Eras, testimony in own	240
Evangel, a different	147
Evangel, my (Paul's)	57
Evangel of Uncircumcision	150
Extricate from present wicked eon	146
Faith OF Christ	180
False teachers, expose	271

False teachers, shun	260
False teaching	247
Firstborn (Christ)	208
Flesh, associated with no one	130
Flesh, confidence in	202
Foundation, building upon	95
Freedom, but consider others	105
Freedom, Christ frees us	156
Freedom not a license	157
Giving gleefully	134
Grace is sufficient	139
Grace, measures of	183
Grace not law	64, 67
Hierarchy, God's	105, 188-9, 216
Image of God	208
Immortality, He alone has	249
In Christ	68
Indignation, Day of	55-6
Indignation, God's	53
Indignation, rescued out of	62, 220
Israel calloused	126
Israel, God's choice of	72
Israel not permanently discarded	75
Israel stumbles	73
Jerusalem council	14
Jerusalem, Paul opposed in	28
Jerusalem, Paul submits evangel	149
Jew & Greek, no distinction	74, 154, 215
Judaizers follow Paul	14
Judge not before the season	96
Judging, admonish disorderly	233
Judging behavior in ecclesia	55, 97-9

Judging, Christ will be	262
Judging, deal graciously w offenders	125
Judging, man not qualified	54
Justification	11
Law	153
Law cannot justify	151
Love builds up	102
Love fulfills the law	79
Love most important	109
Lydia believes	18
Marriage, deal with passions thru	101
Maturity needed	94
Measures of faith	77
Measures of grace	183
Nations, Israel stumbles	73
Nations, to the	21, 34
New creation	130, 163
New humanity	177
None are just	58
Passed over, sin	59
Pattern of sound words	254
Pattern, Paul is a	236
Paul's early ministry	6
Paul's last days	36
Paul's 1st journey	9
Paul's 2nd journey	16
Paul's 3rd journey	22
Peddling the word of God	125
Prayer	50, 71, 216, 232
Progressive revelation	270
Propitiatory shelter	59
Quiet life	238

Ransom, correspondent	239
Realization of God, coming to	173
Realization of His will	208, 212
Reaping what is sown	161
Redemption, awaiting	70
Resurrection, how?	115
Revelation, Paul's evangel thru	148
Revelation, progressive	270
Schisms	92
Secret made known by revelation	83, 178
Secret of the evangel	191
Secret of His will	171
Secrets, God's	96
Seek that which is above	214
Severed	9, 48
Shipwrecked	33
Snatching away	223
Sons of God	69, 154
Specially	162
Spiritual forces, armor	190
Spiritual gifts	107-111
Spiritual warfare	136
Stumbling blocks	80-81, 102, 133
Systematizing of the deception	184, 191
Temple of God	96
Test things of consequence	198
Timothy	17
Tradition, beware of philosophy and	213
Tradition, festivals and sabbaths	213
Tradition, observing the elements	160
Tradition, one day over another	80
Unveiled in his own era	231

Walk as children of light	187
Walk in spirit	68, 158
Walk respectably	79
Walk worthily	182, 199-201, 208, 257
Walking in Him	212
Women in subjection	240
Word of God, Paul's word is	221
Work	27, 233

This overview contains the thoughts and opinions of the author and is a work in progress as his study of the Scriptures continues. Some things that God has revealed are very clear. That Christ died for our sins; that He was entombed; and that He was roused (1 Corinthians 15:3) is clear. That all are to be ultimately reconciled to God thru the work of Christ is also very clear (1 Corinthians 15:20-28). But on many specifics in the Scriptures there are a variety of interpretations and opinions, and none should conclude they have the complete and final understanding on these matters that are less clear. The reader is encouraged to consider various opinions, but to study and to think for himself. Within the Body of Christ we should study and discuss our understandings so as to mutually reach a more complete understanding of that which God has revealed.

Unless otherwise noted, Scriptures are taken from the Concordant Literal
New Testament and the Concordant Version of the Old Testament.
Concordant Publishing Concern, 15570 West Knochaven Road,
Santa Clarita, CA 91387 (www.Concordant.org)

Grace Evangel Fellowship:
P O Box 6, Wilmore, KY 40390
www.GraceEvangel.org

About the Author

Bob Evely is Vice President with a national company, overseeing sales, sales training, servicing, marketing, and special projects. He is a graduate of Oakland University (Rochester, Michigan) and has a Master of Divinity (M.Div.) Degree from Asbury Theological Seminary (Wilmore, Kentucky). For three and a half years Bob served as pastor of the Canton and West Point United Methodist Churches in Salem, Indiana; and for five years he served as pastor of the Open Door Free Methodist Church in Nicholasville, Kentucky. Both were bi-vocational positions, with Bob supporting his family through full time employment.

In May 2002 Bob resigned as pastor of Open Door Free Methodist Church to found Grace Evangel Fellowship, an independent ministry/church based in Wilmore, Kentucky. His ministry includes writing, speaking, teaching, and corresponding via email.

Bob resides in Wilmore, Kentucky with his wife Jill (since 1975). Originally from the Romeo, Michigan area the Evelys have five children: Cris (Jen), Dusty (Sharon), Chad (Molly), Kari (Jason), and Scott (Martha). As of this writing they are blessed with 7 grandchildren (Elinor, Allison, Abby, Lilli, Livi, Annabelle, and Alex).

Jill homeschooled all five children, and for 20 years represented Sonlight Curriculum as a consultant. Besides staying busy as a wife, mother, and grandma, Jill is an accomplished soap maker (PrairieKari.com) and she continues to encourage parents interested in homeschooling their children.

The author can be contacted at Grace Evangel Fellowship, P O Box 6, Wilmore, Kentucky 40390; or via email bob@GraceEvangel.org

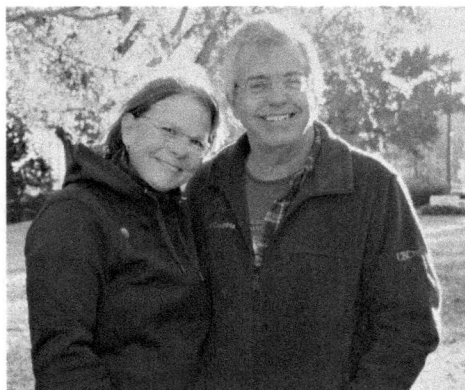

Books by Bob Evely

At the End of the Ages; the Abolition of Hell (2002)

The Visitation; An Overview of the New Testament, Part One (2018)

The Waiting; An Overview of the New Testament, Part Two (2018)

The Pause; An Overview of the New Testament, Part Three (2018)

The Return of the King; An Overview of the New Testament, Part Four (2018)

Many shorter writings can be found at GraceEvangel.org

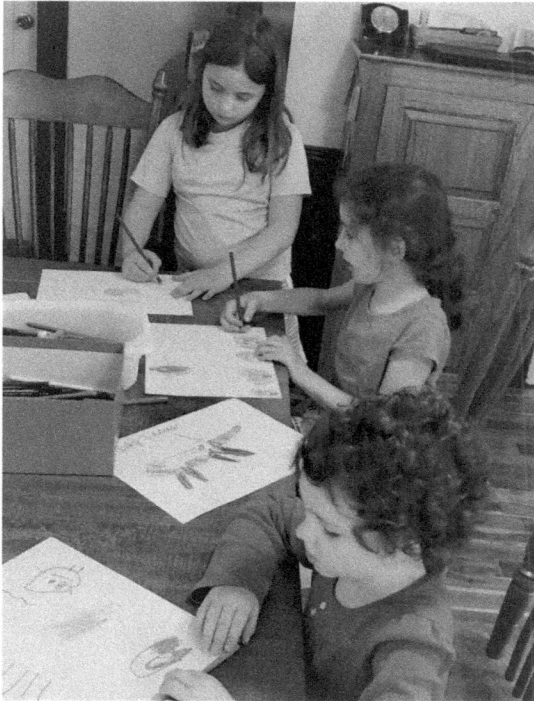

Book Artists at Work
Allison, Elinor & Lilli Evely

www.ingramcontent.com/pod-product-compliance
Lightning Source LLC
Chambersburg PA
CBHW031945080426
42735CB00007B/264